Sultanate Architecture of Pre-Mughal India

The Mughals ruled a united north India for over three centuries, but the roots of the glorious monuments they built are found in earlier provincial styles of architecture. In this richly illustrated work, Dr. Elizabeth Schotten Merklinger presents the first comprehensive study of the architecture of the Sultanate period. During the pre-Mughal centuries provincial Islamic styles of architecture developed, some of great importance and originality, each a spontaneous movement arising from its respective rulers and the desire to express particular aesthetic ideals. Many factors influenced these regional styles, the most important being the indigenous arts prevailing in the region prior to Islam, the technical ability of the craftsmen, the climatic conditions and the strength of the bond each province had with the capital, Delhi.

In *Sultanate Architecture of Pre-Mughal India* Elizabeth Schotten Merklinger traces the architectural development of each Sultanate. She shows that each provincial style is a synthesis between opposing spiritual and aesthetic concepts faced by the early Muslims in India. Nowhere else in the Islamic world was the clash of values more pronounced. But it is precisely these counteracting forces which released the enormous energy that resulted in the construction of the splendid monuments of the Mughal age.

This book evolved out of a series of lectures on Indian Islamic architecture given at the Oriental Institute, Oxford, in 1991. There has been no update on Indo-Islamic architecture since the definitive work, Percy Brown, *Indian Architecture: Islamic Period*, Bombay, 1956, reprint, 1968.

Elizabeth Schotten Merklinger obtained her BA and MA degrees from Cambridge University (UK) and her PhD from Delhi University (India). She has held research grants from the Social Sciences and Humanities Research Council of Canada, the Aga Khan Program for Islamic Art and Architecture (Harvard University and M.I.T.) and the Shastri Indo-Canadian Institute. Among her publications is *Indian Islamic Architecture: The Deccan 1347-1686*, Warminster, 1981.

Sultanate Architecture of Pre-Mughal India

Elizabeth Schotten Merklinger

with 23 plans and 188 b & w illustrations

Munshiram Manoharlal
Publishers Pvt. Ltd.

ISBN 81-215-1088-0
First published 2005

Typeset, printed and published by
Munshiram Manoharlal Publishers Pvt. Ltd.,
Post Box 5715, 54 Rani Jhansi Road, New Delhi 110 055.

Contents

List of Illustrations

List of Plans

Preface

This book evolved out of a series of lectures on Indian Islamic architecture I gave at the Oriental Institute, Oxford, in 1991. To my utter surprise, I could not find a suitable text on the monuments of the pre-Mughal period to assign to the seminar students. Julian Raby, Lecturer in Islamic Art and Architecture and organizer of the seminar suggested that I gather together my lectures in book-form and have them published. Since over the years I had done extensive research in India and had taken a large number of photographs of the Islamic monuments, the project seemed feasible. I decided, therefore, to do just that—to expand into book-form the lectures given at the Oriental Institute, Oxford, in 1991.

There has been no update on Indo-Islamic architecture since *Indian Architecture: Islamic Period,* the definitive work by Percy Brown written in 1956. In this book there are sixteen chapters devoted to the pre-Mughal period of Islamic architecture in India and I have followed that general division. I decided, however, to condense the monuments of Gujarat into one chapter and to eliminate the chapter on the monuments of Shīr Shāh Sūr, fitting the material in elsewhere in the text. Also, I have regrouped the Deccan chapters and rectified an unfortunate lacuna, the omission of the monuments of Sind (Pakistan).

A project of this scope is not possible without financial help. I would like to thank the three institutions that helped with financial support: the Social Sciences and Humanities Research Council of Canada, the Aga Khan Program for Islamic Art and Architecture at Harvard University and the Massachusetts Institute of Technology, and the Shastri Indo-Canadian Institute in New Delhi and Mr. Malik in particular for his continued interest over a period of more than twenty years.

I would like to thank many friends and colleagues for the help they have given me over the years. The work began thirty years ago when I was living in New Delhi. Anita Gold-Pearlroth walked into my house and then and there changed the future course of my working life. She lured me first to the splendours of Rajasthan and Gujarat but then saw her life's path lead elsewhere. She gave me a copy of her unpublished PhD dissertation with the hope that it might be useful. For chapter 3 on the Slave Dynasty I am deeply indebted to her early research. I thank her now for giving me that initial push all ventures need. It was also in India that I first met George Michell whose "mittel-europaeische" love of Brahms ignited the fledgling musical aspirations of my older daughter Catherine. With him I have shared countless evenings indulging in a mutual passion-opera. I thank him now for his enormous enthusiasm and good advice over the years which propelled me on in times of flagging energy. While living in Rome in the eighties I met Roloff Beny, a wonderfully eccentric Canadian photographer who became a friend and whose penthouse over the Tiber was a welcome refuge from the bustle of the Eternal City. Upon Roloff's untimely death in 1984 his entire photo collection went to the National Archives of Canada. I thank the staff of the National Archives for allowing me access and giving permission to reproduce some of these unique views of Indian monuments seen through the eyes of Roloff. Thanks also to Julian Raby and James Allan for their support and encouragement during the crucial year for this book in Oxford. I thank also my younger daughter, Alexandra, who, with utmost dedication, typed and retyped the many drafts of the original manuscript. And finally, thanks to my dear friend, Mary Denton, who accompanied me on most of my working trips to India in 1978, 1979, 1984, and 1985. Her continuous sense of humour and wit in the face of sometimes the most challenging circumstances helped enormously to lift any temporary clouds of darkness and to bring the project to a happy conclusion. And it is to her memory that I should like to affectionately dedicate this book, for it is, after all, full of monuments she would have intimately remembered, having so often nobly held the end of my tape while I measured.

ELIZABETH SCHOTTEN MERKLINGER

Ottawa, Canada
12 June 2004

CHAPTER 1

Historical Introduction

Following in the tracks of many invaders before them, Muslim armies finally conquered Delhi in 1192. India at that time was a wealthy land with a complexly structured society which had evolved out of the religions of Hinduism, Buddhism and Jainism.

India's commercial ties with the Middle East, Iran and Central Asia began in ancient times and were never actually broken, trade bringing economic, cultural and religious changes in its wake. The Muslim political invasions over the Hindu Kush were preceded in the seventh and eighth centuries by an Arab and Persian intellectual and political drive (the first Arab military action occurred in Sind in 712, but its efforts were confined to a small area). When they began their invasions again in the eleventh century under Maḥmūd of Ghaznī, the Muslim invaders followed a different route and persisted in their drive over the following centuries until almost all India was in their hands. Permanent Muslim rule in northern India was finally achieved under the Ghūrīds in the last decade of the twelfth century.

The Aryans were the first invaders who poured into the subcontinent, displacing the native Dravidian peoples, pushing them south to the tip of the peninsula. Between the sixth and fourth centuries BC the Persian Achaemenid Empire stretched into the Indus Valley and from here stone masons were sent to the Mauryan court at Pataliputra. And with them came the art of large-scale stone building and carving hitherto unknown in India. Alexander the Great led his armies in the direction of India and after him, in 183 BC the Bactrian Greek Demetrius conquered parts of the Punjab. The fruits of this civilization lived on in Roman and finally Gandharvan culture, perhaps the finest consequence of this intermingling of Greek and Indian elements. In the third century AD India began to absorb many Sassanian motifs from Persia which flowered in the classical Gupta period in the sixth and seventh centuries.

The southerly migration of the Muslims across the Khyber Pass in the tenth and eleventh centuries was of great significance to the Caliphate. On the fall of the Umayyad dynasty the seat of government was moved from Damascus to the new capital of Baghdād, founded by the successor Abbāsid rulers. Persian ideas now began to infiltrate into the Arab political structure. Persian officials took over government posts and Persian governors acquired almost independent power in the more distant provinces and began to establish hereditary dynasties.

The Caliphs needed a guard of mercenaries and for this purpose the warlike young Turks captured on the northern frontier were chosen. The Turkish guard soon ruled the Caliphs, acquiring control of distant provinces. Turks overflowed into Persia and this scramble led to the invasion of India.

In 962 one of these Turks, Alptagin, settled with his followers in the fortress of Ghaznī in the heart of the Afghan mountains. Here he established a small kingdom, where he ruled until his death and was then followed on the throne by one of his slaves, Sabuktagin, father of the future Sultan Maḥmūd. Sabuktagin was the first Muslim who attempted the invasion of India from the north-west, which eventually paved the way into Hindustan.

The new invaders brought their religion, Islam, which first appeared in south India, having entered by way of the Arabian Sea. Traders and missionaries found their way to the Malabar Coast centuries before the actual occupation of Hindustan by Muslim armies. In the Indus Valley Islam was first implanted by the governors of the Umayyad Caliphs. In 711 the province of Sind at the mouth of the Indus was conquered by the Abbāsid General Muḥammad-ibn-Wasim, at the same time as Arab-armies were sweeping across the heartland of Christian Europe into Persia, Transoxiana and Central Asia. By 871 Sind (now in Pakistan) had become an independent Muslim province. However, the vast western Rajasthan desert prevented the conquerors from pushing eastward and in later centuries an alternative land route via Persia and Afghanistan had to be found.

In the tenth century the fabled riches of India fired the imagination of the world and envious eyes turned towards the plains between the Jumna and Ganga rivers. Between 1001 and 1026, Maḥmūd of Ghaznī made seventeen raids into India from his capitals of Ghaznī and Qal'ah-i Bust in present day Afghanistan. The conquerors managed to subjugate some Rājpūt rulers of north-west India, penetrating as far as Varanasi in the east. In his drive for the bigger spoils of the city of Mathura, birthplace of the god Krishna, where supposedly legendary idols of gold and sapphire awaited, Maḥmūd skirted Thomar Delhi, continually returning to Lahore, the Ghaznavid capital in India in the eleventh century. From there he managed in 1026 to sack and loot the fabled shrine of Somnatha in Saurashtra on the west coast of India. To the Ghaznavids India was mainly a source of booty and wealth to enrich their coffers and the raids only stopped when the Seljuq Turks finally took Ghaznī in 1038.

The Ghūrīds who next overran Hindustan at the end of the twelfth century were Afghan highlanders with their capital at Jam, in an inaccessible central region of Afghanistan. Their zeal carried them west and east, finally absorbing the remnants of the Ghaznavid Empire. In 1175, Muḥammad, brother of the ruler of Ghūr, annexed Sind and Punjab. In 1191 the conquerors thrust into the plain of Hindustan. The turning point from exploitation to settlement came in 1192, when Muḥammad defeated Prithviraj Chauhan, the last Rājpūt ruler of Ajmer and Delhi on the battlefield of Tarain and made Delhi the centre of Muslim India. The battle of Tarain was one of the major turning points of the early medieval history of India because, at last, a Muslim over lordship was established in Qila-i-Rai Pithora, the Hindu stronghold. Quṭb al-Dīn Aybak, a general raised and elevated to rank by Muḥammad, was left in charge when the ruler returned to Lahore. The campaigns of Aybak were soon to cut across the entire subcontinent. By 1200 Ghūrīd military outposts had been set up and fort commandants appointed from Benares to Punjab and to Gujarat. Only Bihar and Bengal, ruled by the renegade Ikhtiyār al-Dīn Muḥammad bin Bakhtiyār, a Khaljī Turk from Ghūr, remained outside this new empire.

Quṭb al-Dīn was the real builder of the first Muslim empire in Delhi, although his master, Muḥammad Ghūrī, continued to visit India until his death in 1206. When the Ghūrīd ruler was removed from the scene, Quṭb al-Dīn declared himself independent in Lahore and became the first Muslim sultan of Delhi.

The rulers of the Delhi Sultanate used the title of "sultan," which they borrowed from Maḥmūd of Ghaznī, who had assumed the title when declaring his independence from the Samanīds. It had been conferred on Maḥmūd by the Caliph of Baghdād. The Shannsabani ruler of Ghūr, 'Alā' al-Dīn Ḥusayn, was the first of that line to call himself sultan when he stopped paying tribute to the Seljuq Turks in 1152. His nephews, Ghiyāth al-Dīn and Mu'izz al-Dīn, became joint rulers after the final occupation of Ghaznī in 1173. Both used the title "sultan." Under Mu'izz al-Dīn the Ghūrīds conquered northern India (1192-1206). While the newly independent Delhi Sultanate was considered legally a part of the Eastern Caliphate, it was always an independent state and was never conquered by the Caliph or in his name. In reality the Delhi Sultanate was never actually an imperial state, such as the later Mughal Empire. As before, it was a conglomeration of various provinces, where political and military power depended on the capabilities of the individual ruler.

The real importance of Quṭb al-Dīn's brief reign (1206-10) lies in the fact that an independent Turkish political authority, cut off from Afghanistan, was established in India. But Quṭb al-Dīn was not able to become master of all the Turkish territory in northern India and had to leave Bengal and Bihar to Bakhtiyār Khaljī.

The day Quṭb al-Dīn conquered Delhi a new chapter in the history of Hindustan began. All felt the impact of the new culture and religion which was to remain dominant for the next six centuries. The Hindus were reduced to tributary status under the rule of the new dynasty. Quṭb al-Dīn, the most successful of all the commanders of Muḥammad of Ghūr, was appointed governor and placed in charge of his master's conquests in India. But the premature and unexpected death of the Ghūrīd ruler prevented the nomination of a successor. Foremost among Ghūrīd officers, Quṭb al-Dīn seized the throne with the support of the nobles of Lahore, then the centre of Islam in India. The newly formed empire laid the foundations for the establishment of Muslim power in northern India. Five Muslim dynasties ruled in Delhi from 1206 to 1526, but eventually they were supplanted by a new group of invaders from the west, the Mughals.

Merciless to their enemies and tyrannical overlords to their subjects yet, paradoxically, like the great Tīmūr whose hordes were to threaten the very gates of their capital within two centuries, these harsh rulers revelled in constructing monuments which may be listed among the finest and most civilized in the entire Muslim world. Everywhere throughout their realm, they have left eloquent records of their power.

At length in 1206 India had a Muslim sultan of its own, ruling not from an outside capital but from Delhi. Muḥammad Ghūrī's viceroy, Quṭb al-Dīn Aybak, was the first of thirty-four Muslim sultans who ruled in India from the beginning of the thirteenth century to the invasion of Bābur in 1526. These thirty-four rulers fall into five successive dynasties: the so-called Turkish Slave dynasty, descended from Aybak the slave of Ghūrī; the Afghan Khaljīs; the Tughluqs; the Sayyids who claimed Arabian descent from the Prophet; and the Lodīs, the last dynasty to rule a much diminished realm until its defeat by the Mughal Emperor Bābur on the field of Panipat in 1526.

The caste system had accustomed Indians to immovable barriers between classes and in a way the new conquerors formed a new caste of Islam, a brotherhood based on equality. The great power of Islam as a missionary influence, especially among the lowest in the caste structure of India, has been due to the benefits of this new caste system. In Islam there is no class distinction in the sight of God and all are therefore able to advance in both rank and marriage.

The essential unity of all was the chief cause of Muslim success over the Hindu masses they governed. Muslim rule in India was essentially that of an armed camp, within which all are brothers and might call for help to the Islamic community of the west. The solidarity and zeal of the conquerors, added to their great energy, gave the Muslims an enormous superiority over the natives. The Hindu system, which persists to the presentday, depended on birth, race and class, and hence there was no central loyalty to compare to that of the Muslims, who, inspired by the spirit of adventure and by the word of Allah, had every advantage.

The slave system in the East has produced some great men, slaves who have often proved the equals of their masters. The slave, the most fit to have survived, was chosen for his mental and physical abilities. If ever his great effort for survival relaxed, he would certainly be ousted. The Seljuq and Mamluk systems in Anatolia and Egypt bred equally strong slaves, as did the empire of Muḥammad Ghūrī in India. Quṭb al-Dīn Aybak was only one of the superior results. Brought as a child from Turkestan to Khūrāsān, he was educated by his new owner and sent in a merchants caravan to Ghaznī, where he was purchased by Muḥammad Ghūrī.

In the last decade of the twelfth century Aybak conquered Delhi (1191) Benares (1194), Gwalior (1196), and Anhalwara (1197) with the kingdom of Gujarat falling under his power. At the same time Muḥammad Bakhtiyār, a fellow commander, who carried the Muslim banner across Bihar into Bengal and made Lakhnautī his capital, brought his spoils to the great viceroy. Aybak and Bakhtiyār had completed the conquests of Muḥammad Ghūrī and nearly all of Hindustan north of the Vindhya range was now under Muslim rule.

Aybak survived his master only a few years and his rule ended in 1210 when he died from a fall from a horse while playing polo. A time of confusion followed with rivals appearing on the scene who held Multān, Sind, Lahore, Bengal and Bihar. Shams al-Dīn Iltutmish, a slave of Aybak, seized the Delhi throne and became the true founder of the Slave dynasty, which Aybak did not live long enough to consolidate. Iltutmish, a Turk from Alkbariu, had been taken to Ghaznī in his youth. He was purchased by Aybak, brought to Delhi and made captain of the guard, and later, in 1196 Governor of Gwalior.

The new rule however did not start well. The hordes of Genghis Khān began to threaten all of Asia causing widespread turmoil. But as quickly as these hordes had appeared, they withdrew focusing their attention westwards. Iltutmish marched into Bengal in 1225 and with the submission of Mālwā in 1234, all of India north of the Vindhyas was in his hands.

In 1229 the Caliph of Baghdād sent an embassy of state to invest Iltutmish with the robe of office as recognized sovereign of India, allowing the new ruler to now strike his own coins. Iltutmish was the first to introduce a purely Arabic coinage, such as had been used in Muslim countries further west.

For ten years, after the death of Iltutmish in 1236, the country suffered from the weakness and depravity of his sons. Finally his daughter, Raziyat al-Dīn, was chosen to succeed to the throne and she became sultan. But the rule lasted for only three years (1236-1240) and Raziyat was deposed by a corps of Turkish mamluks known as The Forty, who were convinced that no woman could or should be sultan.

Once again another remarkable slave rescued the state. The reins of power fell into the hands of Balban, a Turk of the same district as Iltutmish, who was kidnapped and brought to India and purchased by the sultan. Balban became a distinguished officer and a member of The Forty and soon emerged as the guiding spirit of Muslim rule, the real holder of power. For twenty years he served the sultan, until 1266, when Naṣīr al-Dīn died and the minister stepped into his shoes.

Balban's one absorbing preoccupation was the danger of a Mongol invasion. To this end he disciplined the army to the highest point of efficiency. He was never tempted by distant campaigns and, when he died in 1267, Delhi lost one of the most striking figures among the many notable men in the long line of its Delhi rulers.

Besides the Turks who had held most of the offices of state since the days of Aybak, there was a large number of adventurers of other races in the service of the slave sultans. Many of these were Afghans or a mixture of Turks and Afghans, known as Pathans, a term for white men from the north-west mountains. The clan of Khaljīs, named after an Afghan village, had conquered Bengal and held many other posts. They now formed a strong party and rallied around Jalāl al-Dīn Khaljī, and on the death of Balban the Khaljīs seized power and placed Jalāl al-Dīn on the throne. The Khaljī dynasty managed to survive for thirty years, and included six sovereigns, amongst them 'Alā' al-Dīn, whose reign of twenty years contributed powerfully to the extension of the Muslim dominion in India.

'Alā' al-Dīn, Jalāl al-Dīn's nephew, assumed the throne in 1296, after slaying his uncle. The historian Baranī writes that 'Alā' al-Dīn, despite his successes, never did escape retribution for the blood of his uncle and could not trick fate, and, in due course, would destroy the Khaljī line. 'Alā' al-Dīn ruled vigorously for twenty years, from November, 1296, when he entered Delhi unopposed and seated himself on the throne. Foremost a soldier, he knew how to command an army, having already made conquests in the Deccan. No Muslim ruler had hitherto dared venture into southern India, the land of the Marathas, seat of ancient monarchs and strange tongues. In 1294 the sultan carried his force to Devagiri, capital of the Maratha raja which he took unresisted. The Muslims had made their first step into the Deccan The way to the south, now opened, was never again closed.

In Delhi 'Alā' al-Dīn settled himself in his new palace—fortress of Sīrī, one of the royal suburbs emerging around the capital. He repaired and added to the forts of Delhi, and resumed his conquests, reducing Ranthambor and Chittor before turning to the Deccan. The northern part of the Deccan now acknowledged the suzerainty of Delhi.

When 'Alā' al-Dīn died in 1316 the hope of Muslims centered on one man, Ghiyāth al-Dīn Tughluq, the man who had defended the frontiers against the Mongols since the great days of 'Alā' al-Dīn's victories, even routing the enemy in a score of battles. Ghiyāth al-Dīn placed himself at the head of all that was left of the old nobility and set out from his frontier post to save Delhi and become the first ruler of a new dynasty.

Disorder followed 'Alā' al-Dīn's death in 1316 and peace only returned in 1321 with the accession of Muḥammad, the second ruler of the Tughluq dynasty. The new sultan appeared to have everything in his favour. He had a fine reputation as a great general, having recovered the distant provinces of the Tughluq dominions lost during the previous reign. Yet, in 1351, at the end of his reign, the vast Tughluq realm which had once extended from Delhi to Lahore in the north and to Dvārasamudra and Mabar in the south, comprising a total of 23 provinces, had been reduced considerably. The people, the nobility and the religious orders had withdrawn their support and all looked with longing for a change of regime.

One of the chief causes of the Tughluq decline was Muḥammad's decision to act on his idea that his territory could no longer be ruled from the northern administrative centre. In 1327 he decided to move his capital from Delhi to a more southerly position. Deogir, renamed Daulatābād, became the focus of these new plans and nobles and officers alike were impelled to emigrate and to settle there.

The next ten years the sultan spent between the two capitals and during this time the land appeared to be stable and prosperous. This was the opinion of Ibn Battūtā, the Moorish traveller when he came to India in 1333. The calm was the superficial lull before the storm which the foreigner did not perceive, but which the sultan definitely sensed. Believing the cause of the unrest to be the loss of central authority, Muḥammad suddenly ordered the return of all nobles and civil servants to the old capital.

The ferocious tyranny of Muḥammad Tughluq drove his subjects to rebellion in all quarters of the realm. In 1347 the large unwieldy Tughluq Empire disintegrated. In the early years of his reign Muḥammad Tughluq had ruled a state wider, larger and more splendid than any of his predecessors. The name and titles of Muḥammad Tughluq shimmered on the coins of Delhi, Āgrā, Daulatābād, Warangal, Lakhnautī, Satgaon and Sonargaon in Bengal. A contemporary writer gives a list of twenty-three provinces subject to the sultan of Delhi, from Siwistan, Uchh, Multān and Gujarat, by the Indus, to Lakhnautī in Bengal and Jajnagar in Orissa, and from Lahore near the Himalayas to Dvārasamudra and the Malabar coast. Never again until the time of Aurangzīb did a ruler of Delhi hold so wide a sway. But piece by piece all dropped away, and one province after another revolted. Although the sultan was usually victorious and punished the rebels without mercy, he could not be everywhere at once, and while one insurrection was being crushed, another sprang up at the other end of his dominions. Some were never suppressed and Bengal and the Deccan were lost irrevocably.

Bengal had first been conquered by Muḥammad Bakhtiyār Khaljī in 1204 and between the initial appearance of Islam and 1338 was ruled by governors of the Delhi Sultanate from their capital of Lakhnautī, in the Delta's northwestern corner. Eastern Bengal remained a political and social frontier zone. Prior to 1338, while Bengal was still ruled as a province of Delhi, Muslim armies had consolidated their grip over much of the Delta, with their provincial capital at Lakhnautī (later called Gaur) and regional capitals at Satgaon and Sonargaon. The expansion of Muslim political power in early Bengal is reflected in the growth of towns where coins were struck; after Lakhnautī, Sonargaon and Satgaon, there were Pandua (1339), Mu'azzamābād (1358), with towns being added in the fifteenth and sixteenth centuries.

Not for long did Bengal remain a mere appendage of Delhi. In 1338 Fakhr al-Dīn revolted against imperial power, declared his independence and became the first Ilyās Shāhī ruler, inaugurating a tradition of independence that lasted until the Mughal conquest in 1576.

In 1347 the amirs of the Deccan successfully revolted against the authority of Muḥammad Tughluq. They elected as their leader Ḥasan Gangu, entitled Zafar Khān, an energetic Persian adventurer who had distinguished himself at the Delhi court and taken a prominent part in the uprising. On ascending the throne of the Deccan, Ḥasan assumed the title 'Alā' al-Dīn Bahmān Shāh and chose Gulbarga, which he had held as *jāgīr* from the Delhi sultan, as capital.

Another province in the northern part of the country attained independence sometime during the reign of Muḥammad Tughluq. Kashmīr had been ruled by a long succession of Hindu and Tartar princes, since the earliest recorded history to the beginning of the fourteenth century. Sometime around 1340 the territory fell into the hands of a Muslim adventurer and from that time on was held by independent Muslim princes until Akbar's invasion in 1586 and the final annexation of the northern land to the Mughal empire a year later.

Too late Muḥammad Tughluq obtained the sanction of the Abbāsid Caliph of Cairo to his title of sultan of India. Even the mantle and diploma of investiture he received in 1343 from the Caliph of Baghdād was in vain. Nothing could restore the loyalty of the people or their governors. The end came while the sultan was quashing an insurrection in Gujarat and Sind, on his way to Thatta.

The death of Muḥammad Tughluq in 1351 for a time halted further dismemberment. A troubled but relieved nation elected his 45-year-old cousin Fīrūz Shāh to the throne. Fīrūz, the son of a Hindu mother, had inherited a religiously inclined disposition abhorring war and being content to ignore the insurrecting provinces, expended little effort to recover them. The Deccan was allowed to become independent under Ḥasān Bahmān, who ruled all the provinces south of the Vindhyas range. Bengal also remained independent, although Fīrūz Tughluq attempted twice to bring it back under subjection, in 1353 and again six years later.

The Arabs had been expelled from Sind in 750 and until the end of the twelfth century it remained in the hands of the Sumra Rājpūts who held fast until, with the end of the line, the land fell into the hands of another Rājpūt tribe, the Sammas. From about the twelfth century onwards the Hindu leaders paid tribute to Muslim overlords, first to Shahāb al-Dīn Ghūrī and then to his successors. In 1361 Fīrūz Tughluq tried to annex Thatta and to consolidate the realm where his predecessors had failed, but famine and illness foiled his plans and after the ensuing battle with the independent Samma Jam of Sind, Fīrūz retreated to Gujarat from where, after a six months hault, he attempted a second successful invasion. The captive Jam was brought to Delhi, leaving the power of Sind in the hands of his son who succeeded to the throne. This was the only victorious exploit of the reign of the gentle Tughluq ruler.

The Sammas thereafter were converted to Islam and kept the reigns of power, until they in turn were expelled by the next rulers, the Arghuns. When Akbar succeeded to the throne he tried to recover the lost territory of the former Delhi Sultanate. In 1592 he was successful in lower Sind with the capture of the key town of Sehwan.

The remaining years of the reign of Fīrūz were uneventful politically, and the sultan left the headaches of governing to his very able minister, Khān-i Jahān, who thus held power until his death in 1371. Tragedy struck again with the death three years later of the heir-apparent, the prince Fath Khān. For the rest of his life, a saddened and severely grieving sultan then surrendered all authority into the hands of his late minister's son, the second Khān-i Jahān.

The long reign of Fīrūz Tughluq which only ended in 1388 with his death had not strengthened the crown. And in the last decade of the fourteenth century, during the minority of his son, Maḥmūd, the last Tughluq sultan, Jaunpūr, Gujarat and Mālwā proclaimed their independence.

Jaunpūr was formed of the territory on the Ganges from Bengal to the centre of Oudh. And here Khaja Jahān, vizier at the time of Maḥmūd's accession, declared his independence in 1394. Four of his family followed in succession, all preoccupied with the wars they continually waged against Mālwā and Delhi. In 1476 Bahlol Lodī restored the province briefly to Delhi, but it was conquered shortly thereafter by Bābur, and then by Sher Shāh. With the fall of the Sūr dynasty, Jaunpūr passed through various other hands until finally conquered by Akbar early in his reign.

The territory of the rulers of Gujarat, though rich, was small, and surrounded by forests, hills, predatory tribes and political enemies. But, despite these obstacles, Gujarat became one of the most powerful provincial dynasties. Twice its rulers marched successfully against Mālwā and in 1531 annexed the territory. The rulers of Mewar were frequently defeated and Chitor, their famous capital fell. A supremacy over Khandesh was established in 1399 and the rulers of Aḥmadnagar and Berār were forced to pay homage. Although Humāyūn occupied Gujarat in the ensuing confusion, the province succeeded in regaining its independence which it did not again lose until Akbar's occupation in 1572.

Ten years after the death of Fīrūz a storm burst which bent and finally broke the Delhi Sultanate. During those ten years Delhi was ruled by incompetent sultans and when Tīmūr attacked with his "ninety-two regiments of a thousand horse each" it had no chance to survive. An advanced force under Pīr Muḥammad, Tīmūr's grandson, descended upon the Indus at the close of 1397 and besieged Multān. Tīmūr followed and on 17 December 1398, the conqueror crossed the Jumna. In the ensuing battle the Indian army was routed and crushed and finally fled to the mountains. The victory was complete and Tīmūr pitched his camp by the Tomb of Fīrūz. But the world conqueror continued his plunder for only another two months and by March, 1399, he departed as quickly as he had appeared. But Delhi would not again regain her old ascendancy until the days of the Mughal Empire.

One of Fīrūz Shāh's fief-holders, Dilāwar Khān, a descendant of the Ghūrī rulers, made himself independent in Mālwā in 1401 during the confusion that followed Tīmūr's invasion. He extended his authority over the greater part of the ancient Hindu kingdom of Mālwā, which had up to now been more or less subject to the ruler of Delhi. Dilāwar's successors founded the capital, Māṇḍū, and ruled from there until its annexation to Gujarat in 1531. Mālwā was engaged in frequent wars with all its neighbours in Hindustan and the Deccan. The most remarkable event in its history was the ascendancy of a Hindu at court who eventually usurped all the powers of state, and was only deposed when the sultan of Gujarat came to the rescue of his fellow Muslim.

When Sultan Maḥmūd died in Delhi in 1412 there was no Tughluq successor to follow. The government was conducted by the Lodī amīr Daulat Khān, but neither he nor his successors made any assumption of royal title. Khizr Khān, founder of the Sayyid dynasty supposedly descended from the Prophet Muḥammad, also made no further royal pretension and contented himself in being Tīmūr's deputy in Hindustan.

The history of the four Sayyid rulers consisted mainly in perpetual struggles to retain the remaining feeble control of the small territory still attached to the Delhi Sultanate. The murder of Khizr's successor, Mubārak Shāh, led to further anarchy and paved the way for the accession in 1451 of the Afghan, Bahlol Lodī, the first ruler of a new line, which for a time restored something of the faded splendour of Delhi.

The rest of India was split into numerous independent states. Petty rulers held the land to within a few miles of Delhi to the south. There were independent chiefs in the doab and the Biana, and Hindu rajas at Kampila and Patiala and in other places which formerly belonged to the Delhi Sultanate. Of the Muslim dynasties only a few distinguished themselves: Bengal, the Deccan, Mālwā, Gujarat, and for a time Jaunpūr, Sind, and Kashmīr.

Chapter 2

Architectural Forms

Islamic architecture in India falls into three broad phases. To the first belong the monuments erected by and for the patronage of the five Muslim dynasties which ruled Delhi from the assumption of power by Quṭb al-Dīn Aybak until the Mughal conquest: the so-called Slave dynasty (1206-90), the Khaljīs (1290-1321), the Tughluqs (1321-1414), the Sayyids (1414-44) and the Lodīs (1451-1526). To this period also belongs that short but brilliant postscript, the rule of the Afghan Sūr dynasty (1440-55) which interrupted the rule of the second Mughal emperor, Humāyūn. New cities built mostly in the Tughluq period like Daulatābād, Hissār and Jaunpūr, spread the Delhi Sultanate style beyond the capital and had a lasting effect especially on the Sharqīs of Jaunpūr and the Bahmānīs of the Deccan. These and other monuments constructed by other Muslim provinces, often originally ruled by governors appointed by the Delhi sultans, but which later declared their independence, formed the second phase. This distinctly separate development is known as provincial architecture. To the third phase belong the monuments of the Mughal emperors who, by the end of the sixteenth century had united northern India, finally conquering the last independent provincial Sultanates, Bījāpūr and Golkondā in the Deccan, in 1686 and 1687. The monuments of the Delhi and Muslim provincial sultans, those belonging to the first two phases, are collectively known as Sultanate architecture.

Initially, during the early period, Islamic monuments in India were constructed from the material of demolished Hindu and Jaina temples. This reshuffling of demolished elements lasted about thirty years and during this time the Muslim overlords adopted a purely makeshift and temporary building technique. As construction methods improved, mosques, tombs and other monuments were planned and built with newly-quarried material, manufactured and ornamented as necessary.

The Hindu workman was much in evidence. Pointed ogee-shaped arches, built in the indigenous overlapping corbel technique appear everywhere. Spaces were spanned by means of beams laid horizontally in the Hindu trabeate or post-and-beam method. The Muslim method of bridging spaces with true arches was finally adopted, albeit slowly, only during the Khaljī dynasty in the thirteenth century. The appearance of the arch in Islamic architecture can be traced to an early contact with the buildings of the Roman period. And with it came the use of a new material, hitherto unknown in India, the cementing agent, mortar. Once the arch had been mastered, it was only one further step to construct hemispherical rather than conical domes as used in temple *śikharas.* And yet, curiously enough, some Islamic structural forms were only rarely used in India. For instance, the barrel vault and the *īwān* form were almost totally ignored except for a few isolated cases which were inspired by foreign examples.

In Persian vault construction, centering was rarely if ever used. Instead a quick-setting gypsum plaster found favour. While this method worked successfully on Iranian brick vaults it could not so easily be transplanted to India and stone construction.

It must also be kept in mind that especially during the early Sultanate period Islamic monuments were built by Hindu artisans. But, whereas Hindu religious monuments were generally built communally, by groups and not individuals, each member contributing what he could, in the Islamic world building was a more private and individual affair. The Hindu mason had to adjust to a new set of circumstances while the Muslim patron, in turn, was forced to modify his demands and to utilize in a positive way the superior skill of the local workers. The balance was not easily found but eventually the Muslim patron demanded more carved surfaces and fewer soaring internal members. A compromise had been reached between the ability of the native builders and the requirements of the Islamic patron.

The types of buildings built during the Sultanate period in India include both religious and secular examples, the former being much the more important. The religious structures include mosques, tombs, *madrasas* (schools), *dargāhs* (shrines), and *khānqāhs* (monasteries). In that part of India where the ruler was a Shī'ā Muslim rather than a more dominant Sunnī, buildings especially constructed for the use of this sect, *āshūrkhānas* and *ta'allum* were built. The few secular structures which remain are mostly palaces. In India, unlike most of the rest of the Islamic world, there is no evidence that caravanserais were ever built.

During the early centuries of Islam the mosque became more than merely a place for prayer. Mosques were centres of community life and nearly all activities were conducted there. Often schools were attached, as were rooms for travellers known as *sarāīs*. Mosques were also used as courts of justice and were, in fact, the centre of religious and secular life.

But a mosque is primarily a religious building for the performance of daily prayers, one of the five pillars of Islam. It is thus the most important building for Muslims. The plan of the mosque as developed in the earliest mosques in India was maintained throughout the centuries with relatively minor changes.

Early mosques in India were generally built along traditional Islamic lines: an hypostyle plan, a large open court surrounded by colonnades, the prayer hall facing Ka'ba (in India to the west) of greater depth than the other three. In the middle of the *qibla* wall facing Ka'ba is a niche, the *miḥrāb*, indicating the direction of prayer. In the open court there is generally a fountain for ablutions. But a new somewhat advanced plan was introduced during the reign of Muḥammad Tughluq in the fourteenth century. While the Begampūr Mosque is built in an hypostyle plan, it also has four typically Iranian *īwān*, one in the centre of each courtyard side. This four-*īwān* plan was later to become important in the mosques of Jaunpūr.

Other mosques were built in different plans. For instance, a series of mosques remain from the reign of Fīrūz Shāh Tughluq, the work of his minister Khān Jahān. All have high walls around the court, arcades of arches on the interior and a number of small domes. None have minarets. The stonework is rough with no ornament, only a coat of plaster. All have arch-and-beam doorways. The interior cloisters are formed of square bays each roofed by a dome.

Two mosques built for different patrons define another mosque type, the two-storeyed plinth mosque, standing on a substructure of arches, where worship took place in the upper storey. In addition to the half-ruined mosque in the Kotilā Fīrūz Shāh, the Kalān Mosque also follows this plan.

A third type of Tughluq mosque is in a cruciform or cross-axial plan, representing a striking, shortlived innovation. The earliest example of this type is the Khirkī Mosque, a very large monument in the south-eastern part of Jahānpanāh. A second mosque built in 1370-7, the Kālī Mosque in the Dargāh of Niẓām al-Dīn, completes this series.

In Tughluq Delhi and elsewhere in the provinces, a number of mosques consist simply as prayer halls, occasionally with one or two projecting arcades partially enclosing an open courtyard. Some such mosques were built under the patronage of Fīrūz Shāh Tughluq, such as the Mosque of Makhdūm Shāh Ālam at Wazīrābād.

Yet more an unusual plan was developed in Gulbarga in 1367 where the Jāmi' Mosque has no courtyard, the entire structure is merely covered by a series of domes, sixty-three over the centre, four medium-sized ones over the corners, and one larger stilted dome on a square clerestory over the *miḥrāb.* Although the plan of the Gulbarga Mosque was eventually discarded, some of its innovations were incorporated into mosques in Delhi, Bīdar and Bījāpūr.

Not all mosques are used for congregational prayer. *'Īdgāhs* or wall mosques, used primarily on the two 'Īd festivals, have no enclosed courtyard. Other non-congregational mosques follow another plan: single or double aisled, with three, six or more bays and no courtyard. In Bījāpūr, in the Deccan, there is even a mosque located on the upper storey of a *sarāī* and another, actually two-storeyed, intended for prayer on both levels.

In the early centuries of Islam it was forbidden to glorify a grave by constructing a building over it. All men were considered equal in death and any veneration of tombs was thought to derive from improper Christian and Jewish habits. But eventually in the Islamic world great tombs were regarded the prerogative and duty of the ruler, a personal statement of his power, personality and taste. Islam conveyed this notion to India where the tomb became eventually one of the most popular and lasting results of the personality cult.

When the Muslims invaded India in 1192 all parts of the Islamic world already had some mausolea. The conquerors were therefore able to introduce tomb construction into India. A tomb in India usually consists of a single-domed chamber in the centre of which is the cenotaph. The mortuary chamber with the grave in the middle is on a lower floor, beneath the cenotaph. In small tombs a niche, the *miḥrāb* in the middle of the western wall marks the direction of Ka'ba, but in larger monuments mosques are often attached as separate buildings.

Most of the early tombs in Delhi are square with thick sloping walls, flat domes and corner finials. There is at least one most unusual funerary monument in this early period. The Tomb of Sultan Gharī has an octagonal underground chamber with a roof projecting in the centre of the courtyard. The *miḥrāb* in the west wall below the dome is preceded by a small columned prayer area. In Tughluq times the octagonal Tomb of Khān Jahān in Niẓāmuddīn served as a precedent for later Lodī tombs. During this time began that proliferation of tombs which characterizes later Sultanate architecture under the Sayyids and Lodīs, ending with the splendid Mughal tombs which became the most important structure of Islamic architecture in India.

Scattered throughout Delhi there are also canopied tombs, a dome supported on six, eight, ten or twelve pillars. This plan served as a model for some later Gujarātī and Sindhī tombs.

In the Sayyid and Lodī periods the mausoleum became all important. In plan these funerary monuments were either octagonal and surrounded by an arched verandah or square with a façade of two or three storeys of blind arches. Many fine mausolea were built in Delhi following both these plans but the most splendid examples are in Sassaram, capital of Shīr Shāh Sūr in Bihar, where a series of octagonal tombs show the final development of the Lodī style.

In the provinces tombs are generally square in plan with regional variations. For instance, in Aḥmadābād Gujarat the Tomb of Aḥmad has projecting porticos on the sides, the one on the south entrance. In plan the tomb chamber is surrounded by a pillared aisle and four square corner rooms. An original feature was the use of perforated stone screens to join the pillars. But in this western part of India tomb construction did not evolve along the lines set out by the conquerors. By the mid-fifteenth century at Sarkej, the tomb of Shaykh Aḥmad Khattrī is composed of a dome supported on twelve pillars, as earlier in Delhi, with four concentric aisles of slender pillars on each side, roofed by smaller domes. Nor are there any minarets on this purely indigenous monument.

Other plans were also followed in tomb construction. In Bīdar the Bahmānī sultans experimented with an undomed octagonal shell around a square tomb built for the Saint Hazrat Khalīl Allāh. There is also a true octagonal fifteenth-century tomb in Holkondā known as the Tomb of Dilāwar Khān. This is the only domed octagonal tomb erected before the sixteenth century, when in Golkondā, Jamshīd Qulī, the second Quṭb Shāhī ruler, was buried in an octagonal tomb. It has been suggested[1] that the Tomb of Dilāwar Khān is a tomb tower such as may be found in all parts of Iran. The Barīdī sultans, who succeeded in Bīdar, built a series of memorial structures which followed a plan with an arched opening on each side.

The 'Ādil Shāhīs of Bījāpūr built tombs with single or double arcades surrounding the square tomb chamber. In addition a plan was developed in which the mosque and tomb are placed together on a plinth with an ablution tank. These ensembles are known as *rawzas.*

Institutions for the teachings of various Sunnī rites, *madrasas,* sprang up in the ninth and tenth centuries, primarily to fight the Shī'ā heresy. They first appear in the lands of the Seljuq Turks and in Egypt, in the parts of the Islamic world where orthodox religious education was at that time most needed. In eastern Islamic lands *madrasas* spread in the wake of the Seljuqs, who had probably learned the art of proselytizing from Buddhist and Nestorian Christian neighbours in their Central Asian homeland. The Turks brought with them to the west an ardent desire to use the *madrasas* for teaching purposes. And from their inception, therefore, *madrasas* were propaganda platforms for the Sunnī religion. Men trained in the traditional doctrines of Islam became the bulwark through which orthodox Islam intended to fight the new popular movement. The *'ulamā* with the help of the *madrasas,* was thus able to hold the Sunnī community together.

No standard plan appears to have evolved for *madrasas* in India. Fīrūz Shāh Tughluq built a *madrasa* in Delhi consisting of a range of low rooms along the southern side of Hauz Khās tank. But the exceptional Madrasa of Maḥmūd Gāwān in Bīdar resembles Tīmūrīd *madrasas* in Khūrāsān and Transoxiana. The plan consists of four *īwān* axially placed in the centre of the forecourt façades. Each *īwān* is flanked by cells and living rooms for teachers and students in three storeys.[2]

[1]E. Schotten Merklinger, "Seven Tombs at Holkonda: A Preliminary Classification," *Kunst des Orients,* vol. X, no. 1/2, p. 195.

[2]E. Schotten Merklinger, "The Madrasa of Maḥmūd Gāwān," *Kunst des Orients,* vol. XI, no. 1/2, p. 153.

Ṣūfism is Islamic mysticism and from about the tenth century it has led men yearning for a personal communication with God away from the strict laws of orthodox Islam. Ṣūfism teaches that to reach God directly it is necessary to awaken the usually dormant intuitive spiritual forces latent in all men, to induce them to "travel the path."

From earliest times ṣūfis have gathered around men endowed with spiritual gifts to form religious orders. There are many ṣūfī orders, all differing in name and in some customs but all agree upon the necessity of submission to a guide or *pīr*.

The orders through which Ṣūfism has been introduced into India have a long history. Early ṣūfī missionaries came with the first Muslim armies over the Khyber Pass. They became very popular with the people and their rulers, serving often as both spiritual and political guides at court.

The oldest of the ṣūfī orders in India is the Chishtīyā which dates back to 1142. Khwājā Mu'īn al-Dīn Chishtī of Sistan came to India with the Ghūrīd invaders in the last decade of the twelfth century and settled in Ajmer, in Rajasthan, where he remained until his death in 1236. His tomb is still an important attraction for pilgrims who come yearly during the time of the *'urs,* the festival which celebrates the death anniversary of the saint.

Spiritual descendants of Khwājā Mu'īn al-Dīn Chishtī have been among the most famous saints of India. Important Chishtī saints include Khwājā Quṭb al-Dīn Bakhtiyār Kākī, whose shrine is near the Quṭb Mīnār in Delhi, Chiragh-i Delhi also buried in Delhi, and Shaykh Niẓām al-Dīn Awliyā buried in the *dargāh* which bears his name.

After the death of a ṣūfī Shaykh he was usually buried in an enclosure known as a *dargāh,* which became a place of pilgrimage on the death anniversary of the saint. Spiritual descendants and disciples of the Shaykh sought to be buried near their master and thus one finds a clutter of tombs and graves about that of the Shaykh. Buildings are often crowded together and it is difficult to get an idea of individual monuments. Many different styles exist side by side, varying in dates. Disciples of the saint have often reconstructed the actual tomb along modern lines. When good examples of architecture do exist, as, for instance, the Jamā'at Khāna Mosque in the Dargāh of Niẓām al-Dīn Awliyā of Delhi, they are often hidden among the surrounding buildings. To add to the confusion, many graves of rulers and courtiers are scattered about, not to mention the many more humble graves which are generally unidentified.

The Dargāh of Niẓām al-Dīn Awliyā in Delhi is probably one of the most famous shrines in India. The saint had a long life, from the reign of Balban to the first year of Muhammad Tughluq (1324). The Jamā'at Khāna Mosque, built by 'Alā al-Dīn Khaljī, is the earliest structure in the *dargāh.* The highly ornate tomb of the saint is of much later date. Buried here are the poet Amīr Khusrau, a contemporary of Niẓām al-Dīn, Jahānāra Begum, daughter of Shāh Jahān, and Jahāngīr, son of Akbar II, the last but one Mughal emperor. *Dargāhs* are found throughout Muslim India.

* * *

Architectural decoration in India was used differently by the indigenous and Muslim builders. For the Hindu ornament is inseparable from the structure while for the Muslim it is a thin veneer grafted on an independent monument. A monument without ornament for the Muslim would have been a strange mixture of reused Hindu and Jaina material. Decoration was therefore needed as the unifying element to give the structure its Islamic character.

In the early Sultanate period indigenous decorative motifs were frequently used by the Muslim builders as an overlay, an exterior method of organizing a particular space. Hindu designs used in this way lost their original meaning.

Islamic ornament consists of a flat motif, its organic nature either abstracted or carefully restricted by geometric enclosures. Yet a surprising number of traditional. Indian motifs were given a new life during the Islamic period. Unlike Iran, India was never completely Islamicized and ancient motifs, therefore, often remained totally unchanged. But to the Hindu these symbols were often full of religious and metaphysical meaning, while the Muslim regarded them as mere ornament.

In a mosque the most decorated areas were those of the greatest religious significance: the *qibla* wall and the *miḥrāb* in particular. Quite in contrast to a Hindu temple where the exterior is richly decorated, the outside of a mosque is generally plain. The mosque interior is often covered in ornament, while the *cella* of a temple, symbolizing higher levels of consciousness, is almost bare.

Script had never been used as ornament on pre-Muslim architecture in India. But in early Islam, Arabic inscriptions became a very important form of decoration. Unlike Iran and the rest of the Islamic world, India had very little *kufic* script in the thirteenth century, wherefrom the beginning *naskh* was used for epigraphical decoration, before its general acceptance in the rest of the Islamic world.

Islamic architecture in India is constructed mainly of dressed stone and it is therefore not surprising that carved stone became the major medium of architectural ornament. This preference for stone both for construction and ornament lasted well into the fourteenth century in Delhi and even longer in the provinces.

In Delhi stone carving is used on the Aybek and the Khaljī screens of the Quwwat al-Islām Mosque, as well as on the Quṭb Mīnār with its splendid inscriptions. But the outstanding feature of this tower of victory is the four beautifully designed balconies supported on stalactite bracketing. Stalactites or *muqarnas* were universally used throughout the Islamic world but rarely in India. The Quṭb Mīnār is the rarely exception to this rule in India. Here are clusters of miniature arches, separated by brackets patterned like honey-combing, or *muqarnas.* It is an enigma as to why this fairly common feature of Islamic architecture elsewhere was almost totally ignored in India.

In Gujarat, in particular, stone ornament is used continually and with great success. Excellent stone carvers worked in Aḥmadābād on such monuments as Aḥmad's Tomb and on the Tomb of the Queens, where the carving of the window screens and blind niches is of a very superior quality. But the finest carving perhaps in all of India is the superb stone tracery in the form of trees and branches in the ten semicircular tympani windows of the sixteenth-century Gujarati Mosque of Siddi Sayyid. From Gujarat this style of ornament spread to various areas of Rajasthan, to Jalor, Jodhpur and to Nagaur where the Shams Mosque has some fine carving.

In other part of Muslim India, as in the Deccan for instance, stone is primarily used for mouldings, columns, *miḥrābs,* screens and *chhajjas* (eaves) and remains throughout largely in Hindu hands. In Bījāpūr, in particular, there is some exquisite stone carving in the façade of the Meḥtar Mahāl gateway. In Bengal the fourteenth-century Adina Mosque in Pandua has a *qibla* wall faced with polished black basalt ashlar masonry delicately carved to three-quarters of its height. In Sind the monuments on Makhli Hill near Thatta, constructed of stone and covered in carved stone designs were probably influenced by the contemporary architecture of Akbar's dominions, such as Fatehpur Sikri near Āgrā. The Tomb of Jam Niẓām al-Dīn has a beautifully carved *miḥrāb* with a richly decorated projection on the exterior.

The use of brick as architectural ornament has a long history and may be traced back to the mid-tenth century, when in the Tomb of the Samanīds, in Bukhārā, bricks were first used to achieve a decorative effect. In Delhi decorative use of brick was not known until after the invasion of Tīmūr, when on the cornice moulding of the Tomb of Mubārak Shāh Sayyid (1434) were used diagonally laid bricks decoratively for the first time.

It is, however, in the eastern province of Bengal, where brick is the most easily available material for construction, that the finest terracotta decoration may be found. Among these are the splendid floral and geometrical patterns carved into the ornamental panels inserted in the upper storey of the Eklakhi Mausoleum (1431) in Pandua. The finest brick relief ornament of all in Bengal, is perhaps the east façade of the Tantipara Mosque in Gaur.

Stucco carving became popular in Delhi only in the middle of the fourteenth century with the accession of Fīrūz Shāh Tughluq, when it was fashionable to finish poor rubble structures by applying a layer of stucco. In India stucco has been used primarily on the exterior of buildings, often merely as a coat of plaster. It was used to decorate archivolts, crenellations, spandrels and *miḥrābs.* However, in Gulbarga in the Deccan in the first half of the fifteenth century two fine examples of the art were built, the anonymous tomb near the early Bahmānī royal tombs and the tympanum of the Langar kī Mosque. There were probably artisans trained in the art of stucco carving in Gulbarga during the first half of the fifteenth century who seemed to understand the possibilities of stucco as a medium and how well it lent itself to express the endless repetitious designs so often found in Islamic art.

The origin of the use of coloured mosaic tiles as decoration is obscure but in Islamic times the technique was revived in Mesopotamia during the days of the Caliphate and was fully developed during Seljuq rule. In the twelfth century the technique had spread to Iran and by the thirteenth century, cobalt blue, turquoise and yellow colours were in use for tiles on inscriptional panels. By the fifteenth century, in Tīmūrīd times, tile decoration virtually dominated the buildings on which it was applied, so that the walls seemed a mere background on which were mounted the colours of the mosaic cutter's palette.

In north India mosaic faience was virtually unknown until after the invasion of Tīmūr at the end of the fourteenth century. On some Delhi monuments of the fifteenth century, the Lodī sultans used tile mosaics for the first time. There is a series of tombs and mosques built by these rulers which made some limited use of the technique: the Shīsh Gumbad, the Barā Gumbad in the Lodī Gardens and the mosque north of the Tomb of 'Īsā Khān near Humāyūn's Tomb.

In Bengal mosaic faience is used on two mosques built in Gaur towards the end of the fifteenth or early sixteenth century. On the Chamkattī Mosque in Gaur (1475), mosaic tile borders are added to decorative panels on the façade. The best preserved example in Bengal is the Lattan Mosque which had the interior walls decorated with a rich display of mosaic faience—mostly blue, white, yellow and green. The exterior was once also covered in tiles.

In south India the technique is used for the first time on the Madrasa of Maḥmūd Gāwān in Bīdar towards the end of the fifteenth century. But this monument is no feeble attempt at a new medium but rather the sudden appearance of a masterfully-worked ornamental style. The colour scheme here is unusually rich: white, yellow, turquoise, light and dark blue, and green. The decoration is in Tīmūrīd style and the whole monument might be classified as a Tīmūrīd monument in India.

The Tomb of 'Alī Barīd in Bīdar marks yet another stage in the development of mosaic faience in India. But the palette here is more limited, mostly white, turquoise and cobalt blue. There are no yellows or greens as on the Madrasa of Maḥmūd Gāwān. It is obvious that the Tomb of Alī Barīd belongs to a different tradition than this great *madrasa.*

In addition to mosaic faience, fitted together to form a whole, each colour fired individually, another technique also appears in India during this time. In Sind, in the Punjab and in Kashmīr different colours were fired together on one tile. In Multān, in the Punjab, tiles are used as early as the thirteenth century but the best preserved example is the Tomb of Shāh Rukh-i Ālam (1320-24) which was originally erected by Ghiyāth al-Dīn Tughluq as his own tomb but later given to the sultan's spiritual guide. The sloping walls are decorated with carved brickwork and coloured and raised tiles in white, dark and sky blue and turquoise.

In Sind there is a type of memorial structure built entirely of brick covered with coloured tiles. Little has survived intact but it appears that the colours used were chiefly two transparent blues, a cobalt and a light turquoise, and white. Sindi tiles were always laid in a flat surface with a binding agent generally cement. Most of the tiles were manufactured in Halla, 35 km north of Thatta. The Tomb of Mīrzā Jānī Beg (1599), the last independent Tarkhan ruler of Thatta, is covered in blue tiles which alternate with unglazed red bricks. The most colourful and best preserved of the brick-and-tile monuments is the Tomb of Dīwān Shurfa Khān (1638), originally covered in light blue tiles.

In the remote valley of Kashmīr in Srinagar a more colourful variation of the Sindī tiles is found. The Tomb of Madanī had some tile work in the spandrels of the east façade which conformed to some of the pre-Mughal Multānī and Sindī types, but differed from the western Indian variety because of the brilliant use of colour—green, blue, red, yellow, white, and brown. Of great interest also is the subject, an adaptation of what appears to be a Saggitarius figure, an animal body with leopard spots, the face and trunk of a human being, shooting with a bow and arrow at its own tail which ends in a dragon's head. The Tomb of Zain al-'Ābidīn's mother is built of brick, with glazed moulded blue tiles studded at intervals in the exterior walls.

Early Indo-Islamic architecture is a combination of Hindu and Islamic forms and ideas. But as Muslim rule progressed, a compromise and balance of the two systems is eventually found. The success of this fusion may only be measured when we realize that India produced more notable Islamic buildings than any other Muslim country.

CHAPTER 3

The Slave Dynasty (1193-1290)

The last Hindu king of Delhi, Pṛthvīrāj, died in the Battle of Tarain in 1191 opposing the advancing armies of Muḥammad Ghūrī. This defeat led to the Ghūrīd rule of northern India and in 1192, to the occupation of Delhi, which became the centre of Muslim India. From legendary times to the Mutiny of 1857, the possession of Delhi has spelt dominion. It was no idle chance that led the British to cling to the Ridge, for they knew, as others before them had known, that rule was theirs only as long as they held fast to these rocky heights. The number of cities which flourished on the banks of the Jumna is not exactly known but among the earliest was Indraprastha, capital of the Pāṇḍavas of *Mahābhārata* fame. When it comes to Muslim cities, our knowledge is not quite as sketchy. The defeat of the Hindu forces in 1191 led to nearly eight-hundred years of Muslim rule in Hindustan, when Delhi was the seat of one Muslim dynasty after another. In 1191 the captured city became the capital of the Delhi Sultanate and Muslim India. Various cities, abandoned one by one, were situated on a broad plain on the west bank of the Jumna until New Delhi was finally built on their old sites.

After the Muslim invasion, Delhi was no longer the small provincial city it had been under Hindu rule. Here and in a few other cities in the north, the Ghūrīds and their successors sponsored the first monumental architecture of the province. Delhi became the headquarters of the army of occupation during the first two centuries of Muslim rule, while the new state attempted to conquer the neighbouring Hindu principalities and to keep the ever-threatening Mongol hordes at bay. By the thirteenth century, after Lahore, the first Ghūrīd capital had been abandoned, Delhi became and remained for nearly four centuries the religious and cultural centre of the great new Muslim empire in Hindustan, as well as its administrative capital and the residence of the court.

The Quṭb is the most remarkable architectural ensemble of the Slave dynasty, so called because the rulers sprang from the royal bodyguard recruited in childhood in the same manner as the famous Turkish Janissaries. Erected for the most part in the thirteenth and fourteenth centuries on the plinth of an older Hindu temple, it is here that the Muslim conquerors left their most powerful record of the might of Islam. From the time of Quṭb al-Dīn Aybak, appointed viceroy of Hindustan when the Ghūrīd armies returned to Afghanistan, the message of the new faith was spread by constructing mighty monuments intended to fill the hearts of all Hindustanis with awe.

As soon as the Ghūrīds settled in India, the building of mosques became the first necessity. The process was simple, temples were dismantled and the stones rearranged to form the elements of a mosque. Why this was done remains a puzzle. In India masons are plentiful and highly trained in their own tradition and could from the start have easily been enlisted to quarry stone to build the new Muslim monuments.

It appears that the earliest Ghūrīd rulers were uncertain of their own tenure of office and were anxious to build at break-neck speed, even if the monuments were not able to withstand time. No thought, apparently, was given to the future, only to the immediate impression the monuments would evoke.

The Quwwat al-Islām Mosque and its surrounding buildings become known as Old Dillī, the first Muslim capital, and are the work of three rulers: Quṭb al-Dīn Aybak, the first Ghūrīd viceroy and subsequently the first sultan of Delhi (1206-11), his son-in-law Shams al-Dīn Iltutmish (1220-36), and 'Alā' al-Dīn Khaljī (1295-1315). With the exception of some later repairs carried out by Fīrūz Shāh Tughluq and Sikandar Lodī, the history of the Quṭb then comes to an end.

The central structure of the entire complex is the Quwwat al-Islām (Might of Islam) Mosque [Ill. 1], which, with the attached tombs and the Quṭb Mīnār is the only monument in Delhi of the Slave dynasty and nearly the only surviving example of the following Khaljī period. The original mosque, the inner court, the surrounding colonnades and the sanctuary, were all built in the last decades of the twelfth century by Quṭb al-Dīn Aybak most probably to celebrate the victory over the Rājpūt forces.

The Quwwat al-Islām Mosque, the earliest mosque of the Sultanate period and the first congregational mosque in Delhi, was built on a temple plinth. An inscription on the eastern gateway bears testimony that the Hindu fort was conquered and the mosque constructed in the year 1191-92 by Quṭb al-Dīn Aybak.[1] Built in the traditional hypostyle plan, the mosque has a rectangular courtyard and surrounding pillared cloisters, those on the north and south two bays deep, on the east three, and the western prayer hall four and is roofed by shallow corbelled domes. Quṭb al-Dīn Aybak built the inner court and surrounding colonnades in 1191 while still Ghūrīd viceroy of Hindustan. Four hundred and seventy Hindu or Jaina pillars from twenty-seven temples were used in the construction of the cloisters around the courtyard. The pillars of differing shapes, sizes and designs were arranged so as best to support the ceiling, even if this meant setting one upon another to achieve the necessary height. The Hindu figural representations were covered with plaster or chipped clean to make them acceptable to the new religion. Islam forbids the destruction of old mosques but allows the dismantling of Jaina, Hindu and Buddhist monuments to obtain building material.

The entrance opposite the sanctuary has generally been the most important in mosque construction and in the Quwwat al-Islām Mosque the builders adhered to this tradition. The city was to the south and for practical reasons the main entrance ought to have been in that direction.[2]

In the centre of Aybak's court stands an iron pillar, one of the most interesting relics of pre-Islamic times. According to the inscription it was built by a fourteenth-century king called Chandra. The question as to why this huge bar of iron, nearly 8 m. in height and weighing over 5000 kg. was placed in the middle of Aybak's court remains unanswered but it appears to have been used as a symbol of Muslim triumph in India.

It soon became obvious that the mere rearrangement of temple spoils did not satisfy the Muslims for long. The mosque had little to indicate its Islamic character. To rectify this work began in 1199 on a great arched façade screen (Ill. 2) to front the

[1] J.A. Page, *Guide to the Qutb*, Delhi, 1938, p. 2.

[2] Anita K. Gold-Pearlroth, "The Formation of Islamic Architecture in India: 1192-1235," unpublished doctoral dissertation, Institute of Fine Arts, New York University, 1976, p. 8.

qibla side of the court. The development of Indian Islamic architecture had started.

Here in the middle of Hindustan a very Iranian tall *īwān* arch flanked by two shorter arches was constructed in the ancient stone corbelling technique of India. Except for the ogee curve at the apex of each arch, the Aybak screen resembles other *maqsūra* screens in the Islamic world.

The need for a façade screen is obvious to hide the Hindu low-pillared sanctuary at the rear and to make the whole scheme appear more Islamic. It has even been suggested that the interior might have been totally hidden from view by screen arches that were each completely closed by a now missing tympanum screen wall and an inset doorway, as in the Cambay Jāmi' Mosque (1325) in Gujarat.[3]

The Aybak screen points to some conflicting ideas. The screen was to be a series of five arches but the indigenous masons had no idea of how to accomplish this structurally. Nor could the Muslim rulers solve the dilemma, their instructions apparently only dealing with the appearance of the final monument. Up to now Indian masons had simply added successive courses of stone in corbelled form and they continued to built such semi-voussoired arches here. This type of construction is not structurally sound and most of the earlier corbelled arches have collapsed.

Attempts at dome building were even less successful. Small corbelled domes were built during the first period of Muslim rule in India. The dome of the Tomb of Iltutmish is an example of one unsuccessful attempt of such an effort on a larger scale.

Decoration on the Aybak screen is sparse and carving appears only on the outer courtyard side. But here the entire surface of the screen is covered with calligraphic and floral designs (Ill. 3) which are naturalistic and Hindu in feeling. For instance, convoluted flower stems may appear as buds or in full-bloom, from various vantage points, an old Indian tradition dating back to the ninth-century ceiling paintings of the Sittanavasal Temple in Tamil Nadu.[4]

Although we associate geometric patterns with Islam, a variety of such designs found on the Aybak screen have a different origin. Gold-Pearlroth has shown that grid patterns and diamond flowers, for instance, had an Indian origin and were found in the ninth century on some pre-Islamic structures such as the "Ath Khamba" (eight pillars) at Gyraspur in Madya Pradesh.

The inscriptional panels of *Qur'ānic* verses written in *naskh* and *tughra* were executed by Hindu craftsmen with little knowledge of Arabic script. The importance of the inscribed quotations lies in the fact that they were used at all. The Aybak screen is the earliest example in India of the use of calligraphy for ornament on a religious monument. Script was never used in pre-Muslim times as ornament and is therefore not found on temple walls.

The Aybak screen, the earliest known monumental corbelled arches, was an Islamic creation introducted into the Quwwat al-Islām Mosque to impress the Hindu and Muslim population of Delhi by its sheer size. The conquerors must also have had in mind, whether consciously or not, the desire to blend the style of the screen with the more Hindu aspects of the rest of the mosque. Whatever their aims might have been, Aybak managed to create an Indian masterpiece full of naturalistic life and movement and able to fit into the dignified and conservative atmosphere of a mosque.

The screen does not yet represent a true synthesis of the Hindu and Muslim styles

[3] Ibid., p. 71.

[4] Ibid., p. 81.

of architecture, but is rather an early attempt by the Indian mason to come to terms with Islamic architectural forms. The Aybak screen influenced the development of mosque construction in many areas of provincial Muslim India. Jaunpur, Gujarat, Mandu and the Deccan Sultanate styles copied the form. Near Delhi two similar screens were commissioned by the next ruler, Iltutmish, one in Ajmer (1217), the other in the Quwwat al-Islām Mosque (1229).

* * *

During the last years of Quṭb al-Dīn Aybak something still more monumental seemed necessary to exalt the growing power and omnipotence of the new faith. In the last years of the twelfth century the foundation of a structure was laid, which, when completed, would become one of the most effective Islamic monuments ever constructed. A tower from which the Muslims may be called to prayer is an important feature of any mosque and although the Quṭb Mīnār is unique, its elements may be traced in later *mīnārs* for more than three-hundred years. The actual design of the Quṭb Mīnār, a cylindrical upper storey on a stellate lower course, comes from the brick towers of Persia such as those of Maḥmūd and Masūd III near Ghaznī. The closest prototype is the great Ghūrīd Mīnār of Jām in the highlands of Afghanistan. The Quṭb Mīnār is an Iranian type adapted to the stone technique of India. But unlike the Jam minaret, the Quṭb Mīnār in its final form represented a double function, that of a *ma'dhana* and a victory tower. There is also the question whether the ultimate purpose of the Quṭb Mīnār was funerary or symbolic. The suggestion first made by von Berchem and later supported by others that the Quṭb Mīnār was originally intended by Aybak to be his tomb-tower and not a *ma'dhana* but that, on his death, after the completion of the first storey, it was converted by Iltutmish into a tower, rests on its close similarity to the tomb-tower of Kishmār in Khūrāsān, perhaps built in the same period. In a convincing analysis of this hypothesis,[5] it has been shown that in the Quṭb Mīnār the structural positioning of a spiral stairway in the interior of the first storey appears to be part of the original plan and not an after-thought. There would thus have been no room for the tomb, whereas in Kishmār and in all the tomb-towers of Persia the grave occupies the centre. Whether the function of the Quṭb Mīnār was funerary or symbolic is still uncertain but there is no doubt that the immense structure proclaimed the might of Islam to the whole world.

In the lands of western Islam minarets are used for the call for prayer.[6] Derived from the Syrian church tower they are generally square or polygonal. In eastern Islamic countries, on the other hand, minarets or *manāra* are usually free standing and cylindrical with or without a square or polygonal lower course. Often they have balconies, which at first were constructed of wood but which later were replaced by stone platforms supported by projecting brackets protruding beyond the cylindrical

[5]A.B.M. Habibullah, *The Foundation of Muslim Rule in India*, Allahabad, 1961, p. 366, n. 19.

[6]The most complete monograph on the minaret is Hermann Tiersche, *Pharos in Antike, Islam and Occident*, Berlin, 1909. There is some other important bibliography: M. von Berchem in E.Diez, *Khurasanische Baudenkmaler*, Berlin, 1918; K.A.C.Creswell, "The Evolution of the Minaret with Special Reference to Egypt," *Burlington Magazine*, vol. XLVIII, 1926, pp.134-40, 252-58, 290-98; E. Diez, *Kunst der Islamischen Volker*, Berlin, 1917, pp. 23-24, 87-88; E. Diez's article, "Manara" in *Encyclopaedia of Islam*, vol. III, Leiden, 1936, pp. 227-31; R.J.H. Gotteil, "The Origins and History of the Minaret," *Journal of the American Oriental Society*, vol. XXX, 1909-10, pp. 132-54; Joseph Schacht, "Eintarchaische Minaret-Typ", *Ars Islamica*, vol. V, 1938, pp. 46-54; "Further Notes on the Staircase Minaret," *Ars Orientalis*, vol. IV, 1961, pp. 137-41. For an entire study on the minaret in India see A.B.M. Husain, *The Manara in Indo-Muslim Architecture*, Dacca, 1970.

drum. Due to their often excessive height these eastern *manāra* are not used for the call to prayer but are rather symbols of Islam. The former western type of minaret is not found in India, where minarets in general are confined to certain areas. In Aḥmadābād, Gujarat, for instance, they are used primarily to flank entrances and facades.

Diez[7] maintains that cylindrical freestanding minarets were evolved from the indigenous wooden tree pillar which became the Buddhist stone pillar of Aśoka's reign (272-232 BC). However, the minaret in eastern Islamic countries is more than just a pillar: it is and has always been a symbol of Islam, a spiritual tower which soars to heaven as a confession of the faith without the human proportions of western minarets, but with an almost unimpeded strength.

Freestanding cylindrical minarets were not built in Persia during early Islamic times, the first known examples are of the eleventh century.[8] The Seljuqs, it appears, brought the *manāra* with them from Central Asia for in shape the Persian examples are not unlike the Qalyan Minaret of Bukhara and other towers of Turkestan. By the twelfth century, the tapering minaret had completely replaced the earlier octagonal and square towers in Iran. This new type of minaret is generally found outside the mosque walls, near the main entrance often opposite the *qibla* wall (the direction of prayer), viz., the Ibn Tulun Mosque, Cairo (876-79) and the mid-ninth century Mosque of al-Mutawakkil at Samarra, which served as its model.

In north India there is only one *manāra* of the freestanding type, the Quṭb Mīnār in Delhi. However it is possible that others were attached to some early Pathan mosques, although there is no literary or archaeological evidence of their existence.

Originally the Quṭb Mīnār[Ill. 4] had four storeys, diminishing in circumference as they ascended, the lower three still in their original form but the fourth a fourteenth century replacement. As seen today the tower is the product of several different building periods and restorations. The lowest stage of twenty-four flutings [Ill. 5], alternating round and angular, was built by Aybak in 1202; the second and third storeys have respectively only round and angular flutings; the fourth and fifth stages[Ill. 6] were built by Fīrūz Shāh to replace an earlier top storey composed of a circular kiosk with domical roof which was apparently struck by lightning. Including the round pavilion at the top, the Quṭb Mīnār was originally 72.5 m. in height and thus the highest freestanding minaret in the Islamic world.

The lowest storey bears an inscription with the name of the first ruler of Delhi, Aybak, and two inscriptions containing the name of his master, Muḥammad Ghūrī [Ill. 7], dating it therefore to about 1202, before Muḥammad's death.[9] The second, third and fourth storeys bear inscriptions with the name of Iltutmish, dating them therefore to some decades after the lowest storey. The top storey has an inscription relating that Fīrūz Shāh in 1367 restored and rebuilt the top upper storeys with original materials.

Four beautifully designed and corbelled balconies supported on stalactite bracketing divide the separate storeys. Stalactite vaulting, although universally applied in other parts of the Islamic world, especially in Persia where it is used in the phase of

[7]*Encyclopaedia of Islam*, vol. III, Leiden, 1936, p. 228.

[8]Arthur Pope, *Survey of Persian Art*, London, 1939, Sanghbast (Plate 260C) and the Jāmi' Mosque, Damghan (Plate 359).

[9]The inscriptions have been fully published most recently by A.B.M. Husain, *The Manara in Indo-Muslim Architecture*, Dacca, 1970, Appendix I, pp. 201-15.

transition of the dome and is called *muqarnas*, is rare in India. In the Quṭb Mīnār the bracketing consists of a cluster of miniature arches separated by brackets patterned like honey-combing. Probably this decoration was constructed from descriptions of true stalactite vaulting such as found in other parts of the Islamic world and was an attempt to reproduce the true geometrical stalactite effect. Wide encircling bands with *naskh* inscriptions provide a handsome relief to the plain fluted red sandstone and grey quartzose of the great *mīnār*.

The Quṭb Mīnār stands outside the enclosure of the original mosque in the southeast corner but within the Iltutmish phase of construction. Being adjacent to the original structure it is in about the same position as the *mīnārs* of some of the most venerated mosques of earlier times—the Mosque of al-Mutawakkil in Samarra, the Mosque of Ibn Tulun in Cairo and the Mosque of Raqqa in Syria, all dating from the eighth-ninth centuries.

The lowest storey doorway faces north, giving it access from the east (main) entrance of the Aybak phase of the mosque. The four upper doorways face west in the direction of the mosque and the site of the early sultanate palace behind it. The arched doorways of the later fourth and fifth storeys have true voussoirs, while the three on the lower levels are built in the corbelled technique.

The lower three storeys are built of grey ashlar quartzite on the interior with rubble and mortar facing. The exterior of the *mīnār* is faced with various shades of sandstone, a pale pinkish-buff on the lower two storeys, a darker red on the third, while the fourth and fifth are a combination of red sandstone and white marble. This is the earliest known use of red sandstone facing in India, a technique to become extremely popular under the later Mughals.

* * *

Quṭb al-Dīn Aybak was succeeded by his son-in-law, Shams al-Dīn Iltutmish, a Turk of the Albari tribe, who enlarged the Quwwat al-Islām Mosque by surrounding and enclosing the older Aybak structure on three sides, extending the *qibla* wall to the north and south and including the Quṭb Mīnār within the walls. The north and south extensions had been roofed each by three corbelled domes now fallen, and each had three *miḥrābs* in the *qibla* wall.

On the south side of the exterior part of a colonnade remains. Similar to the adjoining Aybak work, the pillared cloisters consist of three rows of two bays on the north and south, four rows of three bays on the east and five rows of four bays on the west sides. The more simply carved granite pillars are also raised one on top of the other to attain height.

Iltutmish also extended the arched screen (1229) which in design followed the adjoining Aybak screen. The extant two arches show that the indigenous corbelling technique of construction was also used here. Yet, a change has taken place in the arch shape. The ogee curve has gone and the arch has become more pointed. But the most significant change is in the carved decoration. While the earlier screen had floral and vegetal designs naturalistically rendered, Iltutmish's extension substituted Islamic patterns, the ensuing arabesques and calligraphic designs hardly to be distinguished from ornament in other parts of the Islamic world. Instead of high relief-cut carving there now appears a flat shallow design. The Arabic script is no longer the work of unskilled Hindu masons working in an alien medium, but that of master craftsmen familiar with the intricate characters of the letters [Ill. 8].

The original screen of Sultan Aybak has purely Hindu naturalistic ornament—flowers, buds, vines, in fact foliage of all sorts. Interwoven are quotations from the *Qur'ān*. An Islamic *maqsūra* screen has been made into an Indian monument, an all too brief balancing of two opposing architectural styles which would soon part permanently.

The screen extended by Sultan Iltutmish displays the same leaves, buds and flowers as the Aybak screen but the treatment is entirely different. Nature, seen here in another way, is no longer a copy of the physical world. The artist is now free to compose and recompose the vegetation in anyway he wishes and the resulting composition is known as an arabesque. What could have caused a change of such magnitude in one generation?

The thirteenth century was an age of violence and disruption with Mongol hordes sweeping across Central Asia devastating one Muslim state after another. Even the important artistic and cultural centres of Bukhārā and Samarkand fell in 1212 causing an exodus to parts of the Muslim world relatively safe from the scourge. One such haven was Hindustan and it is precisely this dispersion of religious and artistic forces which nurtured the nascent Muslim state. Among the refugees were many ṣūfīs and their arrival brought to India something of the religious mysticism of western Islam. The mystically inclined Sultan Iltutmish was not immune to the religious fervour surrounding him and soon became a devotee of the great Chishtī saint, Quṭb al-Dīn Bakhtiyār Kākī, whose shrine was a great centre of spiritual activity in thirteenth century Delhi. The great saint never really associated himself with the ruler but extended his moral support in the construction of public works and centres of cultural activity.

In comparing the decoration of the screens of Aybak and Iltutmish a considerable difference is noted. The latter appears to be the work of Central Asian artisans steeped in the Islamic tradition and their underlying ideas as well as the story of their flight is written in the carved ornament. Sultan Iltutmish encouraged the refugee artists for he recognized that they saw life and nature much as he did himself. The spiritually inclined sultan was greatly influenced by holy men and they, in turn, supported him. It is therefore not surprising that the doctrine of the ṣūfīs is also written in the stone. In analyzing the ornament of the two screens of the Quwwat al-Islām Mosque, a new Muslim identity is revealed in the later work and this changing aspect of Islam continued to evolve in Hindustan during the entire thirteenth century.

* * *

One further important structure attributed to Quṭb al-Dīn Aybak is not in Delhi but in Ajmer, Rajasthan, where a congregational mosque was built in 1199 shortly after the Muslim conquest. Known as the Aḍhāī Din kā Jhoṃparā or Two-and-a-Half-Day Mosque, it was probably so named because it was built on the site of an annual fair which lasted that length of time.[10]

Ajmer, capital of the Hindu Chauhan dynasty, was one of the earlier cities captured by Muḥammad Ghūrī. The son of the Chauhan ruler, Pṛthvīrāj, was allowed to govern the city as vassal until 1194, when, after a rebellion by his uncle, a Muslim was put in charge for the first time. Aybak himself spent considerable time in Ajmer during the

[10]For an interesting contemporary view see Michael W. Meister, "The Two-and-a-Half Day Mosque," *Oriental Art*, vol. XVIII, no.1, Spring 1972, pp. 57-63.

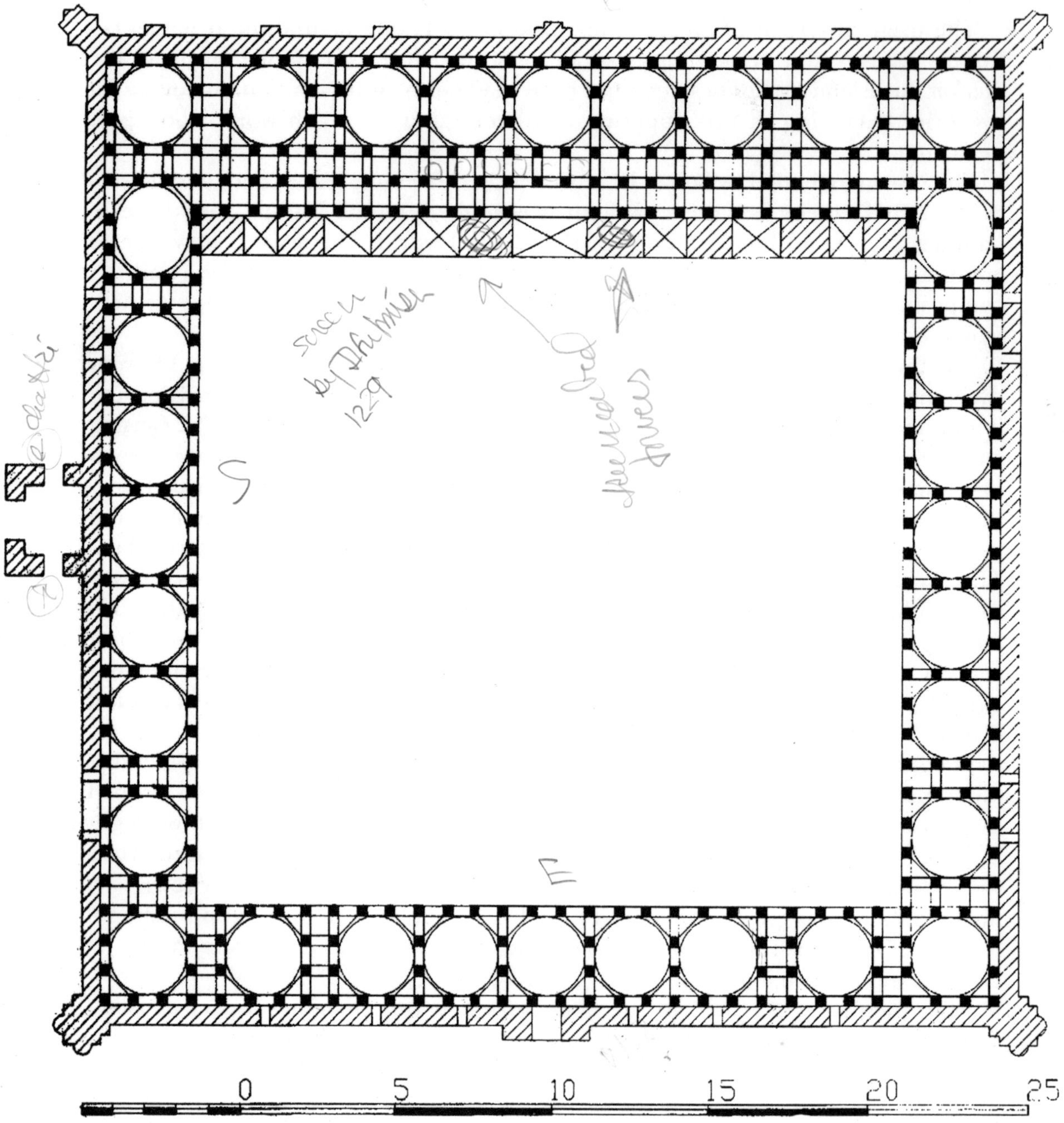

Plan 1. Ajmer, Aḍhāī Din kā Jhoṃparā Mosque (after James Fergusson)

year 1197 but the city and its territory was transferred in 1242 to a Turkish officer, the future sultan of Delhi, Balban.

Ajmer became famous when the mystic Shaykh Mu'īn al-Dīn Chishtī settled here sometime before 1192, the date the city was first captured by Muslim forces. Noted for his deep humanism and pious way of life, the saint's influence on and importance to early Muslim civilization in India was to be considerable.

The Aḍhāī Din kā Jhoṃparā Mosque [Plan 1] is raised on a high plinth, the main approach on the east side leading up a steep stairway to a domed arched gateway flanked by two porches. All corners except the north-west, which abuts on a rocky outcrop, have projecting towers. What remains of the interior is a hypostyle hall roofed on the *qibla* side by five large and five small corbelled domes[Ill. 9]. The ceilings show details which indicate newly quarried Muslim work combined with reused temple material.[11] The central lotuses in the ceilings, while certainly made by Hindu workmen, are not used as they would have been in Hindu structures, but are substituted for the deep sometimes figured pendents of the Hindu. Even the great central ceiling might have been a work commissioned for the Muslim overlords, for no provision is made for the bracket figures required of any Hindu ceiling of this dimension. The use of certain Hindu motifs, such as the diamond and its placement are not consistent with pure Hindu tradition. The cusped *miḥrāb* is exuberantly decorated with vegetal and epigraphic ornament carved in shallow relief.

In Ajmer, as in Delhi, indigenous materials and techniques of construction are combined with a hypostyle plan. But in Ajmer the mosque was not only built from temple spoils but also from a new order of shafts called neo-Hindu. The plain shafts of this new order each support Hindu pillars superimposed in twos or threes to achieve the necessary height to form the colonnade and to create the effect of spaciousness [Ill. 10]. That such a new order was created and used in a consistent way to support the Hindu pillars is in marked contrast to the disordered use of temple shafts in the Delhi mosque. The neo-Hindu shafts show the advance made by Hindu masons and their Muslim overlords in the years between 1192 and 1199, the seven years which separate the construction of the Delhi and Ajmer mosques.

A screen of seven cusped and corbelled arches, the central one higher than those on the sides, was added by Sultan Iltutmish in about 1229 in front of the prayer area [Ill. 11]. The central arch is raised above the lateral arches in imitation of the *pishtaq* in front of the *īwān*, and is surmounted by stubs of flanged towers modelled on the Quṭb Mīnār. The arched screen is obviously copied from the Quwwat al-Islām Mosque, but its carved relief decoration [Ill. 12] is a reworking in stone of brick and stucco ornament typical of Ghūrīd architecture in Afghanistan. In the character of this decoration the greatest change is noted. The floral designs of the indigenous Delhi workmen are gone and in their place there are conventional patterns of stylized flat designs.

Beautifully set against a mountain range, the Ajmer mosque, built entirely of local yellow limestone, is the largest early mosque in India, more than double the size of its Delhi prototype.

* * *

In the Bayana region about 160 km south of Delhi, in the state of Rajasthan, there are two mosques and an *'īdgāh* belonging to the earliest phase of mosque building in Sultanate India. The Chawrāsī Khambha (Eighty-four columns) is in the village of Kaman, the Ukha Mandir and its Khaljī extension, the Ukha Mosque, and a praying wall are in the town of Bayana.[12]

[11]Ibid., p. 57.

[12]On the architecture of Bayana and Kaman see Mehrdad and Natalie H. Shokoohy, "The Architecture of Baha al-Din Tughrul in the Region of Bayana, Rajasthan," *Muqarnas*, vol. IV, 1987, pp.114-32.

Bayana was first conquered by Mu'izz al-Dīn Sam, the Ghūrīd ruler, in 1195 and later conferred on Bahā al-Dīn Tughril, one of the Ghūrīd ruler's senior Turkish slaves, who founded Sultan-Kot, a new Muslim city and made it his headquarters. Baha al-Dīn held the fiefship of Bayana for less than fifteen years (1195-1210), but during that time he ruled as an independent monarch and took his orders directly from Mu'izz al-Dīn Muḥammad ibn Sam. During his tenure of office, Tughril encouraged Indian and Khurasanian merchants to settle in the region which he held until his death, when it appears probable the area fell to the Hindus and was not later recovered by Iltutmish.

Kaman was a town in the Bayana region during the early Sultanate period. Situated on the ancient route that connected Delhi with the south, it was conquered by the Ghūrīd armies as they marched south towards Bayana and Ajmer at the time of the Muslim conquest. Kaman remained a part of the province of Bayana until the time of Sikandar Lodī, when it was included in the newly formed province of Āgrā.

Inside the area of the ruined fortification wall, to the west of the village of Kaman, the Chawrāsī Khambha is dated to the first decade of the thirteenth century. Built in a hypostyle plan, the mosque has two column shafts one on top of the other to achieve the desired height. In the centre of the *qibla* wall is a decorated rectangular *miḥrāb* with a stone *mimbar* [Ill. 13] to the right. Although the stones used here are from Hindu temples, they are laid in imitation of some of the wooden *mimbars* of Iran. In the north-west corner is a women's gallery, a small balcony with its own entrance at the western corner. The gateway entered from the east projects on the exterior to form a chamber with thick walls and heavy piers and a stairway built on each side.

The Chawrāsī Khambha is the only extant early Sultanate mosque with no later additions. And because it was not in the capital, it was more modestly built with little ornament. Nevertheless it is one of the best examples of a provincial mosque of the Sultanate period.

The Ukha Mandir in the town of Bayana is another monument associated with Bahā al-Dīn Tughrul[Ill. 14]. Originally a Hindu temple, it was converted into a mosque and then reconverted back to a Hindu temple. Part of a complex which includes the Ukha Mosque (1320), a later extension, and the unfinished sixteenth-century Ukha Mīnār, the large Ukha Mandir is situated to the west of the town. Built in a hypostyle plan, like the Chawrāsī Khambha, it was originally walled on the north, south and west sides, and only open to the east, where the monumental entrance gateway is located. Among the changes made when it was reconverted back to a temple two centuries ago was to wall up the eastern arcade. As in the Kaman Mosque, a women's gallery with its own entrance is in the north-west corner. There are three *miḥrābs* in the *qibla* wall with a fourth in the *zanāna*.

The standard plan of a Tughril mosque appears to have had the same number of bays on the east and west sides, an unusual feature since generally the *qibla* side is deeper. The Ukha Mandir in Bayana has four bays on each side and the Chawrasi Khambha, three. In both mosques the main entrance as usual is on the east side, where the exterior wall was an open colonnade.[13] In both mosques the east sides are more than a metre above ground level and may have been used to cool the interior colonnades. In the Kaman Mosque the north side is also open. These open arcades

[13]Gold-Pearlroth, op. cit., pp. 19-20.

are later also found in the Ukha Mosque in Bayana, no doubt modelled on the earlier monuments.

The Ukha Mosque is attached to the south side of the original mosque and is very similar to the earlier structure, with the same hypostyle plan and surrounding pillared colonnades. Somewhat narrower the eastern elevation corresponds to that of the Ukha Mandir. However, the Ukha Mosque has some more advanced features which were in use during the early fourteenth century. Among these are newly shaped arches, such as the four-centered true arch of the gateway, as well as the small dome in the roof in front of the *miḥrāb,* a true ribbed dome of a type unknown in India in the early Islamic period.

The Ukha Mīnār is an unfinished round tower located north-east of the mosque. Dated 1519 it belongs to the reign of Ibrāhīm Shāh Lodī. The entrance on the south-east side leads to a spiral staircase. The *mīnār* was apparently left unfinished when Bābur attacked the region.

Also belonging to the early centuries of Muslim rule is the *'īdgāh* of Bayana. Two round towers originally roofed with corbelled domes strengthen the structure which has a central *miḥrāb* flanked by four smaller niches. The *'īdgāh* is one of the earliest buildings constructed in Bayana and one of the earliest prayer walls still standing.

* * *

Iltutmish was a stern soldier who made the Delhi Sultanate independent by severing relations with the Ghaznī empire and creating a new state in north India with Delhi as capital. Iltutmish became the first real Delhi sultan by striking his own coins, having the *khuṭba* read in his name and receiving the Patent and Investitute from the Abbāsid Caliph in Baghdad. Delhi became the most important centre of political and military authority in India. Iltutmish created a governing class consisting of two principal groups, the Turkish slave officers and the non-Turkish (*tazik*) foreign officers of high lineage. In addition the military base of the state was strengthened by organizing the army under the direct supervision and control of the central government. The Rājpūts were suppressed and some of their strongest fortresses captured. Iltutmish consolidated the Muslim conquest of India and introduced the dynastic principle into the government of his dominions. Succession was now reserved for only one family, his own. And his children did rule. First Raziya (1236-40), his beloved daughter whom he chose as successor, then two of his sons 1240-46 and finally his grandson, Nasr al-Dīn (1246-66). Nobles played the role of sultan-makers and it was one of them, Ulugh Khān, who murdered the last of Iltutmish's clan, assumed power and took the title of Ghiyāth al-Dīn Balban (1266-87). Then followed three years of weak rule of nobles (1287-90) which eventually led to the Khaljī revolution, the end of Balban's dynasty and the monopoly of the Turkish slave aristocracy.

Iltutmish patronized arts and literature and encouraged all other cultural activities. Central Asian and Iranian fugitives sought his court to escape from the Mongol hordes. The sultan was very interested in architecture, extended the Quwwat al-Islām Mosque and its *maqsūra,* completed the Quṭb Mīnār and reconstructed the Ajmer mosque, as well as patronizing several other buildings in Badaun and Delhi.

Like the Quṭb Mīnār and the *maqsūra* of the Quwwat al-Islām Mosque, another specifically Muslim idea given architectural form for the first time in India was the mausoleum. For the remains of his eldest son and crown prince, Naṣr al-Dīn Maḥmūd, who died in 1229, Sultan Iltutmish built the first monumental Islamic tomb in India called Sultan Gharī (the Prince of the Caves) [Ill. 15] [Plan 2].[14]

Situated in an isolated area on a high square plinth and enclosed by stone walls with circular corner bastions and an impressive eastern portal, the tomb is, however Islamic in conception only. The pillars, capitals, architraves and corbelled pyramidal roofs are purely Hindu. An inscription on the outer eastern gateway of the monument

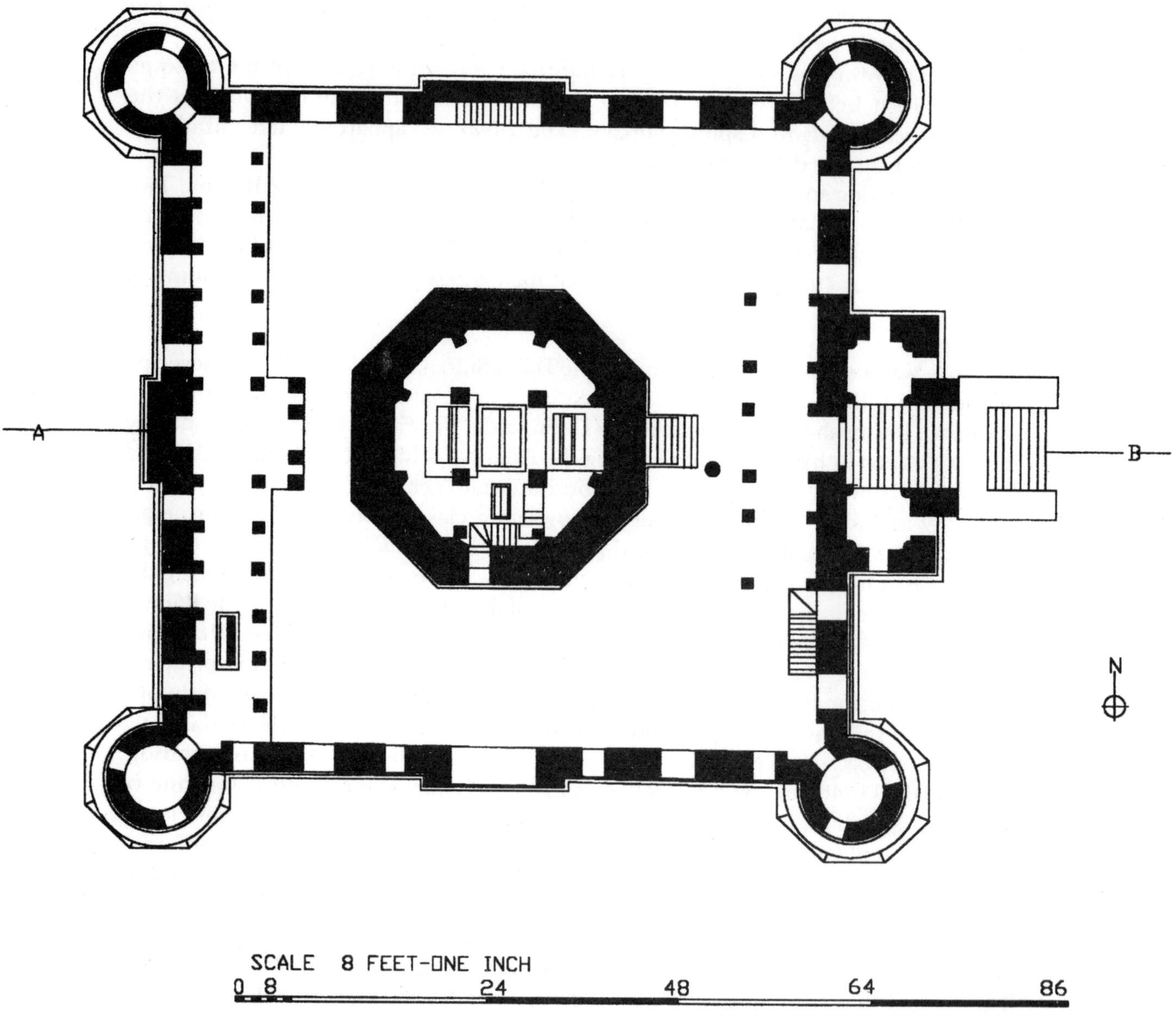

Plan 2. Delhi, Tomb of Sultān Gharī, (after F. Wetzel)

[14]See S.A.A. Naqvi, "Sultan Gharī, Delhi", *Ancient India,* vol. III, pp.4-10.

states that it was built by Iltutmish in 1230 on the site of a Hindu temple and some of its parts were used to construct the tomb. However, the builders also chiselled their own stones according to the new requirements.

The gateway has a staircase leading up through the gate. There are two rooms off the entrance originally used for guardians (*dvārapāla*) figures in temple gates.

As a funerary monument the Tomb of Sultan Gharī differs from any later Indian tombs. This may be seen in the manner in which the tomb is placed in an octagonal underground chamber. Within the walled enclosure is a square courtyard in the centre of which is an octagonal platform forming the roof of the crypt below containing the sarcophagus. Such an arrangement is not found in India again until the seventeenth century, the idea apparently coming from the Seljuq tomb towers of the twelfth century, where there is a basement story for the body and only a memorial stone in the upper chamber to mark the position.

There is a cusped *miḥrāb* in the west wall below the dome and a small columned prayer area in front of it, and along the east wall a double row of columns, and an inner portico. The idea of incorporating a *miḥrāb* in the western wall of a tomb is seen here for the first time. The *miḥrāb* was intended to give the tomb a religious sanction, and hence security, assurance that future rivals and opponents would not destroy the grave. The foliated *miḥrāb* is of marble as are the eight pillars which make up the colonnade in front of it and the entablature above it. With the exception of the *miḥrābs*, the entire sanctuary including the domed ceilings was built of reused temple spoils.

A narrow staircase leads down to the crypt from the south side. The crypt-chamber itself is supported by twelve tall pillars, each two-tiered. An empty white sarcophagus is in the centre of the tomb (the real one is probably in the crypt below). The *qibla* wall has three carved *miḥrābs*, the central one of which has a series of arches set within four arches.

* * *

For his own tomb Iltutmish chose another unusual plan. Despite its Muslim effect, the structure, the earliest example of a square domed tomb, the roof since fallen, is essentially Hindu in constructional details. The arches, including the squinches, introduced for the first time in India to change the square base to the circular diameter of the dome, are built on the native principle of oversailing courses of stone slabs.

The Tomb of Iltutmish was erected before 1235 behind the north-west corner of the Quwwat al-Islām Mosque and is square in plan with walls of plainly dressed local red and grey stone decorated only in the shallow bays with red sandstone. Three entrance portals on the south, north and east sides lead to the interior. The exterior is plain except for inscriptions on the arch frames of the portals. The main entrance is on the east side according to the inscription which begins there and goes around the entire interior of the building. The area around each arched opening is of carved red sandstone and is set in a larger arch.

The interior is profusely ornamented like a Hindu temple with carved geometrical and inscriptional panels interspersed with Hindu motifs [Ill. 16] over the entire wall surface. The roof, although now fallen in, shows there to have been a dome constructed in the local corbelled technique of concentric overlapping masonry rings supported on a semi-domed squinch found in this form for the first time in India, but a method of transition common in early Islamic buildings in other countries. This is an Indianized version of the same theme containing neither a true vault nor a true arch, planned rather on the traditional system of overlapping courses, technically unscientific, yet artistically most effective.

Beneath the tomb is a crypt which was originally entered by a still accessible stairway leading down in front of the north door. An empty white marble sarcophagus is in the centre of the tomb. The *qibla* wall has three carved *miḥrābs* originally coloured green and purple. The central *miḥrāb* has white marble decoration and is of the same height as the doorway arches and occupies the entire height of the wall to the zone of transition.

The Tomb of Iltutmish is the first tomb known to have been built by a Delhi sultan except for the so-called "Sultan Gharī" tomb. The conception of the monument is therefore new for India. Yet the feeling of the monument with its emphasis on interior decoration and disregard for external effect remains Hindu. The tomb was obviously built and decorated by artists who had been trained in the Hindu tradition and shows the difficulties facing them in executing an aniconic ornament.

* * *

Other monuments of the period erected in provincial cities follow more or less the same lines of development. Most of them have been either repaired or restored so many times subsequently that their original details have almost entirely disappeared. This is the case with the Jāmi' Mosque (1223) Iltutmish built at Badaun,[15] Balban's Mosque at Jalālī (1266) and the Tomb of Bahā al-Dīn Zakariyā in Multān (1262) and believed to have been built by the saint himself. In Multān there are two other tombs, one of the saint named Shams al-Dīn, locally known as Shams-i Tabrīzī, which has received extensive renovations from devotees. Only the comparatively insignificant tomb of another saint, Shadna Shāhīd (d. 1288) has preserved its original fabric.

The lofty gateway at Nagaur, Rajasthan, known as the Atarkin kā Darwāza [Ill. 17], has retained the original surface ornament [Ill. 18] which is similar to that on Iltutmish's screen at Ajmer and ought, therefore, to be attributed to that reign. Muḥammad Tughluq, however, is known to have extensively renovated the original structure. Finally, the *mīnār* of Balban at Kol (Aligarh) erected during Maḥmūd's reign, but destroyed by the British in 1861, was in point of time and style the second *mīnār* in India and possibly meant to serve as a pillar of victory.

* * *

Sultan Iltutmish died on 30 April 1236. He was the greatest ruler of thirteenth century India and a wise statesman who transformed Mu'izz al-Dīn's Indian conquests into a cohesive hereditary monarchy. The receipt of the Deed of Investiture from the Abbāsid Caliph in 1229 gave legal status to his realm. The sultan was welcoming and generous to refugees, Turkic and non-Turkic, driven from their homeland in Iran and Central Asia by Chingiz Khān's invasions. The many different sectors of society all supported Iltutmish, the Turkish military commanders helping to extend the boundaries of the state. The sultan organized court etiquette on the Samanīd and Ghaznavid patterns, which made special provisions for the *'ulamā* (scholars of Islamic

[15] On Badaun see A. Fuhrer, *North West Provinces and Oudh,* p. 523; J.F. Blakiston, *The Jami Masjid at Badaon and Other Buildings in the United Provinces,* Calcutta, 1926; A. Cunningham, *Report on Tours in the Gangetic Provinces, 1875-6,* pp. 1-11.

theology) and ṣūfīs. Therefore, Iltutmish's relations with the ṣūfīs of his realm were good and he was able to count on their support.

But with the sultan's death, the Delhi Sultanate suffered severe reverses. Hindus reasserted themselves and the Mongols pressed forward to attack Lahore in 1241. With the accession of Naṣīr al-Dīn Maḥmūd I, the period of confusion ended but real power was in the hands of Ghiyāth al-Dīn Balban, a Turkish nobleman, who became sultan in 1266, and whose tomb (d.1280) in Delhi, now in ruins, shows the earliest use of the true arch with radiating voussoirs. The Slave dynasty came to an end in 1290, when the last of the line, the profligate Kaykubād, was replaced by Jalāl ud-Dīn Firoz Shāh, who would himself be brutally removed from office six years later to make room for his nephew, 'Alā' al-Dīn Khaljī.

* * *

The early period of architectural construction under the Slave dynasty is one of uncertainty and improvisation. The monuments illustrate a general feature of Islamic architecture—as Muslim culture establishes itself in new areas, it takes over local traditions and modifies them according to its own needs and habits. In India the Muslims of eastern Iran and Central Asia assimilated the techniques of construction and decoration of indigenous architecture. This fusion produced only two outstanding monuments, the Quṭb Mīnār and the Tomb of Sultan Gharī. Many of the structural problems are solved clumsily, if at all. For instance the arch remains only a visual form and the zone of transition has not as yet been expertly handled. Nevertheless, the Muslim conquerors were so strongly affected by the indigenous monuments they found that the result was perhaps the most original architecture produced in the entire Islamic world.

CHAPTER 4

The Khaljī Dynasty (1290-1320)

The so-called Slave dynasty came to an end in 1290 and was followed by a short period of amazing splendour under the Afghan Khaljī dynasty. 'Alā' al-Dīn Muḥammad (1296-1316), the third of the line, is considered the greatest and most energetic sultan of the dynasty, under whom the Delhi Sultanate reached its peak. Apart from his continually successful campaigns against the incursions of the Mongol hordes and his conquests of the subcontinent, from the Rājpūt forts of Ranthambor and Chitor to Madura in the south, 'Alā' al-Dīn had enough energy remaining to conceive and initiate a number of building projects of gigantic scale. Extant structures of this period are few but what remains is obviously of a highly developed and vigorous school of architecture.

In 1303, as a defence against the incessant Mongol attacks, 'Alā' al-Dīn founded Sīrī, a new city of Delhi, about 4 km north-west of the earlier city around the Quṭb complex.[1] The remarkable Khaljī experiment in urban design and planning was destroyed by Shīr Shāh Sūr in 1548 and its materials were reused for the new sixteenth-century city of Shīrgarh. The walls of Sīrī apparently enclosed an irregular oval which had seven gates.

What is not clear is whether Sīrī was a walled military camp or whether it was intended as protection for the newly constructed palace, the legendary Hall of a Thousand Pillars, of which no trace remains.[2] Whatever its function might have been, the fortifications indicate the sense of insecurity produced by the Mongol incursions.

The Slave dynasty, with the exception of Kaykubād, the last member of the line, held court and issued commands from the Quṭb complex. Jalāl al-Dīn Khaljī completed the city-fortress of Kaykubād at Kilokheri, which was subsequently known as Naya Shahr. His nephew and successor, 'Alā' al-Dīn built the fort and city of Sīrī, the capital of the Delhi Sultanate until 1321 when Sultan Ghiyāth al-Dīn, Tughluq constructed a new city and a citadel he called Tughluqābād.[3]

Under the Slave dynasty Delhi had been a fortified Turkish camp, but now it became the effective capital of India, where the great poet Amīr Khusraw and the celebrated saint Niẓām al-Dīn Awliyā mingled freely.

The next project undertaken was the construction of a large tank, the Hauz Alā' i (1295), enclosed by a stone and masonry wall at a site which became known as Hauz

[1]Carr Stephen, *Archaeology and Monumental Remains of Delhi,* Allahabad, 1967, pp. 33-36.

[2]Ibid., pp. 36-38.

[3]For the early cities of Delhi see H.C. Fanshawe, *Delhi: Past and Present,* London, 1902; Gordon Risley Hearn, *The Seven Cities of Delhi,* Delhi, 1974; H.G. Keene, *Handbook for Visitors to Delhi,* third edition, Calcutta, 1876; Y.D. Sharma, *Delhi and Its Neighbourhood,* New Delhi, 1964; T.G.P. Spear, *Delhi and its Monuments and History,* Oxford, 1943; Carr Stephen, *Archaeology and Monumental Remains of Delhi,* Allahabad, 1967.

Khās. Fīrūz Shāh Tughluq, later in the fourteenth century, restored the tank and built a *madrasa* (1352) along its banks.

The area around the Quwwat al-Islām Mosque reasserted its importance when 'Alā' al-Dīn decided to double the existing mosque. Six arches were added at the northern end of Iltutmish's extension to the screen, and the new version was intended to be twice the width of the two earlier screens combined. In addition to the *madrasa* and his own tomb, 'Alā' al-Dīn proposed to build a colossal new *mīnār* intended to rise 145 m. with a diameter twice that of the Quṭb Mīnār. The sultan's death in 1316 ended any hopes of completing this enormous project. Only the plinth of the great mosque and some of the main walls are visible. Of the great new *mīnār* only the rubble lower-storey core still stands. These were the architectural aspirations of a forceful and relentless monarch who tried thus to express his success and long-term ambitions.

The whole grand design of the powerful sultan survives only in one gateway, the only part of the great Khaljī scheme completed. The domed entrance gateway in the south arcade of 'Alā' al-Dīn Khaljī's extension to the Quwwat al-Islām Mosque, known as the Alā'i Darwāza (1310), was probably the city gate of the mosque [Ill. 19]. Originally, it was one of four almost identical gateways, two on the eastern side, and one each on the north and south sides. While ordinarily it is difficult to speculate on an isolated monument, since its original meaning in the whole concept is lost, the Alā'i Darwāza is different. In structure, plan and decoration this gateway was conceived to stand independently of any other monument. The most perfectly preserved Khaljī building, the Alā'i Darwāza shows that Islamic architecture in India had come of age and found its distinct expression. The importance of the gateway lies in the fact that so much is new here and that these innovations will reappear frequently until the end of the creative phase of Islamic building in India.

The square Alā'ī Darwāza stands outside the enclosure wall of the Quwwat al-Islām Mosque, its immensely thick walls supporting a shallow dome supported on squinches. The walls are faced with red sandstone inlaid with white marble richly carved with arabesque and inscriptions in shallow relief. The contrast between the red sandstone and white marble on the sides and around the arches and rectangular panels is most effective, and is to develop later in the seventeenth century into the exquisite *pietra dura* work of the Mughals.

Tall pointed horseshoe-shaped arches with a "spearhead" fringe in the intrados open on the south, east and west sides. This is the first major appearance in India of the true arch formed of voussoirs, hitherto only modestly noted in the Tomb of Balban (1280) in Delhi. It is also the first appearance of the *pishtaq,* the front arch so typical of later Iranian architecture.

The façade is double-storeyed, each central *īwān* flanked by upright rectangular panels and false arched recesses with stone grills, only the inner pair on the lower storey open windows fitted with screens [Ill. 20]. The arched panels are decorated with rectangular bands of red sandstone and marble containing *Qur'ānic* inscriptions. In fourteenth century India the double-storeyed treatment is unusual but it becomes popular in later Sultanate and Mughal architecture. Only the north entrance has a semicircular Hindu corbelled arch with a shallow trefoil outline. This opening originally led into the pillared arcade of the enlarged mosque.

The interior of the Alā'i Darwāza has squinches in the zone of transition resembling those of the entrance arches with a fringe of "spearheads" in the intrados. These are the first squinches in India to have radiating voussoirs. The interior walls are decorated profusely in a broad flat diaper pattern and sinuous tendrils and rounded lotus buds on the inscribed pilaster panels [Ill. 21]. The entire monument is surmounted by a semicircular dome with an *amalaka*[4] finial at the crown.

There is no known monument in India which might have suggested the design of the Alā'i Darwāza. Blind arcading used on the façades of ceremonial buildings was known in the lands of western Islam on buildings such as the Hārūn al-Rashīd, the eighth century Palace of Raqqa. But the most logical prototype was probably the palace of Ctesiphon, the Taq i-Kisra (531-79), where a central *īwān* rises the full height of the façade and is flanked by a series of blind arcading. The *īwān* appears to have been popular even earlier in Iran, since it is found in Ardashir's Palace at Fīrūzābād. When finally incorporated in mosque design, it became the most prominent feature of the facade in the Jāmi' Mosque of Zawara (1136). Subsequently, it predominated the façade and became a characteristic feature of all Islamic construction—religious, funerary and secular. Most probably the anonymous architect of the Alā'i Darwāza derived his inspiration from these Persian sources.

The Alā'i Darwāza might also have been conceived as a monumental gate, such as those of mausolea which extend something of the grace and holiness of the person buried within. Monumental entrances became a standard feature of Islamic building from the eleventh century on and both secular and religious structures were provided with them.

It is not clear whether the Alā'i Darwāza is a new flowering of Islamic talent, perhaps due to the artists who sought political asylum in Hindustan in the wake of the Mongol hordes, or whether it shows the last effort of the Hindu workman. In either case, this splendid monument is built in a traditional style which does not survive the onslaught of Tīmūr into the Tughluq period.

Under 'Alā' al-Dīn Khaljī and his son the area around the residence of the Chishtī saint, Niẓām al-Dīn Awliyā (1236-1325)began to be developed. Niẓām al-Dīn's prayers were said to have protected the city from Mongol attack. A congregational mosque was built in the shrine, and after the saint's death, the area known as Nizamuddin became a *dargāh*, following a pattern common in other regions of the Islamic world in the fourteenth century.

The Jamā'at Khāna Mosque[Ill. 22] is a small five-domed red sandstone structure. The façade has a wide central entrance arch and two flanking narrower arches with perforated stone screens. On the sides are two wings each with two domes and an entrance arch on the façade. The central arches resemble the arches of the Alā'i Darwāza, with the same "spearhead" fringe in the intrados, recessed planes and nookshafts. Squinches with "spearhead" fringes are also used in the interior. The entire central portion of the mosque is richly carved, in contrast to the wings which are undecorated and probably a later Tughluq addition. Inscriptions have led to the conclusion that the central portion of the mosque was intended as the tomb of the saint Niẓām al-Dīn Awliyā.

'Alā' al-Dīn left no worthy successor and the reign of Khusraw Khān, the "sweeper king," provoked a military revolt in 1321 led by the governor, Ghiyāth al-Dīn, who ushered in the Tughluq era.

[4]A round ribbed motif at the top of a temple spire.

CHAPTER 5

The Tughluq Dynasty (1320-1414)

In 1320 the Turkish governor of the Punjab, Ghiyāth al-Dīn Tughluq, defeated 'Alā' al-Dīn Khaljī, the ruler of Delhi, proclaimed himself sultan, and ushered in the stern soldier's reign with which his name is associated. The Tughluqs assumed control over an area that included much of the subcontinent, but during the century of their rule, their territory diminished as one provincial governor after another declared independence from the central government, leaving the Delhi sultan little more than the capital and its surroundings. The dynasty survived nominally until 1412 but the death blow had been dealt in 1399 by Tīmūr who sacked and destroyed Delhi.

Determined to restore order after years of anarchy, Muḥammad Tughluq faced great difficulties in trying to set about his new task. Revolts threatening on all sides and the Mongol hordes became an increasingly more formidable menace. Despite these constraints, during his short reign (1320-25) Ghiyāth al-Dīn managed to do a considerable amount of building in the capital. His greatest accomplishment was the construction of a huge new garrison city, the third of the seven cities of Delhi, which included a royal quarter and accommodation for his retainers, the army and the administration. The mighty sloping walls of Tughluqābād[Ill. 23] with their enormous bastions and battlements still frown down today, although the melancholy fortress-citadel lies abandoned. Deserted just fifteen years after its completion, a legend ascribes this to the potent curses of the Saint Niẓām al-Dīn who predicted that the city would never be inhabited by humans but only by wild animals. This prophecy proved true since shortly after the accession of the next ruler, Muḥammad Tughluq, the capital for some years was transferred to Daulatābād in the Deccan. When Muḥammad eventually returned to the Delhi region in 1334, a new site between the Quṭb and Sīrī was selected for Jahānpanāh, the new capital.

Although completely in ruins today, the fortified city of Tughluqābād was the first of the great Indian Islamic complexes to combine a city, a fort and a palace, an architectural scheme to be frequently followed in later times. In Roman fashion, the complex was in two parts, a citadel, the equivalent of the castle in the occident, and a city with heavily sloping defensive walls. The ground plan was an irregular rectangle due to the rocky outcrop on which the entire compound stood. There were seven km of walls with circular two-storeyed bastions and fifty-two gateways all surrounded by a moat. This huge fortified city was one of the most impressive schemes of the Sultanate period.

The austere square Tomb of Ghiyāth al-Dīn[Ill. 24] immediately to the south of Tughluqābād is as isolated and fortified as the city itself. Originally standing in the midst of a lake, the mausoleum is separated from Tughluqābād by a narrow causeway. A warrior's grave in every respect, the tomb is a self-contained miniature castle with prominently sloping walls. It has been suggested that the structure was a donjon which could readily be put into a state of defence. The entrance is cunningly placed at the end of the causeway, a death trap to an invader. Within the courtyard are several massively built underground vaults not connected to the mortuary chamber below, which the Moorish traveller Ibn Battūtā maintained were used by the sultan for storing his great treasure.

In India there is an architectural tradition of building fortified tombs, the earliest of which was the twelfth-century brick mausoleum of Khālid Walīd near Multān. In Delhi there followed the Tomb of Sultan Gharī (1231) constructed by Sultan Iltutmish over the remains of his son, Naṣīr al-Dīn, which stands on a high plinth with sturdy enclosing walls and round corner bastions. After the Tomb of Ghiyāth al-Dīn, Sikandar Lodī built his own mausoleum with fortified walls in the Lodī Gardens. Daryā Khān followed this plan in 1520 and 'Īsā Khān also placed his tomb in a walled garden. During Mughal times fortified tombs are less fashionable and garden mausolea, such as the Tomb of Humāyūn, become the vogue.

The inclined walls of the Tomb of Ghiyāth al-Dīn are faced with red sandstone up to the springing of the arches, then with a combination of the red stone and white marble. The dome, faced with white marble, is in the popular "tartar" shape of later monuments and is crowned by a Hindu *amalaka-kalaśa* finial, associated with fertility and good fortune.

There are tall recessed arched entrances on the north, east and south sides and a plain exterior wall on the west to accommodate the *miḥrāb* in the interior. The pointed arches with their "spearhead" fringe resemble those of the Alā'i Darwāza, but the keel-shape arches of the earlier monument have been modified into a "tartar" outline, with a slight ogee curve at the crown. The central arched openings are also flanked by ornamental arched niches as in the Alā'i Darwāza.

The Tomb of Ghiyāth al-Dīn introduces an unusual treatment for the arched entrances. A lintel is thrown across the base of the arch, the first example of the use of the arch and beam-and-lintel together in Islamic architecture in India[Ill. 25]. The fusion of the two systems of building, the indigenous trabeate and the Muslim arcuate, robs the beam of its structural property and makes it a purely ornamental device. The tomb also introduces a support bracket under the ends of the beams, a device to be used frequently in subsequent periods.

The interior of the tomb is a square chamber faced with red sandstone up to the squinches, and then with white marble. Light is admitted through the three arched openings. The domed ceiling is supported on four squinches similar to those of the Alā'i Darwāza, but with the addition of three projecting blocks of stone acting as brackets in the angles between the octagon and the sixteen-sided figure.

The tomb contains three graves, the central one belonging to Ghiyāth al-Dīn. The second probably holds the remains of the sultan's second son, Maḥmūd Khān, picked to succeed him to the throne, but slaughtered together with his father under a wooden pavilion at Afghānpūr. Father and son were interred together after the tragedy. The third grave belongs to Maḥmūd's wife, Makhdūm-i Jahān, who was buried at a later time.

The Tomb of Ghiyāth al-Dīn marks the beginning of a new phase in the Sultanate architectural style, in which sloping walls appear and persist for a long time. The slanting effect blossomed from the architecture of Multān and was a blending of the indigenous Indian building tradition and that of Iran. Ghiyāth al-Dīn, while governor of Multān, constructed a tomb there with sloping walls for his own use, but when he became sultan he built another mausoleum for himself in Delhi and gave the Multān tomb to his spiritual guide, Rukn-i Ālam. The octagonal shape, the sloping walls, the slanting tapering buttresses, which rise to become domed turrets above the parapets, and the ornamental finials were all features which influenced the development of Islamic architecture in Delhi. The Tombs of Ghiyāth al-Dīn and Rukn-i Ālam introduce the two major Tughluq tomb plans, square and octagonal, and are the prototypes on which later Sultanate tombs would be modelled.

Closely following the Tomb of Ghiyāth al-Dīn in plan, elevation and construction, is the Lal Gumbad, built earlier by probably the next sultan, Muḥammad, in his new capital of Jahānpanāh. On a low plinth, the square monument also has sloping walls faced with red sandstone and white marble courses and a white marble-faced dome with a finial. If the structure does belong to the end of the fourteenth century it would show that a trend for the earlier animated style of the Khaljīs persisted almost to the end of the Tughluq era.

Muḥammad Tughluq, son of Ghiyāth al-Dīn and the next ruler (1325-51), tired of the grim security of Tughluqābād, adandoned it in 1327 and transferred his capital to Daulatābād in the Deccan for seven years. Literary accounts indicate that the southern capital was a major architectural showcase, although its present state of ruin provides little information about the types and styles of buildings constructed there under Muḥammad.

* * *

On returning to Delhi in 1334, the sultan began to construct an eight km long wall with thirteen gates, linking the two older cities of old Delhi, the area around the Quṭb and Khaljī Sirī, and enclosing the suburbs that had grown up between them. The new royal city of Jahānpanāh (Refuge of the World) is now in total ruin, with only one surviving structure, the terraced tower-like Bijay Mandal [Ill. 26], probably a part of the once legendary palace known as the Hall of a Thousand Pillars, so splendidly described by the Moorish traveller Ibn Battūta.

To the south-east of Tughluqābād and linked to it by a bund and a causeway is Ādilābād, a similar but smaller fort also built by Muḥammad Tughluq, with sloping walls and two gates leading into the lower keep while the upper has two fortified gates on the east and west and in addition contains an inner court.

Events did nothing to make the image of Muḥammad Tughluq more popular. Severe famines and the plague ravaged many parts of India during the reign and unsuccessful military campaigns weakened the army and made it more rebellious. The rage directed at the tyrannical sultan resulted in many provinces declaring their independence, the first of which was Bengal in 1338. A resurgent Hindu ruler in Vijayanagar added further problems until at the end of Muḥammad Tughluq's reign, the large unwieldy Delhi realm finally disintegrated, the sultan's authority now being confined largely to northern India.

The third ruler of the Tughluq line, Fīrūz, ascended the Delhi throne in 1351. Greatly interested in the cultural history of his country, Fīrūz was also an enthusiastic patron of the arts, repairing and restoring many monuments. In 1354, as his predecessors had done before him, he built a new capital, the citadel of Fīrūzābād, around which the fifth city of Delhi was to grow. Contemporary chronicles which give much information about the first four cities, Old Dillī, Sīrī, Tughluqābād and Jahānpanāh, are silent on the subject of Fīrūzābād. The actual size of the new capital may only be estimated by examining the architectural remains and inscriptions.[1]

The architectural style of the period of Fīrūz cannot be mistaken, since it grew out of the conditions that prevailed in the capital. There was a scarcity of skilled stone masons and experienced workmen primarily due to their dispersal on the transfer of capital from Delhi to Daulatābād in 1325. This together with the reduced finances allowed only limited construction. The material used was generally the least expensive possible, put together in the quickest manner, in a plain serviceable style. There are no well-finished ashlar blocks fitted squarely, so characteristic of earlier Islamic architecture in India. Walls are of plain rubble, the untrimmed surfaces covered only in plaster, dressed stone being used only for doorposts, pillars and lintels. Decoration is limited and when it appears is mostly of moulded plaster and colour wash. For these reasons, it is not surprising that the architectural style of this era has been labelled puritanical.

The walled enclosure which remains today on an extensive plain once bordered the Jumna River on the Mathura Road. The Kotlā [Ill. 27], was the fortress-palace of Fīrūz which became the official residence in 1354. The new city of Fīrūzābād was originally surrounded by high battlemented walls with tall bastions at intervals. Roughly rectangular in plan, the citadel's palaces and residences were on the east side which was protected by the Jumna River. The space within the enclosure was divided into three rectangular areas. In the centre stood the great Jāmi' Mosque, now in ruins. It had a hypostyle plan, an open central courtyard surrounded by arcades on all sides. The columns of the prayer hall and the side arcades are gone today, but the roughly-tooled stone blocks which supported them, spaced at regular intervals in the paved floor, still indicate where they once stood. The main entrance was through a domed porch on the north side and a private entrance leading to the royal apartments was located on the south side at the bank of the river. In the centre of the open court was a sunken octagonal structure around which a record of the public works of the reign was engraved.

Near the Jāmi' Mosque stands an unusual stepped pyramidal-shaped structure [Ill. 28] of three terraces of decreasing size. A series of vaulted cells on each level surround the solid structural core into which a pillar known as the Lat of Ashoka is built. This quite un-Islamic monument was probably part of the private apartments of Fīrūzābād and the pillar, which had been standing near Ambala since the days of the Pāṇḍavas, was known as *mīnāra-i zarin*, the golden column. It was brought to Delhi by Fīrūz and Shams-i Sirāj Afif, one of the sultan's biographers, describes in detail how the monolithic pillar was transported.[2] Another similar column from near Meerut was set up in the Kushak-i Shikār Palace on the Ridge.

When entering the Kotlā,[3] courts of various sizes and the halls of Public and Private Audience were on the right side, while the large open space on the left was open to the public. The residences were aligned on the banks of the Jumna, the most pleasant and desirable location, in much the same fashion as in later Mughal monuments in Āgrā and Delhi. The Kotlā with its palaces, gardens, baths, tanks, barracks and administrative offices was a fully self-contained royal residence.

And yet the defences of the citadel could not have been very strong. Tīmūr relates

[1]See E. Schotten Merklinger, "Fīrūzābād, Capital of the last Turkish Dynasty in India," *Akten des VI. Internationalen Kongresses fuer Turkische Kunst*, Ars Turcica, Munich, 1989.

[2]Afif, in H.M. Elliot and J. Dowson, *History of India*, Calcutta, 1960-63, vol. III, p. 303.

[3]J.A. Page, *A Memoir of Kotla Fīrūz Shāh*, Delhi, 1937, pp. 33-42.

that Sultan Mahmūd and his son, Mallū Khān, took refuge in Jahānpanāh and not in Fīrūzābād during the 1399 siege of Delhi. The mighty conqueror mentions the Kotlā, but only as a fort which stands on the banks of the Jumna.

According to Shams-i Sirāj Afif, Fīrūzābād had three palaces, but the ruins have not been identified. However, the system of dividing the audience into three classes according to rank, each with its own *durbār* (assembly) hall, as introduced by Fīrūz, obviously appealed to the Mughal emperors who adopted the system in both Āgrā and Delhi.

The *Tārikh-i Fīrūz Shāh* makes mention of eight public mosques each able to accommodate up to ten thousand worshippers, one private mosque, a hunting lodge called the Kushak-i Shikar near the northern Ridge in Delhi and numerous other large structures. Ferishta[4] records a large number of public works constructed during the reign including a hundred hospitals. While the numbers cited create some suspicion, historians all appear to agree that Fīrūz was interested in the welfare of his subjects. He improved living conditions in the capital and, built mosques, schools, hospitals, and other public works of which few traces remain.

The Kotlā was the fortress-palace of the sultan and the city of Fīrūzābād grew around it. The urban heart, however, remained at the old site around the Quṭb complex in Old Dillī, which continued to be used for state functions. The Quwwat al-Islām Mosque also retained its central position. Fīrūz obviously wanted to preserve the earlier capital, for he replaced the damaged top storey of the Quṭb Mīnār by two new higher storeys. There is further evidence that Old Dillī with a population Cunningham estimated at ten-thousand at this time, remained important. And within the walls of the fourth city, Jahānpanāh, at least the Khirkī Mosque was built during this era.

Other important southern population centres existed during the reign of Fīrūz. One of these evolved around the Hauz Khās tank built by 'Alā' al-Dīn Khaljī in 1305. Fīrūz repaired and refaced the tank and once finished, constructed a large college on its banks. The site appears to have held special appeal for the sultan for he selected to build his own tomb southeast of the lake. During the lifetime of Fīrūz, Hauz Khās must have been a lively place, for Ibn Battūtā refers to forty pavilions on the shores of the tank where musicians lived, even calling it the City of Music. The Moorish traveller also mentions an extensive bazaar and several mosques. The Hauz Khās area remained important during the latter half of the fourteenth century, since Tīmūr encamped here after he had finished with Delhi, recording in his *Memoirs* that around the reservoir were many buildings. According to Baranī, Fīrūz built thirty *madrasas* throughout the lands of the Delhi Sultanate, but the one in Hauz Khās constructed in 1352 was the most important.

Moving further south, a population centre probably existed around the Dargāh of Niẓām al-Dīn Awliyā [Ill. 29], the Chishtī saint whose burial ground has become the most famous shrine in Delhi. Fīrūz himself mentions that he repaired the tomb of the saint, although the present structure is of a later sixteenth-century date. The sultan also repaired the east wall of the tank, where, according to an inscription on the southern arch of the entrance to a passage leading to the tomb of the saint, the date 1379 and the name Malik Sayyid al-Hujjab, the Chamberlain of Fīrūz, are cited.[5]

In the village of Niẓāmuddīn there are two additional monuments from the reign

[4]Mahomed Kasim Ferishta, *History of the Rise of the Mahomedan Power in India*, vol. I, New Delhi, 1981, pp. 269-70.

[5]*Epigraphia Indo-Moslemica, 1909-10*, p. 71.

of Fīrūz. In the south-east corner is the Kālī (Sanjar) Mosque and in the south-west corner, in an extensive enclosure surrounded by battlemented walls, the octagonal Tomb of Tilangāni, prime minister of the sultan.

North of the Kotlā there is one further population centre near where the Turkman gate stands today. The Kalān Mosque was constructed here and might have served the northern population in this part of the city.

Between the recognized population centres and sometimes beyond the city walls were the suburbs. Some of these were built around the shrines of holy men, such as the Dargāh of Shāh Ālam, a local Muslim saint, in Wazīrābād, at the northern edge of the Ridge. A gateway, a courtyard, a mosque, a tomb and a bridge are found here all apparently dated to the reign of Fīrūz. Wazīrābād was probably an important suburb in the late fourteenth century, for Tīmūr and his horde encamped here, having crossed the Jumna River on 1 January 1399 after destroying the greatest Muslim power in India, the Sultanate of Delhi. Shāh Ālam was not a famous saint, and thus no rulers or their retainers sought to be buried near him. The shrine is therefore not crowded with the usual later structures added to the famous *dargāhs*, such as the Niẓāmuddīn shrine. The Tomb [Ill. 30] and Mosque of Shāh Ālam stand in their original form in near total isolation, an interesting example of an almost forgotten ensemble.

Another suburb built around the shrine of a holy man was located south of where the Lahore Gate stands today. Here Fīrūz constructed the Sacred Enclosure of Qadam Sharīf (1374), known as the Holy Footprint, as a final resting place for his eldest son, Fatah Khān. The tomb is surrounded by an enclosing wall, probably constructed against the attacks of the Mongols, since the shrine was outside the walls of the city of Fīrūzābād. There are two gateways to the arched enclosure built around the grave of the prince, over which the sacred footprint, sent by the Caliph of Baghdād to Fīrūz, was placed in a trough of water.

A third suburb, southeast of the ruined city of Sīrī, within Jahānpanāh, was centered around the Dargāh of Roshan Chirāgh-i Dillī, the Bright Light of Delhi, a disciple of Niẓām al-Dīn Awliyā, who died in 1356 during the reign of Fīrūz. The modernized tomb [Ill. 31] bears an inscription which states that Sultan Fīrūz built the eastern gateway in 1373.

Another inscription dated 1373 records the construction of the Tomb of Mīrzā Qāzī Hāmi al-Dīn Nagaurī, towards the south of the Tomb of Khwājā Bakhtiyār Kākī, indicating that at least a small suburban settlement existed around the *dargāh* of this saint, south of the Quṭb complex.

Finally, a suburb must have existed along the northern Ridge, where the Kushak-i Shikar, the famous hunting lodge of Fīrūz, stands. On the highest point was the Observatory, a tower on which the sultan erected a chiming clock. Popularly known as Pīr Ghaib, the Hidden Saint, this tower had underground galleries connecting it to the plain to the west. A tank with a long flight of steps of the same period was also here. Other hunting lodges and palaces were probably located on the southern Ridge.

The boundaries of the city of Fīrūzābād may best be seen by looking at the monumental remains of the reign of Fīrūz. The monuments the sultan built and restored are found from Wazīrābād in the north to the Quṭb area in the south. The Kotlā was the citadel around which a city grew extending over a semi-circle, with a radius of about 1 km. The population area extended north to where the Lahore Gate is today, the land still further north probably being uninhabited. The population then bent south, between the Qadam Sharīf and the walls built later to include the area around where the Turkmān Gate is today and here the Kalān Mosque was constructed. The Jumna River apparently formed the eastern limit of the city, giving protection in the event of a siege. The Ridge naturally protected Fīrūzābād on the western side. There were large population centres in the south, in Khirkī, Begampūr and Lado Sarai, as well as around the area known as Hauz Khās.

The residential quarters were scattered over a wide area, as the architectural remains of the period testify. The whole plain between the Kotlā and the northern Ridge, between the Jumna and Hauz Khās, might have been a great centre of population scattered about the recognised cities. In between were the more sparsely populated suburbs, generally formed about a shrine of a holy man. During the reign of Fīrūz, a "holy suburb" existed in the north, around the Shrine of Shāh Ālam in Wazīrābād and around the Shrine of Qadam Sharīf near the Lahore Gate. In the south there were others around the Shrine of Chirāgh-i Dillī and Bakhtiyār Kākī.

The remaining monuments of Fīrūzābād help to reconstruct the limits of what must have once been an extensive city with characteristics of other medieval Islamic cities in the fourteenth century. The features Fīrūzābād shared with other more typical Islamic cities were a citadel place on a naturally defensive site, a royal compound grouping residences, administrative offices and army barracks, and numerous urban complexes around the citadel, and suburbs, some outside the city walls, built around the shrines of holy men.

The monuments of this age were constructed in a manner little understood by local Indian masons. The true arch with a keystone was used extensively but alongside this Islamic method of bridging openings the more ancient system of laying a stone or beam horizontally across two upright slabs to form a window or door was also employed. On arched arcades heavy bracketed cornices were introduced. Curiously, no free-standing or attached minarets were added to mosques.

The standard congregational mosque of the Tughluq era is built in a hypostyle plan, an open court surrounded by arcades on all sides. The congregational mosque of Jahānpanāh, the Begampūr Mosque, built by Muḥammad Tughluq, is the earliest of the series. The projecting entrance gateway combines both a dome and an interior *īwān* in Iranian fashion, a plan perhaps brought to India by Muḥammad's architect, Zahīr al-Dīn al-Jayush.[6] The main domed gateway and the two subsidiary gateways on the north and south sides are approached by a flight of steps on the east side.

The large central court is surrounded by single-bayed arcades on the south, east and north sides and by a three-bayed prayer hall covered by low domes on the west. The Begampūr Mosque is the earliest example of the four-*īwān* plan used in India, with an *īwān* and a dome in the centre of each court façade. The pylon-shaped *qibla īwān* is a tall arched tower with three openings and engaged tapering turrets of three storeys at each of the quoins creating a sloping appearance. In shape the turrets have one polygonal and two circular stories. A large dome rises in the earlier *maqsūra* screen. The arcades are encircled by deep stone cornices on brackets and the bays are crowned by sixty-four low domes. A slightly projecting entrance on the north side leads to a royal *maqsūra* three bays square, with its own *miḥrāb,* located at the north end of the *qibla* wall. The rubble walls of the mosque are sloped and covered with thick plaster relieved by tesserae of blue enamel tiles, occasionally still visible.

[6] A. Welch and H.Crane, "The Tughluqs: Master Builders of the Delhi Sultanate," *Muqarnas,* vol. I, New Haven, 1983, p. 130.

A second plan used by builders during the Tughluq period is that of the two-storeyed mosque situated on a high plinth. The earliest example of this type is the Jāmi' Mosque in Fīrūzābād built by Fīrūz in about 1354. The mosque for prayer was situated on the upper floor, while the ground storey contained arched cells probably intended as a *sarā'i* or for shops rented as *waqi* properties for the upkeep of the mosque.[7] A projecting domed gateway on the north side was the main entrance. The court is enclosed by domed arcades of the usual type. Eight pillars supported a dome over a pool in the centre of the court and on them was inscribed the text the sultan's *futūhāt.*

The minister Khān-i Jahān Shāh in 1387 commissioned the Kalān Mosque [Ill. 32] to be built in the northern part of the city. This structure follows the same plan as the Jāmi' Mosque of Fīrūzābād and is also built on a plinth of arcaded cells and is entered by a domed entrance gateway on the east side over which is the patron's dedicatory inscription. Around a central open court are domed arcades one bay wide [Ill. 33] and a prayer hall divided into fifteen bays, three by five. The *qibla* wall has five *miḥrābs.*

The cruciform or cross-axial[8] mosque plan is the third variation found only twice in Tughluq architecture. The first example is the Khirkī Mosque in Jahānpanāh, a large square structure situated on a high plinth[Ill. 34][Plan 3]. Three projecting domed gateways, one on each side, are each flanked by tapering engaged turrets, similar to those of the Begampūr Mosque. But their shapes differ, those of the main entrance on the east side are four storeys high with stellate flanging on the second resembling the Quṭb Mīnār. On the north and south sides the turrets are three-storeyed and circular.

On the upper level, above the basement storey of vaulted cells, are pointed arched windows with pierced screens. Two domed aisles, each three bays wide, divide the interior into four squares, each with an open square court. An arcade three bays by fifteen runs around the interior on all four sides of the mosque. When seen from above, the mosque [Ill. 35] is composed of nine bays each with high domes on drums including the decorated central dome, and twelve with lower domes and flat roofs. The projecting *miḥrāb* is a domed chamber with engaged *mīnārs* which resembles the gateways.

The Khirkī Mosque is generally dated to the latter part of the reign of Fīrūz Shāh, but there is no epigraphic or literary evidence to support this claim. It has recently been suggested[9] that the mosque was built before the foundation of the city of Fīrūzābād and that it was, in fact, Fīrūz's contribution to the capital where he lived from 1351 to 1354. If this is so, the Khirkī Mosque is the earliest example of the architectural patronage of Fīrūz.

The new dating would also explain the relationship between the Khirkī and Kālī Mosques [Plan 4], the second example of a cross-axial plan, the latter in the Dargāh of Nizāmuddīn. An inscription over the eastern door of the Kālī Mosque states that it was built by Fīrūz's minister, Khān-i Jahān Junān Shāh, using the same plan, on a smaller scale as the sultan's Khirkī Mosque.[10] The smaller version was also constructed

[7] Ibid.

[8] This mosque plan is called cross-axial by A.Welch and *caturāṅgana* or four-quartered by R.Nath in *History of Sultanate Architecture*, pp. 69-73.

[9] Welch, op. cit., pp. 130, 161, n. 45.

[10] Ibid., p. 139.

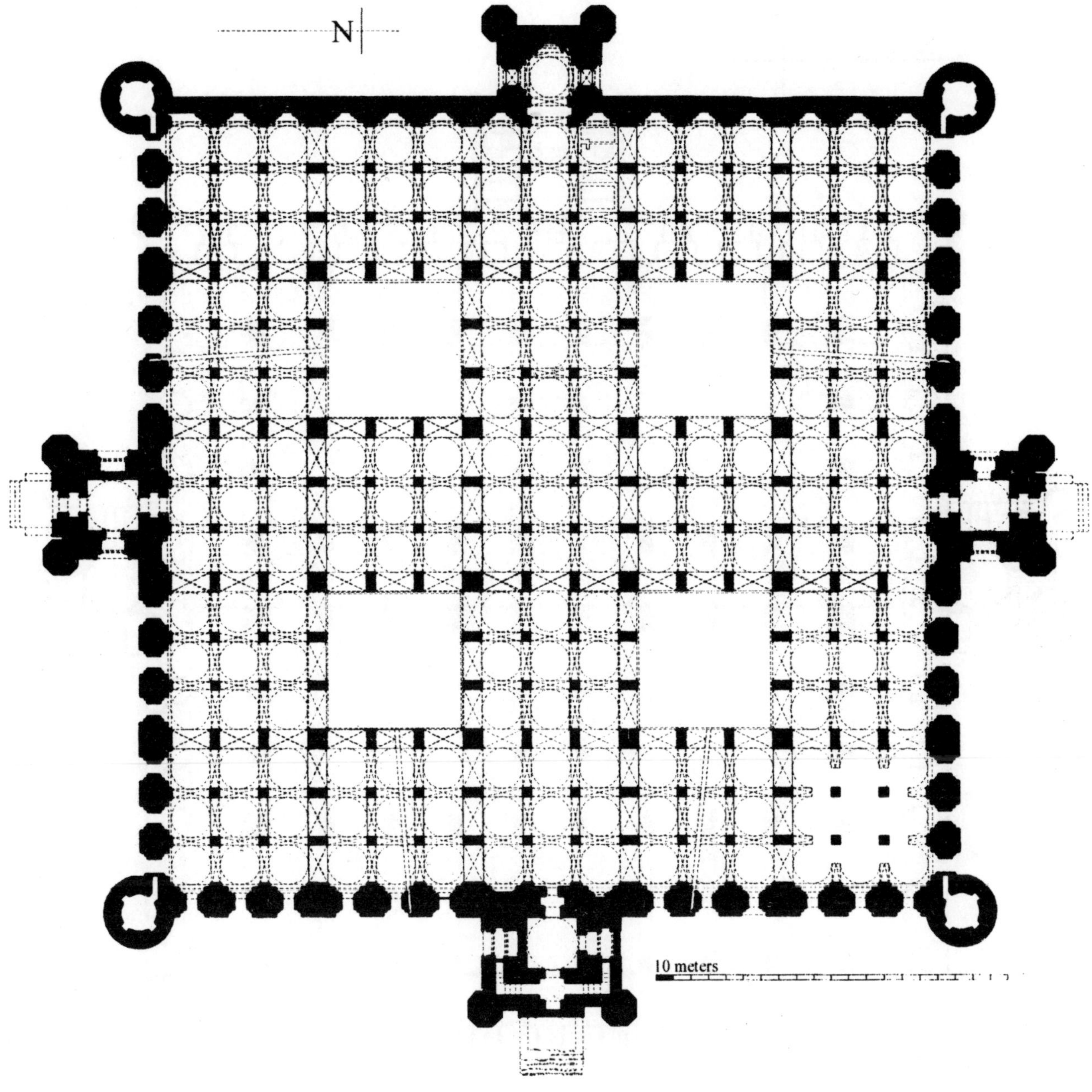

Plan 3. Delhi, Khirkī Mosque (after Archaeological Survey of India)

in a square hypostyle plan, with one-bayed arcades around the open court on the north, south and east sides, and a prayer hall three bays deep. The entrance is through square domed gateways flanked by engaged, tapering circular turrets with no stellate flanging. It has been suggested that copying the design of the great Quṭb Mīnār appears to have been a royal prerogative,[11] and that the Kālī Mosque was the minister's variation on a royal mosque plan.

[11]Ibid.

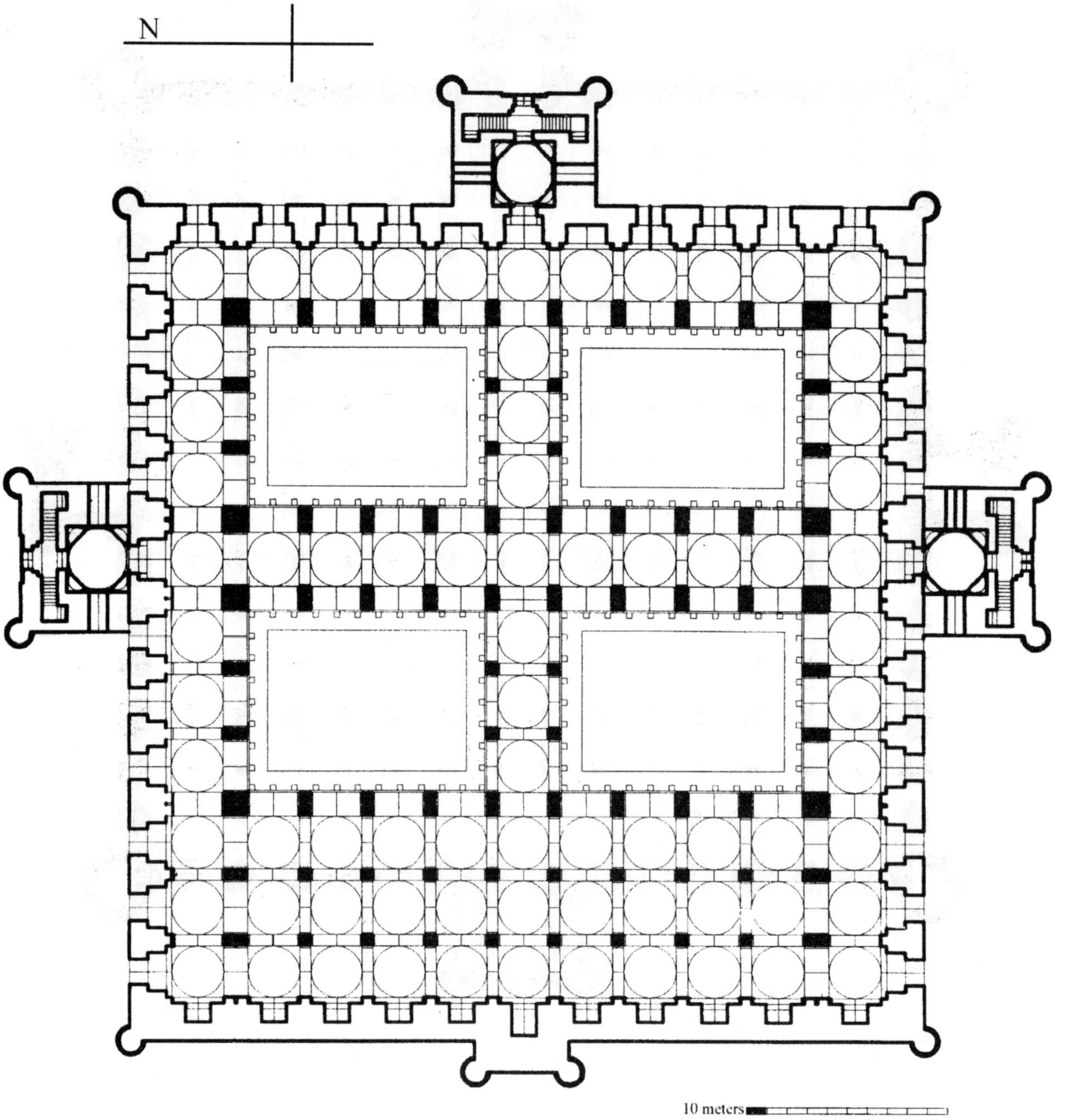

Plan 4. Delhi, Kālī Mosque, Niẓāmuddīn (after Archaeological Survey of India)

Besides those used for congregational worship, mosques were also built by Fīrūz as simple prayer halls without a courtyard. Examples of structures with this plan are found in the Tomb of Naṣīr al-Dīn Maḥmūd known as Sultān Gharī, in the Dargāh of Shāh Ālam in Wazīrābād [Ill. 36], in the Dargāh of Qadam Sharīf (the tomb of sultan's son, Fath Khān), and in a tomb in Hauz Khās near the Madrasa of Fīrūz Shāh.

Four mosque plans were in use during the reign of Fīrūz Shāh. While the hypostyle and the simple prayer hall plan without a courtyard were not exclusively a Tughluq creation, the innovative plans of a two-storeyed mosque built on a high plinth and the remarkable cruciform or cross-axial mosque show the exceptional creative powers of the reign at their best. The genius which produced these masterpieces was almost crushed by the invasion of Tīmūr and his Mongol hordes. However it reasserted itself during the Mughal era in an amazing architectural style which blended foreign and indigenous ideas into a new and glorious Indian idiom.

Only one *madrasa* built by Fīrūz Shāh is extant and it is situated along the eastern and southern sides of the Hauz Khās tank [Ill. 37]. It was built in 1352 for the study of Arabic and Islamic law.

The double-storeyed structure consists of domed rooms and pillared halls, the lower storey used for a residence, the upper for lecture halls. A special garden was built within the complex. Other monuments are also located here, such as a ruined congregational mosque, an open T-shaped structure popularly referred to as the Conventional Hall, which may have served as a debating chamber, and numerous pavilions and tombs. Among the latter the most impressive is the domed Tomb of Fīrūz Shāh located where the southern and eastern buildings intersect. The Madrasa of Fīrūz Shāh is the largest and most complete of its kind in India and during the late fourteenth century it must have been one of the most important intellectual centres in the Muslim world.

The most popular tomb plan in the Tughluq era was the square design introduced in the Tomb of Ghiyāth al-Dīn in Tughluqābād. Fīrūz himself also chose the square plan for his tomb in the Hauz Khās complex [Ill. 38], but unlike the earlier tomb, did not face it with marble but with plaster, probably originally painted. The tomb is approached on the south by a verandah enclosed by a stone railing of stupa prototype. From the west and north walls entrances lead to the *madrasa* complex. The tomb was repaired by Sikandar Lodī in the sixteenth century.

Surrounded by battlemented walls, the last major Tughluq tomb is the octagonal Mausoleum of Khān-i Jahān Tilangānī (1368), prime minister of Fīrūz, in the Dargāh of Niẓām al-Dīn Awliyā. An arched gateway on the north side leads to the domed tomb enclosed by a verandah pierced with three arched openings on each side supported on double square pillars. The sloping walls are relieved by a stone cornice and a domed *chhatrī* over each side of the octagon. Khān-i Jahān died in 1368 and it appears likely that his son, Khān-i Jahān Junān Shāh, built the tomb of his father after his death. The design was probably copied from the Tomb of Zafar Khān in the complex of Ghiyāth al-Dīn Tughluq. The Niẓāmuddīn tomb, however, is the first large octagonal mausoleum which served as a model for the numerous octagonal tombs built by the Sayyid and Lodī sultans.

A third more unusual tomb plan was evolved during the Tughluq period. The domed pavilion (*chhatrī*) began to be used frequently during this time and three different plans are found in the Hauz Khās area. The simplest is a six-sided pavilion supported by six sets of double piers.[12] An octagonal pavilion tomb supported on eight sets of double piers stands near the former. While square pavilion tombs are

[12]For a complete study of the tombs of the Sultanate period and the best classification of pavilion tombs see Friedrich Wetzel, *Islāmische Grabbauten in Indien aus der Zeit der Soldatenkaiser, 1320-1540,* Leipzig, 1918. For pavilion tombs, pp.15-24.

generally supported by twelve piers, the unusual T-shaped structure known as Convention Hall, is composed of three square pavilion tombs, each supported by twelve piers. In this monument a columned hall has a square mausoleum at both ends and a third, a larger tomb in the short axis. Built on a plinth, all these monuments were relieved by stone cornices supported on brackets. The pavilion plan first appears in Tughluq Delhi but becomes increasingly more popular during the Sayyid and Lodī periods, when tombs were combined with mosques and *'īdgāhs* and had the spaces between the piers closed with beautifully pierced masonry screens.

A great variety of tombs were built during the Tughluq period. It has been suggested that the square, the octagonal and the pavilion tombs were each used by certain segments of society.[13] According to this thesis, the three Tughluq rulers were buried in square tombs, associated with kingship. Royal princes, on the other hand, preferred octagonal tombs, while saints and other religious men chose pavilion tombs. While this rule appears not to have been followed during later centuries, under the Tughluqs, apparently, the shape of the tomb indicated the rank of the person baried within.

Four small hunting residences belonging to Fīrūz are located near Delhi: the Kushak-i Maḥāl, the Malcha Maḥāl, the Bhūlī Bhaṭiyārī Maḥāl and the *maḥal* in the village of Mahipālpūr, south of Delhi. All four are temporary rest houses used during the hunt and served as prototypes for the many hunting lodges built under Mughal patronage in the seventeenth century.

The architectural style of the Tughluq period found its way to some newly founded cities like Daulatābād, Jaunpūr, Fathabād and Hissār[14] and served as the prototype on which these new styles of architecture were to evolve. The tomb became the most important structure during Tughlaq times, leading in the later Sayyid and Lodī periods to such a proliferation that Delhi virtually became a royal necropolis. Under the Mughals the tomb was actually glorified and this led to the construction of the magnificent Tāj Mahal. But all these later developments might have evolved quite differently, if the builders of the Tughluq period had not laid the groundwork for the glorious Mughal age.

[13]Percy Brown, *Indian Architecture: The Islamic Period,* Bombay, 1968, pp. 26-27.
[14]Mehrdad Shokoohy and Natalie H. Shokoohy, *Hisār-i Fīrūza,* London, 1988.

CHAPTER 6

The Sayyid (1414-45), Lodī (1451-1526) and Sūr Dynasties (1539-45)

Tīmūr's sack of Delhi in 1398 swept everything before it. No longer the great capital city of an extensive empire, Delhi shrank to the rank of a provincial city, a local capital at times controlling only the immediate surrounding area. The political history of Hindustan from Tīmūr to the first Mughal emperor, Bābur, does not make happy reading. During the first half of the period, despite its struggle for survival, the Delhi Sultanate was shrinking. Some stability was attained in the second half of the period, some lost territory reclaimed, but then, in 1526, all was lost to Bābur at Pānīpat, a battle to cost Ibrāhīm Lodī his realm and his life. In the political sphere, therefore, the fifteenth century was a period of decay and disintegration, although, in the middle of the century, the Lodī sultans (1451-1526) made some vigorous efforts to revive Delhi's status by vanquishing the Sharqīs of Jaunpūr and by starting some extensive building projects in the capital.

During this politically troubled time, however, Delhi became the home of the lovely architectural style of the Lodīs, an unique combination of Hindu and Muslim elements in architecture. In the social and cultural sphere, therefore, the Lodī period was one of sustained progress and more than moderate achievements. In addition to the introduction of a new style of architecture, works of classical and regional languages were produced and social reformers and poets were drawn to the capital. The Lodī age was more than a century of cultural, social and religious reforms and has aptly been called an interlude, an appendix to the Delhi Sultanate as well as a preface to the Mughal period. In architecture the high point was reached in the reign of Shīr Shāh Sūr, whose mosque in the Purānā Qila' is perhaps the crowning achievement of the age.

The successors of the Tughluqs in the shattered and torn capital were the Sayyids, who at first ruled in the name of the Tīmūrīds and whose territory after independence never extended beyond the Punjab. In practice the new dynasty never controlled more than the immediate neighbourhood of Delhi. Four Sayyid sultans hasten across the stage until they in turn are replaced in 1451 by the more powerful and effective Afghan noble, Bahlol Lodī. His son, Sikandar, continued the work and by the conquest of Jaunpūr restored the Delhi Sultanate to something of its former imperial dimensions. The last Lodī sultan was the cause of intrigues which brought the adventurer Bābur to India. But all Lodī hopes ended on that fatal field of Pānīpat where the sultans lost his life amidst his deserting troops, fighting bravely to the end, Richard the Loinheatted of India. The victor on that day was the adventurer Bābur, who brought with him the age of the great Mughals. In its heyday the Lodī Empire extended from the Indus River in the west to the bend of the Ganges River in Bihar in the east and in the north nearly to the Himalayas.

The Sayyid rulers initially attempted to build new capitals as their predecessors had done. The first Sayyid ruler, Khizr Khān, established his court at Khizrābād in 1418. His successor, Mubārak Shāh, started but never finished Mubārakābād, another city in 1433, but the Sayyid and Lodī rulers who followed him built no further cities at Delhi. The second ruler of the Lodī line, Sikandar, lived for some months in the area of the Quṯb, and built the Moth kī Mosque there, however, he later moved the capital to the neighbourhood of Āgrā and started a new city for himself at Sikandarābād, where Akbar's Tomb is now situated.

In addition to the state treasury Tīmūr carried away with him many good craftsmen, architects and stone-workers to his capital of Samarkand to build for him there. Other craftsmen, following the confusion of the carnage, migrated to various provincial capitals. Without money and with no artisans it was impossible for the rulers of Delhi to accomplish anything. Not surprisingly, therefore that during the first decade after Tīmūr's departure only one monument was constructed, an *'īdgāh* whose patron was Mallū Iqbāl Khān. Yet as the fifteenth century moved on, an original style of architecture appeared best seen in the royal tombs. The Lodī architectural style is an unique combination of Hindu and Muslim elements, which reaches its heights in the reign of Humāyūn and Shīr Shāh.

The buildings constructed during the Sayyid and Lodī periods are either tombs or mosques. The mausoleum, in particular, appealed to these rulers and scores of large tombs arose in Delhi, including three for the sultans themselves. Before the Lodīs, elaborate tombs were built only for rulers, their families and saints, but during the time of the Lodī dynasty tombs were constructed not just for royalty, but also for nobles and prominent courtiers. The reason for the proliferation of memorial structures might have been due to the changing attitude towards kingship.[1] Under earlier Islamic dynasties the sultans had been considered an absolute autocrat, but the Lodīs, a settled Afghan tribe, considered the ruler only first among equals in tribal custom. Therefore, the nobles also merited tombs, which had formerly been a royal prerogative. It has been claimed that to distinguish their tombs those of the nobles were built square in plan, rather than octagonal, a shape which was henceforth identified with royal tombs.[2]

Tombs are of two plans, either octagonal surrounded by an arched verandah, one storey in height with a projecting cornice, or square, with two or three storeys of blind arcades on the exterior. Both types are domed and have a range of pillared kiosks rising above the parapet, either at the corners on square tombs, or at the centre of each of the sides in octagonal structures.

Square tombs follow the prototype of the Tomb of Ghiyāth al-Dīn and have a tall projecting central entrance. The outer walls, however, are not slanted as in earlier examples, but vertical. Throughout, the masonry appears rough, originally probably plastered, with dressed stone used only at the entrance. The entire structure is covered by a pointed dome supported on squinches at each corner.

The square-tomb plan is much favoured during the Sayyid and Lodī periods and in Delhi and its environs there are many such mausolea. Now only known by their local names, it is difficult to guess who might be buried within. The most prominent

[1]See Anil Chandra Banerjee, *The State and Society in Northern India: 1206-1526,* Calcutta, pp. 52-53; also Matsuo Ara, "The Lodi Rulers and the Consideration of Tomb Building in Delhi," *Acta Asiatica,* vol. XLIII, 1982, pp. 71-80 as quoted by Catherine Asher in *Architecture of Mughal India,* Cambridge, 1992, p.13.

[2]Sir John Marshall, "The Monuments of Muslim India," *The Cambridge History of India,* vol. III, Cambridge, 1922, pp. 594 ff.

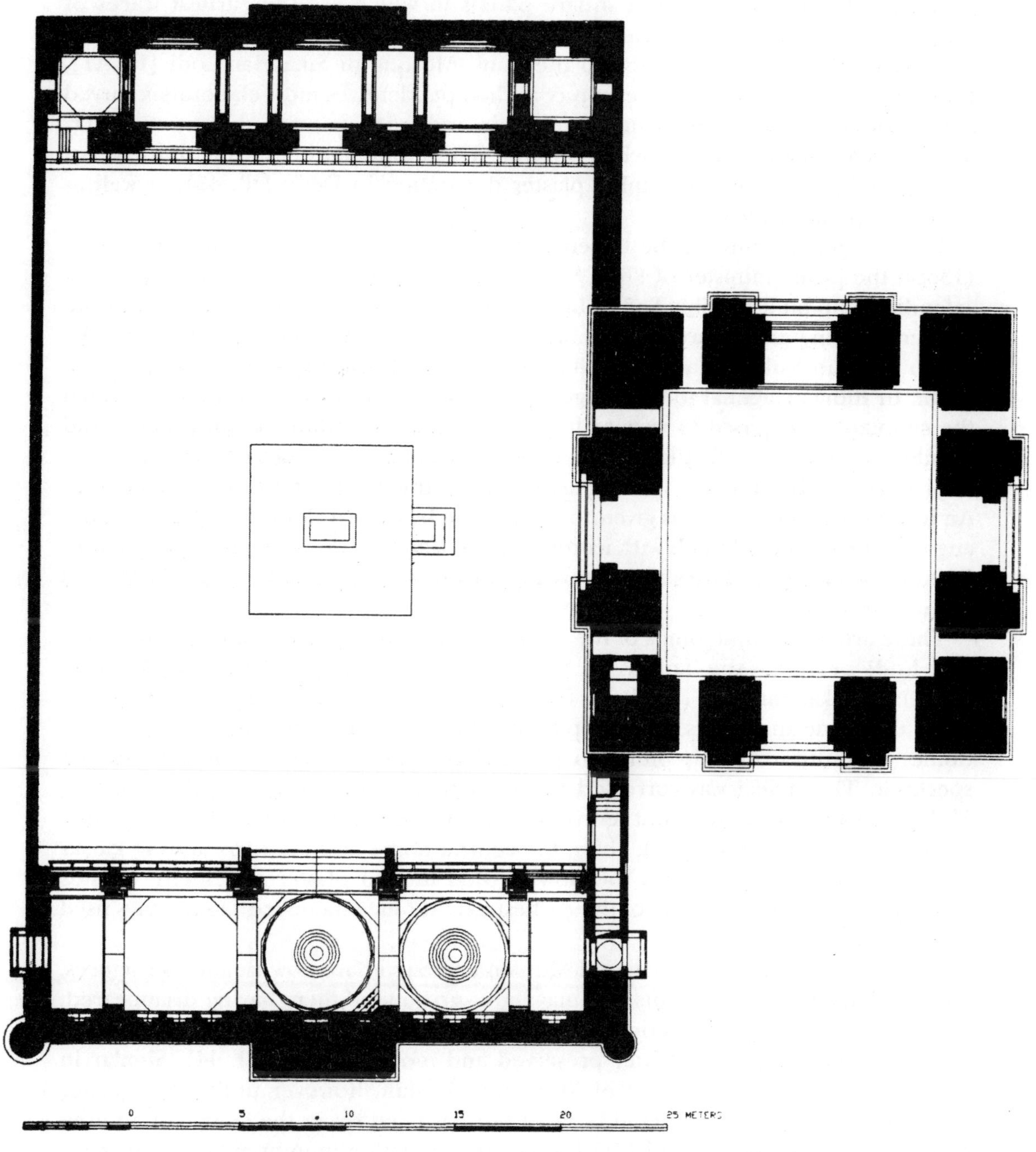

Plan 5. Delhi, Barā Gumbad (after Archaeological Survey of India)

among them are the Barā Khān kā Gumbad, the Chhotī Khān kā Gumbad [Ill. 39], the Barā Gumbad, the Shīsh Gumbad, the Dādī kā Gumbad and the Polī kā Gumbad.

The earliest tomb in the square plan is that of Bahlol Lodī (1488) built by Sikandar Lodī, the son of Bahlol Lodī, outside the western wall of the enclosure of the Dargāh Niẓām al-Dīn Awliyā. The first important square tomb after the invasion of Tīmūr is the Shīsh Gumbad (1490) where the exterior is divided into two storeys of blind arcades with a central frieze of square panels in which are the earliest traces of turquoise blue glazed tiles in Delhi. The second square tomb is the Barā Gumbad (1494)[Ill. 40][Plan 5], attached to the Jāmi' Mosque of Sikandar Lodī [Ill. 41]. Built of grey stone, the domes rest on corbelled pendentives most elaborately carved and finished [Ill. 42]. There is no grave within and for that reason the structure may have been a gateway to the attached mosque. This monument has some of the finest incised arabesque and calligraphic plaster decoration in Delhi [Ill. 43], as well as traces of coloured tilework.

The octagonal tomb can be traced back to the Tomb of Khān Jahān Tilangānī (1368), the prime minister of Fīrūz Shāh Tughluq, and finds its culmination in the splendid tomb built for Shīr Shāh Sūr in Sassarām, Bihar. Octagonal tombs without the surrounding arcades were common in Persia before this period, resembling the Tomb of Shāh Rukn-i Ālam in Multān, suggesting a possible line of influence to Delhi. In India octagonal tombs range from simple open pillared pavilions in which the cenotaph is exposed to view to imposing structures within spacious walled and arcaded compounds with attached mosques. The octagonal tombs in Delhi are built of plastered rubble, the surrounding arcade protecting the plaster from the elements. An impression of battering is given to the outline by inward sloping buttresses at the angles. The octagonal tomb with its roof *guldastas* and merlons remained popular in Delhi for over two centuries and eventually provided inspiration for some of Akbar's monuments.

There are three royal tombs of the octagonal type built in Delhi during the Sayyid and Lodī periods—the Tombs of Mubārak Sayyid (1432), Muḥammad Sayyid (1444)and Sikandar Lodī (1517). In the earliest of the series, the Tomb of Mubārak Shāh, the dome and kiosks, which replaced subsidiary domes and flanked the central dome, were unfortunately built too low and could therefore not be seen by the spectator. This defect was corrected in the next octagonal structure, the Tomb of Muḥammad Sayyid, built about ten years later. While this tomb has about the same dimensions as that of Mubārak Shāh, the central dome and the surrounding kiosks are raised higher. Along with the now refined incised plaster ornament, on this tomb may also be found some of the earliest extant blue enamelled mosaic tiles used for decoration.

The Tombs of Mubārak Shāh and Muḥammad Sayyid are now isolated structures, any supplementary monuments that may have surrounded them having disappeared. The next octagonal tomb, belonging to Sikandar Lodī (1517), constructed by his son and successor, Ibrāhīm, is better preserved and more finished [Ill. 44]. Similar in design and dimensions to that of Muḥammad Shāh, however unlike the earlier examples, since it does not stand isolated but has been set in the centre of a raised and walled garden compound (the Lodī Gardens) with a monumental entrance on the south side and a *qibla* wall on the west. This arrangement paved the way for the splendid Mughal garden tombs to follow. A change may also be noted in the arcade which now has double stone pillars making a pier with a single capital to support the arches. While the shape of the dome is no improvement on those of the earlier tombs, it is supposedly one of the earliest double domes in India, a design to find much favour with the Mughals in the succeeding centuries. Another novel feature is the extended use of enamelled tiles in shades of green, yellow, light and dark blue and in a variety of patterns. In general, the tomb of Sikandar Lodī shows little improvement over earlier octagonal structures, indicating that art evolved very slowly, if at all, during these difficult times.

* * *

Although Bābur founded the Mughal Empire in 1526, it was not really until forty years later that the great period of Mughal building began. The delay was largely due to the unsettled state of the country. Between 1540 and 1555 the government was in the hands of Shīr Shāh Sūr and his sons, who drove the second Mughal emperor, Humāyūn, into Persia for fifteen years, an exile which was to have a lasting effect on Indian art and culture. Humāyūn returned some years later accompanied by two Iranian artists who would irreversably change the now antiquated Lodī architectural style.

The first part of Shīr Shāh's work is at his capital of Sassarām in Bihar where a series of octagonal tombs shows the final fulfilment of the Lodī style on which they have been based. The second part, after having wrested the throne of Delhi from Humāyūn, is in the imperial capital, where Shīr Shāh proceeded by his active patronage to introduce a new architectural style a most important step in the development of the subsequent Mughal style.

In the earlier Sassarām phase there is a group of tombs, three belonging to the Sūr family and one to the architect who built them. And among these tombs are some of the finest examples of the Lodī architectural style. Shīr Shāh's Tomb [Ill. 45] is the most splendid of these monuments and one of the grandest and most imaginative architectural conceptions in India. It is the largest tomb up to that time ever built in India. The tomb is several times larger than an ordinary Lodī tomb and resembles an immense pyramidal structure in five distinct phases, the whole rising 50 m. The tomb stands in the centre of a great artificial lake.

The two lower storeys, a stepped basement rising directly out of the water and a tall terrace above it, are square in plan. The octagonal tomb in three stages stands in the centre of the courtyard. The lowest storey is a verandah with three arches in each of its sides and a projecting eave above. The second storey is a plain wall with pillared kiosks at each angle. And in the third stage, the drum of the dome is relieved by kiosks which break the circular base crowned by a massive lotus finial. The whole conception is really in five tiers—the steps from the water, the high plinth of the stairs, the main storey, the high octagonal drum and the dome set on a sixteen-sided drum. The Tomb of Shīr Shāh Sūr is the culmination of the octagonal mausoleum. The Mughals did not favour this plan and built their memorial structures in the square form.

* * *

The change of political power after the Mughal victory of Pānīpat in 1525 did not close the Lodī architectural period and several buildings were constructed in the old style well into the sixteenth century, when, about 1560, the new Mughal art made its grand entrance. Two of these monuments belonging stylistically to the Delhi Sultanate period are the tombs of the noblemen 'Īsā and Ādam Khān. The Tomb of 'Īsā Khān (1547) [Ill. 46] is an octagonal structure built by the Afghan noble at the court of Shīr Shāh. The design is conventional, three arches in each of the octagonal sides supported by angle buttresses and an eave. The corner buttresses show the remains of the Fīrūzian slope, the last building of its kind to include this structural batter in its composition. *Chhatrīs* are in the middle of each octagonal side over the parapet, below the drum. The drum and buttresses are crowned by a lotus finial. On the western side of the enclosure is a small mosque which is, perhaps, the most successful example of a three-arched façade mosque. The arch shapes are pointed and double recessed and of equal size, outlined with green and blue glazed tiles. The central arch is set in a frame of red stone ornamented with sunk niches and turquoise and green glazed tiles on three sides. The side arches are decorated with stucco carving and there is a single dome over the monument and three *miḥrābs* in the *qibla* wall.

The Tomb of Ādam Khān built fourteen years later gives an elevated effect, since it is built on a hill. In the structure itself additional elevation has been gained by raising the drum of the dome, converting it into an intermediate story, a triforium, quite a prominent part of the structure. An arched recess in each of the sixteen sides of the drum is a skilful device used effectively to create passages of shadow in the composition. This monument is the last example of the Lodī type and its treatment and character indicate that the style, as far as Delhi is concerned, has attained its final expression.

Under the Lodīs a new type of mosque is developed the plan of which became increasingly more important under the Mughals. Instead of large congregational mosques favoured earlier, small private mosques attached to tombs became popular. These generally are single-aisled and have five bays, with a five-arched façade. With the accession of Sikandar Lodī, a devout Muslim, mosque construction is increased throughout the realm. Among the notable structures built during this reign are the mosque attached to the Barā Gumbad(1494)and the Moth kī Mosque (1505-10). These are the first examples of a series of mosques with high entrance portals (*pishtaq*) produced during the next half century, the finest of which is the private mosque of Qila'i Kuhna, the royal chapel of Shīr Shāh Sūr, in the walled citadel of Delhi known as the Purānā Qil'a.

The mosque attached to the Barā Gumbad is more a domestic chapel and represents the origin of the Lodī idea. The façade has five equal arches of an unusually wide span with outlines emphasized by receding planes. The aim of the builder appears to create a surface on which to display the splendid and unusual stucco ornament.

The second example of the series, the Moth kī Mosque (1505) [Ill. 47], while built on the same plan, is more aesthetically pleasing. The shape and proportion of the five facade arches have improved, with emphasis given to the central bay. The three stone and mortar domes on their narrow necks in the usual Lodī style are better spaced over the central and side bays. Vitality is added to the entire concept by the addition of two-storeyed open towers at the rear corners [Ill. 48], with traces of coloured tile decoration.

A tale circulates that the Moth kī Mosque was so named in the reign of Sikandar Shāh Lodī when a poor man picked up a grain of pulse (*moth*), and sowed it in the earth. He vowed to devote its produce to a charitable purpose. The crops multiplied year after year until, after some time, there was enough money to build this mosque.

The mosque stands on the west side of a raised plinth fronted by arched cells and enclosed by a low wall. The entrance is on the east through an ornamental red sandstone gateway inlaid with white marble. The gateway is quite remarkable for its fine carving, mostly in geometrical designs.

The sanctuary consists of a large rectangular hall with five arched openings in its facade. The central arch is enclosed by a high and deeply recessed arch of red sandstone ornamented with marble and a small window under the apex. The support of the central dome is on squinch arches as in most earlier monuments. But the support of the two side domes is unusual for it consists of stalactite pendentives introduced here in the angles for the zone of transition.

The Moth kī Mosque is much larger than the mosque attached to the Barā Gumbad and it therefore provided more scope for the skill of the craftsmen. Red sandstone, white marble and glazed tiles intermingle in the decoration. The spandrels above the arches have arabesque designs of an Islamic character. There was obviously a talented group of artists engaged in mosque decoration in Delhi during the fifteenth century.

Sikandar Lodī is by far the greatest builder of the fifteenth century. Inscriptions on various buildings in northern India indicate his love for architectural activity. He is credited with constructing a canal in 1492-93, a *bāolī* in Rajasthan and mosques in almost all important cities including Lahore, Karnāl, Hansi and Makanpur, besides many in Delhi and Āgrā. There are also the many nameless mosques and tombs belonging to the Lodī period, which from their design and material of construction can be safely attributed to Sikandar's time. Like Fīrūz Shāh, Sikandar Lodī was not only a great builder but also an inveterate restorer. In his reign the mausoleum of the poet Amīr Khusraw (1492) was built. An inscribed frieze at the entrance doorway of the Quṭb Mīnār[3] credits him with repairing this great edifice in 1503. A few other buildings of his son and successor Ibrāhīm Lodī are also extant, such as the Tomb of Khwājā Khizr (1522) and the Rājon kī Bāolī with an attached mosque. But Ibrāhīm's political difficulties left him little time for much building activity.

Before the third of the series of mosques, that of Jamālī Kamālī (1528), is built an epoch making event in the history of India occurred. The decisive Battle of Pānīpat brought the rule of the Lodīs to an end, an episode which also ended the Sultanate of Delhi and ushered in the new Mughal era. One alien adventurer after another had ruled Hindustan, dynasty succeeded dynasty, royal houses had risen, flourished and fallen, but the central power had been consistently maintained in Delhi, in spite of all vicissitudes, for over three hundred years. And now the great Sultanate pageant is finished, and a new dynasty is to fill the stage. The Mughals was founded that day in 1526 by Bābur, prince of the house of Tīmūr.

But in spite of the fundamental changes this movement brought, in mosque as well as in tomb design the original Sultanate style of architecture in the form assumed under the Lodī sultans continues for another half century. This is due as much to its prestige and ancient usage as to the unsettled state of the country under the early Mughals which precluded anything new to replace it. The Jamālī Kamālī Mosque was built during the reign of Humāyūn (1530-40; 1555-56), the second Mughal emperor. Despite political conditions, the art of construction remaines unaffected and continues along its former course.

The Jamālī Kamālī Mosque [Ill. 49] [Plan 6] and Tomb (1528-35) are built to commemorate Fazl Allāh Jalāl Khān, a poet and saint who lived from the reign of Sikandar Lodī to that of Humāyūn. The two graves in the flat roofed tomb enclosure are of Jamālī and his brother, Kamālī. The ceiling is of painted plaster and tile work, filled with Jamālī's own verses. The arches are almost four-centered [Ill. 50], the central one flanked by fluted pilasters and a single dome.

It is apparent that builders were trying to return to the more ornate style of the

[3]J.A. Page, *A Guide to the Qutb*, Delhi, 1938, p. 21.

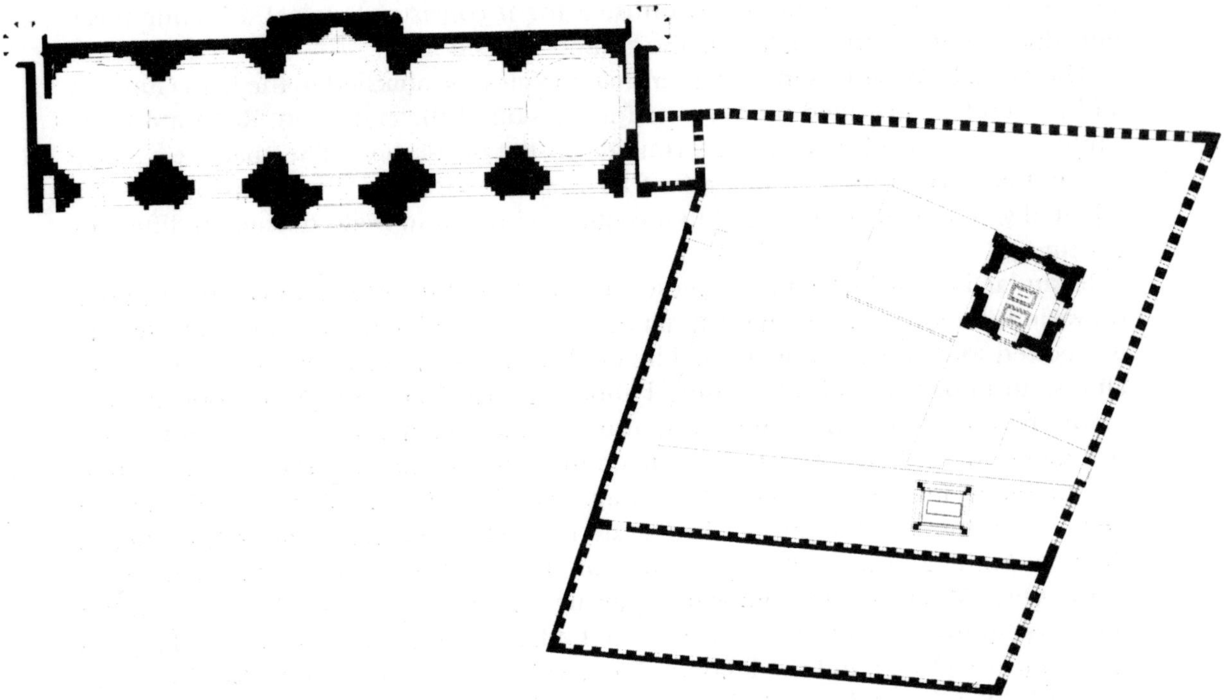

Plan 6. Delhi, Mosque and Tomb of Jamālī Kamālī (after Archaeological Survey of India)

Khaljīs, with its fine ashlar masonry, instead of the rubble and plaster monuments of the Tughluq period. The Jamālī Kamālī Mosque shows that an attempt was made here to achieve a more refined style generally by using better materials and finer workmanship. But the Jamālī Kamālī Mosque, despite its more advanced delicate treatment and fine technique, is in itself merely a preparation for the fourth and last mosque of the period, the Qila'i Kuhna in the Purānā Qil'a. Shīr Shāh Sūr's "chapel royal" not only marks the end of the old Lodī phase but heralds the beginning of a new era in Indian Islamic architecture. The Qila'i Kuhna Mosque[Ill. 51] is the connecting link between the old Sultanate style of architecture and the approaching style of the Mughals.

A large walled enclosure marked the site of Shīr Shāh's citadel, the Purānā Qil'a, around which the new capital, the sixth city of Delhi was to be built. The rectangular citadel has massive corner bastions and an entrance through the north gate.

The site of the new city dates back to Indraprastha, the ancient capital of the Pāṇḍavas in the *Mahābhārata* epic. The present walls and gates, however, were probably started by Emperor Humāyūn in 1530 when he came to Delhi to build a new capital for the Mughal dynasty to be called Dīn Panāh. Humāyūn's scheme was never finished, for in 1540 Shīr Shāh took over the government of Delhi. He strengthened the citadel and built the Qila'i Kuhna Mosque and the Shīr Mandāl, renaming the fort Shīr Garh.

The Qila'i Kuhna Mosque (1541)is the congregational mosque of Shīr Shāh's new city. The façade of the prayer hall is divided into five arched bays, the central one higher than the others, each with an open archway recessed within it. The central arch is flanked by narrower, fluted pilasters and is richly carved in black and white marble and red sandstone. On the interior there are five *miḥrābs* set into the *qibla* wall [Ill. 52]. The arches are ornamented with arabesques and calligraphy and the central bay is crowned by a low dome.

The Shīr Mandal [Ill. 53] is one of the rare secular buildings preserved in Delhi from the time before Shāh Jahān. A small octagonal tower of red sandstone, it is relieved only with white marble and is crowned by a pavilion. Built by Shīr Shāh, it was used as a library by Humāyūn. And here on its steep steps, on 24 January 1556, the Mughal emperor hurrying to obey the call of the *mu'azzin* to prayer, slipped to his death.

* * *

Emerging from the complete anarchy following Tīmūr's invasion of Hindustan is a vigorous new creative energy. The Sayyid and Lodī rulers once again looked to the ancient artistic tradition of Hindustan but simultaneously they also cast a glance westward towards Iran. The fusion of the two styles is responsible for the new spirit of design of the Lodīs best seen in the beautiful ornamental details of the monuments, some inherited from the preceding centuries, but most introduced here for the first time. The use of blue enamelled tiles for decoration, an innovation of the fifteenth century, continues to be popular in later years. Other features the Lodīs contributed to the future development of Indo-Islamic architecture are surface ornament of incised coloured plaster, lotus finials on domes, stunted turrets, *guldasta*, small kiosks, fuller domes and pinnacles. The double domes and the octagonal mausoleum both used by the Lodīs are also adopted by the Mughals. But perhaps the greatest contribution of the Lodī age is the spacious tomb enclosure of the Tomb of Sikandar Lodī which anticipates the superb ornamental gardens of the Mughals.

CHAPTER 7

Bengal (1339-1576)

Muslim armies first reached Bengal in 1202 and under Bakhtiyār Khaljī, the lieutenant of Quṭb al-Dīn Aybak of Delhi, defeated the last Hindu Rājā Lakhau Sen. During the early Muslim period the governors of Bengal attained virtual independence from Delhi and assumed the authority of rulers. The Delhi sultan tried repeatedly to reassert control over the remote region and to prevent it from extending its frontiers, but was not successful. Sultan Ghiyāth al-Dīn Tughluq's decision to divide Bengal into three administrative capitals, Lakhnautī in the north, Sonārgāon in the east and Satgāon in the south, did not achieve the desired result either. Nor was the next ruler Muḥammad Tughluq more fortunate in his efforts to subdue Fakhr al-Dīn Mubārak, who revolted against imperial power in 1338, declared his independence, became the first Ilyās Shāhī ruler and transferred his capital, from Lakhnautī, the early site, to Pandua. It was not until the rule of his foster-brother, Shams al-Dīn Shāh (1345-58) that Bengal was finally united and brought under one rule. In 1352 Shams al-Dīn accepted the title of Shāh. This powerful new ruler rebuked the invasion of Fīrūz Shāh Tughluq in 1345 at Ekdale, giving the Delhi ruler no choice but to recognize the new independent Sultanate of Bengal, which was to flourish until its absorption into the Mughal Empire in 1576.

The majority of Beṅgālī monuments are found in the Māldā district, situated at the juncture of two great rivers, the Ganges and the Mahānadī. Most of the early Muslims settled in this area in which the former capital of the last Hindu Pāla and Sena dynasties had been located and where the two new Muslim capitals, Pandua and Gaur were to follow.

Brick is the most easily available material for construction in Bengal. There is no sandstone or granite, although a limited amount of black basalt is obtainable. The monuments of Bengal are, therefore, primarily built of brick, with only occasional stone facing. While brick is economical for construction, it is porous and allows water and humidity to penetrate. Stone veneer is therefore added, not just as an aesthetic adjunct, but to protect the surface walls from water damage. Lime is used as mortar and as a plaster to make the roof and the dome watertight.

The traditional Beṅgālī bamboo-thatched *chala* roof, with its exaggerated downward curve that so quickly sheds the monsoon rains, influenced the later brick monuments. Bamboo is strong and flexible and was traditionally used in thatched huts to frame roofs, which were given an upward curve to prevent sagging. Curved cornices are later incorporated into the Muslim style of building and emerge first in Pandua on the Eklakhī Tomb (1425). This feature is to become a permanent addition to later Beṅgālī monuments, eventually reappearing in the Mughal cities of Āgrā, Delhi and Lahore.

*　　　*　　　*

The earliest important Muslim buildings in Bengal are not in the capital of Lakhnautī, where nothing remains *in situ* but in the former sacred Hindu ghat village of Tribeni, probably in the fourteenth century the river port of Bengal, from where the Bhagīrathī flowed through south Bengal to the port Satgāon and the open sea.

The Muslim conquest of the region was primarily due to the military commander Zafar Khān Ghāzī (1298-1313) and to the Saint Shāh Saif al-Dīn, responsible for the spread of Islam. A mosque and tomb, commemorating the great military commander, are dated to this early period, as are the beginnings of the Dargāh of ṣūfī sultan.

The early Mosque of Zafar Khān (1298) served as a model for the important later Mosque of Adina (1374-75) in Pandua. It is the earliest surviving example of a rectangular covered mosque where each aisle ends on the west at the *qibla* wall with a *miḥrāb* and on the east with an entrance. The presence on the *qibla* wall of more than one *miḥrāb* is a feature appearing frequently in mosques in Bengal and occasionally, in some mosques in north India. It is likely that the early Quwwat al-Islām Mosque (1192) in Delhi had five *miḥrābs*, since there are five *miḥrāb* projections on the exterior side of the *qibla* wall. In Ajmer the Aḍhāī Din kā Jhoṃparā Mosque also has five *miḥrābs*, not, however, axially aligned with the entrances as in Bengal. Multiple *miḥrābs* as found in India never became a standard practice elsewhere in the Islamic world.

The Mosque of Zafar Khān[1] is divided by large Hindu basalt pillars into two by ten bays, each originally domed. The three extant *miḥrābs* are cusped, the larger central niche set in a rectangular frame surrounded by temple moulding. Cusped arches are very popular in Bengal Islamic monuments. This type of arch may be traced to Buddhist prototypes, since during the Abbāsid period at least, much opportunity existed for the interchange of ideas. Trefoil and quinquefoil arches were known in the Isfahān Jāmi' Mosque and may date back to Samārrā, where a quinquefoil arch spans the inner surface of a window opening. But early western Islamic cusped arches generally had only a few cusps. The multicusped arch assumes distinctive characteristics in the central *miḥrāb* of the Mosque of Zafar Khān to be imitated in the *miḥrāb* of the Adina Mosque at Pandua and in the later Darasbari and Chhota Sona Mosques in Gaur.

The façade of the Mosque of Zafar Khān has five entrance arches springing from large piers. Because of the paucity of stone to form pillars and beams, the post-and-lintel style never became popular in Bengal as it did in Tughluq Delhi. As a consequence, brick was generally used and therefore pointed arches became much the vogue. As in most later Beṅgālī mosques, there are no courtyards, enclosing walls or minarets. But in other respects this early mosque is quite unique, since it has no engaged corner towers and a straight rather than a curved cornice. It is, therefore not built in the typical Beṅgālī style as it was to evolve in the next century.

The Tomb of Zafar Khān (1313), the earliest extant mausoleum in eastern India, has a double chamber. Much of it is built of material taken from a Hindu temple dedicated to Krishna, reassembled here to serve a new purpose. But in addition to temple spoils, the brick work is supplemented and the walls are pierced with the earliest pointed arches in Bengal.

Another monument belongs to this early period. In a village called Chhote Pandua, near Tribeni, are the ruins of the large Barī Mosque (1342). In plan this monument is modelled on the earlier Tribeni Mosque, but instead of two there are three aisles,

[1]Ahmad Hasan Dani, *Muslim Architecture in Bengal*, Dacca, 1961, pp. 40-44.

each divided by basalt pillars into twenty-one domed bays. The court façade has twenty-one pointed arched entrances which correspond to twenty-one brick *miḥrābs.* The earliest known *mimbar* in Bengal, carved of basalt and domed, is found here just north of the main *miḥrāb.* It is to be the model on which the *mimbar* of the great Adina Mosque would be built some thirty years later. In the northwest corner of the interior is the earliest known example of a *takht,* a raised platform, later to become common in many mosques in Bengal. The function of this adjunct is not certain but it has been referred to as *chillah khāna* (meditation chamber) and a *zanāna* gallery. The Barī Mosque has many of the forms Bengal architecture would adopt for the entire Sultanate and part of the Mughal periods.

The most important monument now existing in Chhote Pandua is the minaret standing near the Barī Mosque, a round tower without the usual taper, divided into five storeys, the lower three fluted. Constructed of brick, the monument is plastered and in the interior a spiral staircase leads to a small chamber on the summit, once domed. It is believed that possibly in the native tradition a saint might have lived on the summit. The function of this monument is uncertain, but most likely according to its shape and size it was a victory tower[2] and thus one of the earliest buildings erected in Chhote Pandua.

* * *

Pandua was made the capital of Bengal in 1340 by the founder of the Ilyās Shāhī dynasty, Shams al-Dīn, after wresting sovereignty from the Delhi sultan. Under Sikandar Shāh Ilyās (1358-89)and his family, Pandua became the seat of government until the reign of Naṣīr al-Dīn Maḥmūd (1442-59) when the capital was transferred to Gaur. Sikandar Shāh Ilyās adopted the traditional procedure of starting construction of a congregational mosque. The Adina Mosque (1374-75) was built in a different architectural style than the earlier monuments of Tribeni and resembles in plan and appearance Muḥammad Tughluq's congregational mosque in Delhi built in 1343. In the fourteenth century it was the largest mosque in India, its immense size able to accommodate several thousand worshippers. Probably built by Sikandar Shāh as a symbol of his victory over the Delhi sultan, Fīrūz Shāh Tughluq, the mosque is the most important building in Bengal and gives a good indication of the large Muslim population of Pandua at this time.

The plan of the Adina Mosque is a traditional hypostyle, an open courtyard surrounded by covered arcades on four sides, five bays deep on the *qibla* side, three on the others. Two hundred and sixty thick square pillars divide the arcades into three hundred and sixty domed bays.

The central pointed arch *īwān* [Ill. 54] divides the prayer hall into two symmetrical lateral halls, each consisting of four aisles of seventeen bays. The *īwān* originally had a barrel vaulted roof, now collapsed. In India barrel vaulting is uncommon but it is found in several fourteenth century Tughluq structures in Delhi. The vault of the Adina Mosque served as a prototype for later Beṅgālī mosques.

The central arch of the façade was probably a *pishtaq,* a high entrance similar to the later Mosques of Jaunpūr, and to the Dakhil Darwāza of Gaur, although it might also have been modelled on the Begampūr Mosque in Delhi with its flanking multidomed wings, where, however, the central nave is domed.

[2]Catherine Asher, "Inventory of Key Monuments," *Islamic Heritage of Bengal,* ed., George Michell, Paris, 1984, p. 53.

The *qibla* wall is faced with polished black basalt ashlar masonry exquisitely carved to three-quarters of the height [Ill. 55]; the upper portion is brick. A trefoil *miḥrāb* is set in a rectangular frame and supported on temple pilasters. Large bosses in the arch spandrels are in the form of lotus rosettes. Standing north of the splendid *miḥrāb* is a *mimbar* in design closely following its prototype of the Barī Mosque in Chhote Pandua.

Just north of the formerly high vaulted prayer hall is a *takht* platform on an upper storey, occupying eighteen bays, most of which were once domed. This separate area might have served to ensure privacy for the royal family, or might have evolved from the same tradition as the *maqsūra*, a screen placed around the *miḥrāb* and *mimbar* to protect the leaders of the Islamic community from attack. Some scholars have maintained that this was the grave of Nūr Quṯb Ālam, a local Muslim saint (d.1410). In sixteenth century Bengal the *takht* is to become a prominent feature.

Internally, each arcade [Ill. 56] is fronted by a screen of arches surmounted by a horizontal parapet above which there were originally three hundred and six domes. An impressive advance is shown in the shape of the arches since their first use in the Mosque of Zafar Khān Ghāzī. Instead of clumsily springing from Hindu temple pillars, the arches in the Adina Mosque rise from wide piers forming an unified element in the long screen. The arched façade of the interior of the Adina Mosque is the earliest of its kind in Bengal and is a marked improvement of the pillar-and-post construction of the earlier period. The interior of the flanking wings and other arcades have rows of fluted stone columns originally surmounted by domes supported on brick pendentives of an interesting type. The bricks are built in oversailing courses, those in each alternate course set diagonally so that the corners project. This type of pendentive had earlier been used in both Delhi and Multān.

For the first time in Bengal engaged corner towers are found on the Adina Mosque although they do not rise beyond the parapet wall. The base of the towers is pot-shaped and ornamented with mouldings. The shafts are round and are divided into two sections by an horizontal string course, the lower part of which is fluted. The corner towers are probably copied from Tughluq monuments in Delhi and adopted in a modified form in Bengal. Fluted tapering towers were certainly found in Delhi as early as the Quṯb mosque at the end of the twelfth century, as well as in Ajmer. In Bengal these towers are imitated in the early fifteenth century Lattan Mosque and in the Gumti Gate (1512), both in Gaur.

Externally, the Adina Mosque is surrounded by a brick wall, faced in part with stone. The brick east side has a number of trabeated entrances, each with an arched window above. The north and south sides have moulded basalt plinths, as at the Tomb of Zafar Khān Ghāzī in Tribeni. The better preserved west wall has stone dressing on the lower half and ornamented brick on the upper.

* * *

Just when the danger from Delhi disappeared, the Ilyās Shāhī dynasty was removed from the throne at the hands of Rājā Ganesh, a Hindu chief who installed his newly converted son, Jalāl al-Dīn, in 1415 and established a new dynasty in Bengal. One of the reasons for his eventual defeat in 1433 was the relentless opposition of the famous saint, Haẓrat Nūr Quṯb Ālām, whose powerful influence helped to reestablish Muslim rule in Bengal after the Hindu interlude. The family of this saint supplied spiritual guides to the sultans and the complex where the graves are found is called Chhotī

Dargāh. Jalāl al-Dīn, much like Akbar a century later, steered in a new age of cooperation between Hindu and Muslims, working together to evolve a common culture. This blending of two distinctive traditions may be noted in the monuments constructed during this reign.

The prototype of all subsequent buildings in Bengal and the first monument in the new Bengal style is the Eklakhi Tomb [Ill. 57] [Plan 7] perhaps the only major building in Bengal of the early fifteenth century and the earliest known brick structure. Heavy rains dictate an entirely covered structure and here for the first time are some other characteristics to become a model for later Bengal monuments—heavy walls, octagonal corner towers, terracotta relief decoration and many lines of mouldings. Also seen here is the earliest curved cornice to become a permanent feature in Bengal architecture and later to find its way into Mughal architecture in Āgrā, Fatehpur Sīkrī, Delhi and Lahore. Another innovation on this monument is the use of glazed tiles.

The Eklakhi Tomb is believed to contain the remains of Sultan Jalāl al-Dīn (d.1431) and is therefore assigned to the early fifteenth century. It is a square single domed structure, with squat octagonal towers engaged at corners, possibly earlier covered by cupolas. Unlike the tapering Tughluq towers, tiers of moulding decorate the upper and lower portions, and in each facet is a hanging motif. The curved cornice and parapet allow rain water to run down quickly. There is a small door in the centre of the four sides each with a curved frame from a Hindu temple and a pointed arch above the lintel.

The Eklakhi Tomb is roofed by an hemispherical dome resting directly on the walls, with no drum for additional height. The ceiling of the dome is plastered and painted. The interior is in octagonal plan perhaps to better support the first massive dome constructed in this part of India. The zone of transition to change the octagon into a circular base is filled with squinches.

There is no window in the octagonal tomb chamber and light is admitted only through the four small doors. At each of the corners in the thickness of the walls is a small chamber traditionally believed to be used by the readers of the *Qur'ān* called in to invoke the blessings of Allāh for the deceased.[3] Three graves lie within supposedly belonging to Sultan Jalāl al-Dīn and his family.

The monument shows some foreign influence, probably brought to Bengal by the builders who had worked in Delhi and, in the wake of Tīmūr's invasion, fled to the newly risen Muslim states. From the fifteenth century onwards Tughluq influence is therefore noted in provincial Bengal architecture. But the Eklakhi Tomb also owes much to the local style. It is a brick copy of a bamboo hut constructed on principles known to the masons of Bengal from earliest times. The exterior walls are faced with stone to the string course dividing the wall, which gives the monument the appearance of being a double-storeyed structure. Ornamental panels are inserted in the upper storey and the splendid floral and geometrical patterns recall the terracotta relief carving [Ill. 58] for which the brick temples of Bengal have always been famous.

A monument in Gaur, the Chika Mosque, resembles the Eklakhi Tomb in many ways, since it is also square in plan with a large hemispherical dome. It is, however, believed that this monument is not a mosque because there is no *miḥrāb* on the *qibla* side, but instead an arched opening. Most likely the Chika Mosque it is not a gateway either but one of the few extant secular administrative buildings. The Chika building

[3]Dani, op. cit., p. 79.

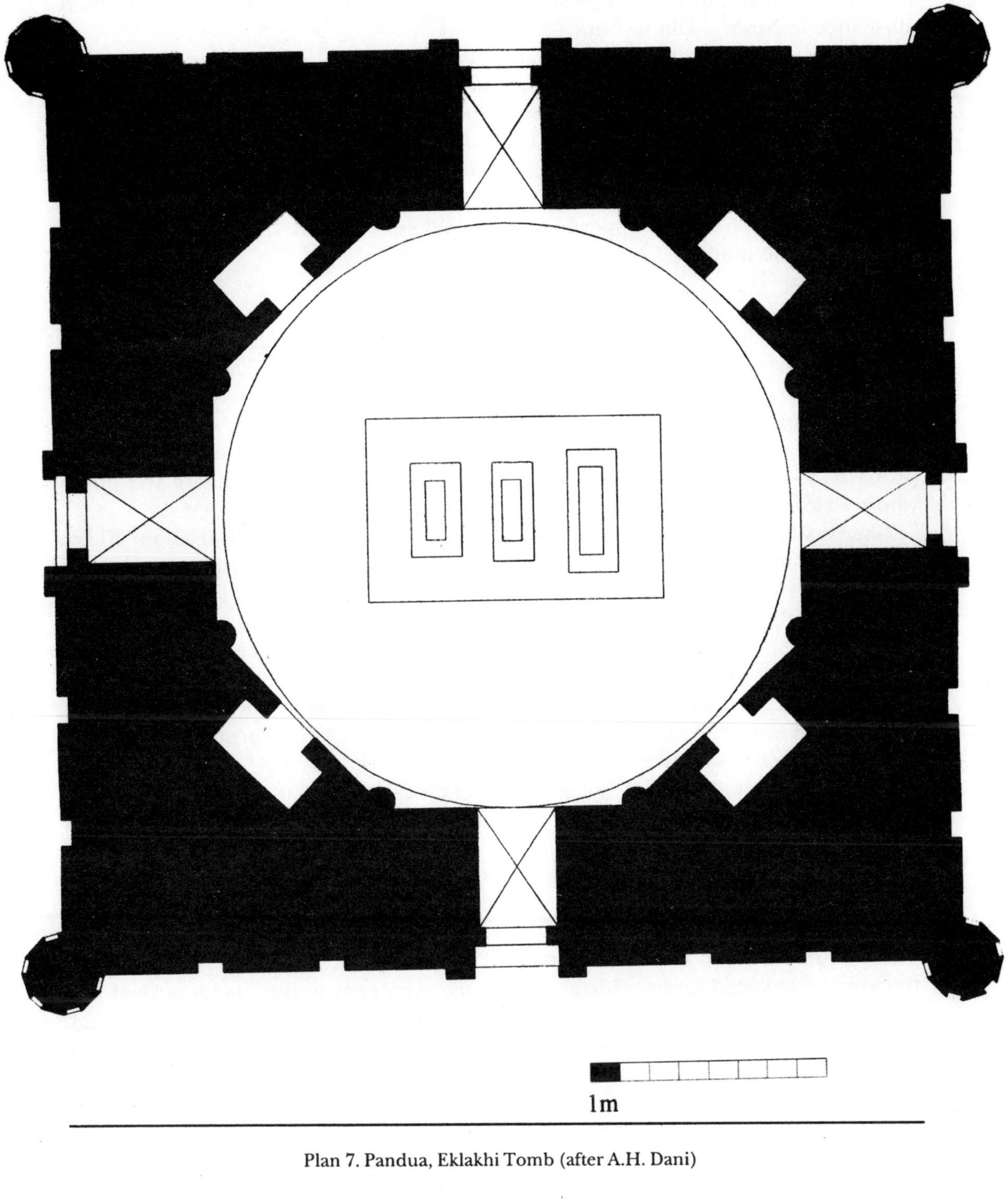

Plan 7. Pandua, Eklakhi Tomb (after A.H. Dani)

must be dated within the reign of Jalāl al-Dīn, when Gaur began to be repopulated.

One further monument might be added here to conclude the series of extant square tombs. While Naṣīr al-Dīn Maḥmūd I, the founder of the restored Ilyās Khān dynasty, ruled in Gaur (d.1459), in the south of Bengal in Bagerhat (now in Bangladesh), there was an independent monarch, Khān Jahān, who never assumed the title of sultan. His titles suggest that he was not an independent ruler but owed allegiance to Naṣīr al-Dīn in Gaur.

The square brick Tomb of Khān Jahān stands within a walled compound and is entered through arched gateways. It is crowned by an hemispherical dome and has engaged corner towers. Stone arch-and-lintel doorways recall Tughluq construction in Delhi. As in the Eklakhi Tomb, the exterior walls are now unplastered and have no ornament. The battlement and cornice have the usual slight curve, and only the engaged towers have string courses dividing them into storeys. The interior is square in plan with stone brackets supporting the squinches. There is a single-domed mosque attached to the tomb.

* * *

Gaur, one the most magnificent medieval cities in India, was celebrated before and after its Muslim conquest in 1198 for its beautiful buildings. The site was the capital of the last Hindu Pāla and Sena dynasties and in the later Muslim era the city became the capital of the new rulers. Its heavy brick citadel now encloses desolation, but from fragments found it is clear that during the Hindu medieval period the site was probably adorned with brick temples decorated with black basalt pillars and doors whose style influenced the later Muslim monuments.

Gaur is situated on what was once the highbank of the Ganges River about 30 km south of Pandua. This location caused concern to early rulers during the time of flooding. Periodically, the capital was shifted to other sites, such as Pandua.

Beginning in the early thirteenth century and lasting for more than a hundred years, Gaur, then known as Lakhnautī, was nominally a provincial outpost of the Delhi Sultanate. As elsewhere on the subcontinent, monuments built during this time reused earlier Hindu temple material. The capital was moved back to Gaur from Pandua in 1433, at the end of the rule of the Hindu usurper Rājā Ganesh (1415-33), when it was ascertained that the waters of the Ganges had found a stable course to the west of the city. Splendid walls more than 20 km in length were built to fortify the city and a great stone embankment was constructed on the east and west side to ensure no further flooding. Cunningham traced the city and stated that it extended for a length of more than 20 km along the east bank of the Bhagīrathī River, from the Pulwari Darwāza to the suburb of Fīrūzābād in the south. A grand thoroughfare was laid out and in about 1465 Barbak Shāh is said to have spanned it with a triumphal arch to face the citadel. The Dakhlī Darwāza [Ill. 59], dominating the now ruined citadel, was probably the principal gateway to the citadel of Gaur and the main ceremonial entrance on the northern side.[4] Originally over 18 m in height, it consisted of a recessed *pishtaq* flanked by buttresses leading to a vaulted passage with vaulted rooms on both sides. From the corners projected engaged round five-storeyed towers, one of which survives. Terracotta bands divide the towers into sections each of which is decorated with a recessed panel enclosing a cusped arch displaying a hanging motif. The walls and turrets are ornamented with terracotta reliefs.

The Dakhli Darwāza is the earliest existing example in Bengal of a complete gate structure. Some elements, such as the tapering towers and their cupolas, may well have been derived originally from the Tughluq architecture of Delhi, but they are modified here and adapted to suit the soil of Bengal. The circular Delhi towers have become twelve-sided, covered and decorated in the typical Beṅgālī manner with

[4]Ibid.

local terracotta relief decoration. The Dakhli Darwāza is one of the finest examples of architecture ever produced in Bengal.

From the northern end of the citadel a road leads to the palace in the south-east corner of the citadel passing through two intermediate gates, now no longer extant, called the Chand Darwāza and the Nim Darwāza (built by Rukn al-Dīn Barbak Shāh in 1466). The most important remains in the citadel are of the palace, probably built by Naṣīr al-Dīn himself. It was divided into three parts, the northern area for use as a *durbār* (reception) hall, the middle division for living quarters, and the rest, for the harem. The *durbār* hall leads to the Chika building, probably attached to it at some later time, where government offices were located.

The southern gate of the city, the Kotwali Darwāza was probably constructed by Naṣīr al-Dīn Maḥmūd I (1435-87) to protect his capital after its transfer from Pandua. Built of brick, the gate, apparently the police station of the city (*kotwāl* means chief of police) once had a lofty pointed entrance *pishtaq* flanked by massive round bastions.

The last surviving gate of the citadel, the Gumpti Darwāza, is the eastern entrance and has a different design than the earlier extant gateways, the Dakhli and Kotwālī Darwāzas. Built considerably later, probably in the reign of Husayn Shāh about 1512, the Gumpti Darwāza is a small square monument with engaged corner turrets of which only the bases remain. Flanking the arched entrances on the east and west sides are fluted turrets which have also lost their superstructures. A single dome supported on squinches rises over the curved cornice. Although the monument is decorated with the usual rectangular panels with a hanging design, an unusual feature appears here, as well as in the nearby Lattan Mosque. Instead of terracotta relief ornament, traces of multicoloured glazed tiles have been found, indicating one of the earliest use of this decoration. It has been suggested[5] that because the Gumpti Darwāza was built in direct alignment with the contemporary Chika monument, probably an administrative building, that it was likely an entrance to the administrative part of the citadel.

The last ruler of the Ilyās Shāhī dynasty, Jalāl al-Dīn Fath Shāh, was killed by the chief of the palace guards, an Abyssinian eunuch. But when the murderer tried to ascend the throne as Barbak Shāh, he was opposed by the Amīr al-Umra Malik Andil, the Abyssinian commander of the forces, who had remained loyal to the uprooted dynasty. The murderer was deposed and the now empty throne was occupied by the loyal commander, who accepted royal power and assumed the title Saif al-Dīn Fīrūz (1487-90). Above all a soldier, the new ruler began his building activity with the construction of a victory tower, the Fīrūz Mīnār, once belonging to a mosque now gone. The Fīrūz Mīnār [Ill. 60] stands south-west of the Dakhli Darwāza, outside the citadel, on a polygonal plinth, and rises five storeys, the lower three polygonal, the upper two circular, and were originally surmounted by a small dome. Brick string courses and shallow niches with a bell-and-chain motif decorate the exterior of the tower. The entrance portal is made of finely carved black basalt, as is the *chhajja* dividing the three lower storeys from the upper stages.

Mosques in Bengal are either built in a square or rectangular plan, in both cases they are crowned by one or more domes. An interesting variation of the square mosque is a plan with an added verandah on the east side. A series of structures following this design were constructed, the earliest of which, the Mosque of Ulagh Nusart Khān in Gopālganj(1460), has a groin-vaulted verandah with three arched entrances leading

[5]Asher, op. cit., p. 74.

to the prayer chamber. The plan is used frequently but reaches its culmination in Gaur with the construction of two fine mosques in the late fifteenth century.

The Chamkatti Mosque(*c.* 1475) is credited to the reign of Yūsuf Shāh. It is a single-domed square prayer chamber with a vaulted verandah on the east side. Built of brick, there are traces of stone facing in the lower courses. At the corners octagonal towers project prominently and three doorways lead into the interior square hall. The dome is supported on squinches and there is a decorated *miḥrāb* on the *qibla* wall.

Many of the features of this mosque are derived from the Eklakhi Tomb but one basic change from the earlier monument is the interior plan of the prayer chamber, which in the Chamkatti Mosque is square rather than octagonal. To help support the dome the builders used eight stone pillars, one at each angle of the octagon on which the arches and squinches rest. The panels have glazed tile borders.

The final pre-Mughal monument following the verandah plan is the Lattan Mosque, dated sometime in the last quarter of the fifteenth or early years of the sixteenth century, and most likely credited to Yūsuf Shāh (1493-1519). It has been suggested that the mosque was built for a favourite dancing girl, Nattan, after whom it was named.

The Lattan Mosque [Ill. 61] is the best preserved example of a covered square mosque preceded by a vaulted verandah. The plan does not differ remarkably from the earlier Chamkatti Mosque. The verandah also has a vaulted ceiling but it differs in this monument since the ribbed vault is flanking by two small domes. The method of vaulting is also different. Instead of the barrel vault found earlier, the central rectangular unit of the verandah vault is covered by a *char-chala* vault, a form of roof found on bamboo and thatched village houses, here translated into brick. Composed of four segments which slope down in the four directions, the longer slopes form a ridge at the top, and the end slopes are triangular in shape. While the *char-chala* vault was used earlier, it is only in the Lattan Mosque that such a vault is found in the verandah.

In the interior the *qibla* wall has three *miḥrābs* and the dome is supported on brick squinches. The interior walls are decorated with a rich display of many coloured glazed tiles, mostly blue, white, yellow and green. Although they are inferior to the tiles of Multān and Delhi, the tiles of the Lattan Mosque are the best preserved found in Bengal. The articulated brick exterior [Ills. 62-63] was once totally covered with glazed tiles, but many of these have now disappeared.

The other type of mosque plan used in Bengal is rectangular and multidomed. The mosques during pre-Mughal times have from two to seven aisles and from ten to seventy-seven bays. The Tantipara Mosque(1480), within the walled city of Gaur, built by the noble, Mirsad Khān, follows the earlier plan of the Mosque of Zafar Khān in Tribeni, and is divided into two aisles and ten bays by squat Hindu temple pillars. Each bay was covered by a now-collapsed dome resting on corbelled brick pendentives [Ill. 64] and there are engaged octagonal turrets at the corners. The heavy moulded and curved cornice has the usual exaggerated downward curve to better shed the rains. String courses divide the walls and corner turrets.

The Tantipara Mosque is outstanding mostly for the brick relief work on its east facade, probably the finest ornament in Bengal. The five pointed arched entrances are set in projecting rectangular frames and are surmounted by elaborate terracotta arabesques in the spandrels. The façade is divided into two storeys on each of which

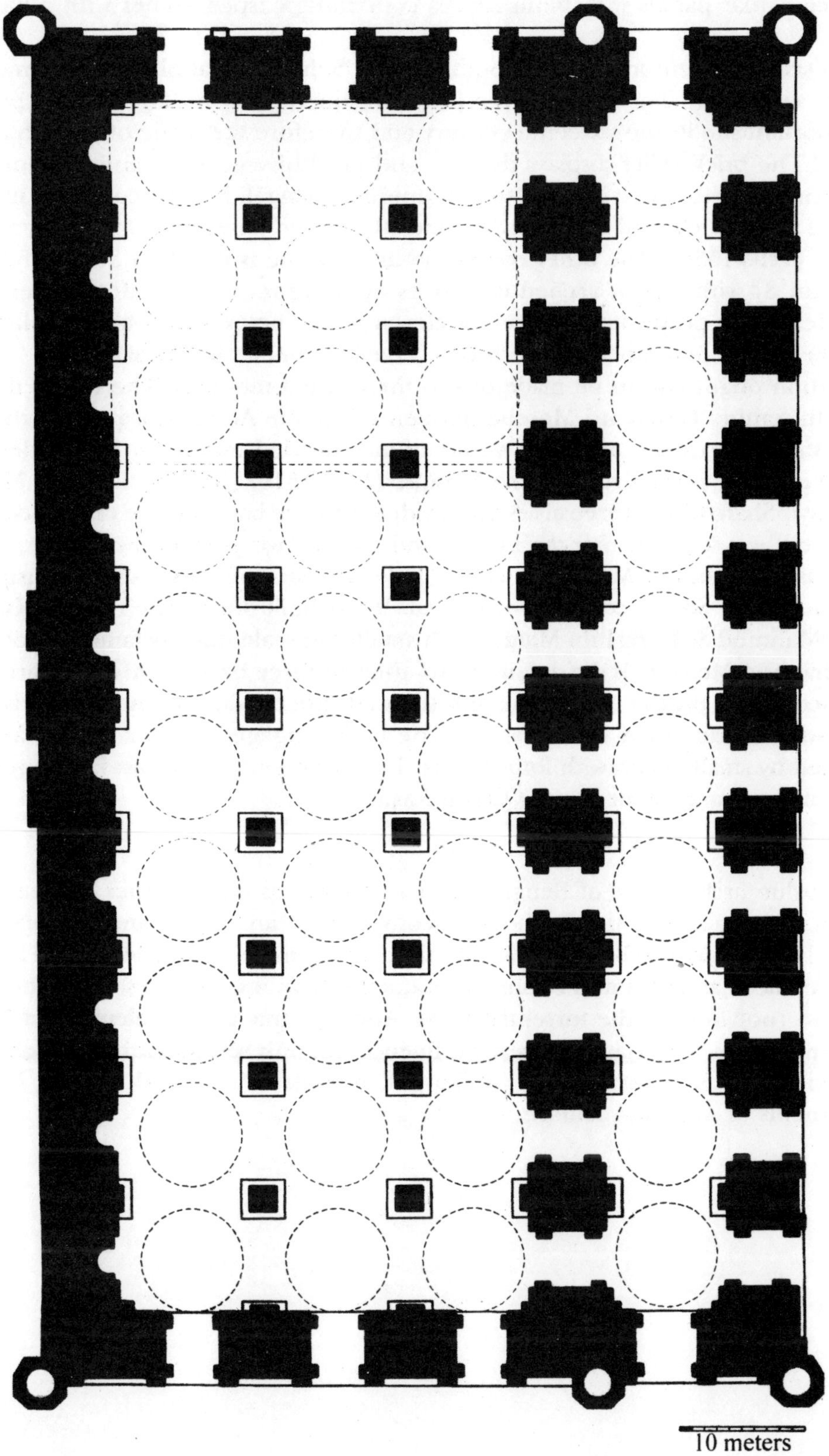

Plan 8 . Gauṛ, Barā Sona Mosque (after A.H. Dani)

are rectangular panels with blind niches containing cusped arches with a hanging motif.

Two sixteenth-century mosques both built by Sultan Nusrat Shāh, follow more or less the same plan. The earlier is the Jāmi' Mosque (1523) in Bagha, quite possibly an important site in the sixteenth century and therefore the scene of some building activity. The brick relief displays delicate and fanciful vegetation and is among the most ornate of the age. It belongs to that uniquely Beṅgālī Muslim culture, a mixture of local Bengal folk and Islamic styles which flourished during the late Husayn Shāhī dynasty (1493-1538). The other contemporary mosque is the Barā Sona (1526) [Ill. 65], [Plan 8] with eleven arched entrances opening into a long domed verandah which leads to a prayer hall of three by eleven bays. The exterior walls are plain and not, like other contemporary structures, carved to imitate brickwork.

Mention ought also to be made of two three-aisled mosques. The first is the late fifteenth-century Gunmanti Mosque, influenced by the Adina Mosque, which has a barrel-vaulted corridor and twenty-four domes divided evenly on both sides. The second example is the Chhota Sona Mosque (1493-1519) [Ill. 66], the Jāmi' Mosque of Husayn Shāh, where three aisles are divided into five bays and the central corridor is covered by a series of *char-chala* vaults and the side wings by twelve domes.

The later Jahāniyān Mosque in Gaur (1535) is a six-domed structure constructed just before Shīr Shāh's conquest of Bengal. It was built during the reign of Ghiyāth al-Dīn Maḥmūd Shāh by Bībī Maltī. Much smaller in scale than its famous prototype, the Jahāniyān Mosque, is divided into two aisles of three bays each. There are three entrance arches on the east façade and the walls are divided by curved bands, each filled with ornamented brick panels. The front engaged corner turrets are surmounted by small *mīnārs* with lotus finials. The ornament of the east façade recalls a very similar arrangement in the Qadam Rasūl (1531).

* * *

The Muslim architecture of Bengal is not as striking as that of other contemporary provincial centres, but the methods of construction are sound and the ornament original. The climate of Bengal, which dictated transient building in wood and bamboo easily replaced and removed in times of natural calamities, also prescribed the use of a curved roof to shed the torrential rains. And it is this unique element of Bengal monuments which was later to greatly influence not only seventeenth and eighteenth centuries temple construction in Bengal, but also the world-famous Mughal monuments of Āgrā and Lahore.

CHAPTER 8

Gujarat(1396-1572)

The largest and most important of the provincial styles of architecture was in Gujarat, centred mostly in the capital, Aḥmadābād. An inaccessible position beyond the great desert and the hills connecting the Vindhyas with the Aravali Range long preserved Gujarat from the Muslim yoke. Only by sea was it easily approached, and to the sea it owed its peculiar advantages, good climate, fertile soil, and the wealth which poured in from the great coastal towns of Cambay, Somnāth and Broach. The greater part of the Indian trade with Persia, Arabia, and the Red Sea passed through its harbours, as did a busy coastal trade. From the earliest days of Islam Muslim merchants followed along this ancient sea route bringing their religion with them. The west coast of Gujarat was therefore introduced to Islam by traders who set up Muslim settlements in the great commercial centres and from there wealth spread to the rest of Gujarat, enriching the coffers of the sultan.

Even after the Muslim conquest of Delhi at the end of the twelfth century, Gujarat remained nominally independent until 1297, when 'Alā' al-Dīn Khaljī's armies first conquered and annexed it to the Delhi Sultanate. Gujarat came under Delhi control at a time when the architecture of the capital had reached its zenith and the builders from the north who chose to live and work in the more temporate climate of the newly acquired province were imbued with the creative spirit of capital. Although there are not many buildings extant from this early date in Gujarat, the influence of Sultanate Delhi is first noted in the Jāmi' Mosque of Cambay (1325), built about a decade after the Jamā'at Khāna Mosque in Delhi. In 1337 a similar mosque was built in Dholkā.

The Sultanate of Gujarat was eventually established in 1396 when Zafar Khān, the governor and son of a convert to Islam, declared his independence and assumed the throne under the name of Muzaffar Khān. From the early fifteenth century onwards there was an impetus to construction which lasted for over a century, ending only in 1537 with the death of the last great Sultan Bahādur Shāh. Then followed a series of puppet rulers each supported by rival nobles, which resulted in virtual anarchy until Akbar's conquest of the province in 1572.

The foundation of the Gujarātī architectural style was laid in the fourteenth century but the political climate was then too unsettled for it to make much headway. But by the early fifteenth century the architectural style developed during the establishment of the powerful Aḥmad Shāhī dynasty. There are numerous reasons why the architecture of the Sultanate of Gujarat is superior to that of other areas under Muslim rule, but the most important is probably the extensive patronage given by both the ruler and the nobles. Almost equally important is the indigenous tradition of building, an art which was never really replaced by the new Islamic forms. This local custom of building was more alive in Gujarat than in other parts of Muslim

India. The undertone of the new style, although Islamic in function, was Hindu or Jaina in feeling. In fact, in many of the earlier examples entire portions of temples were removed and reassembled in their new setting. Not just content with installing temple columns and pillars, entire temple *maṇḍapas* together with domes and ceiling were reconstructed. Also important was the willingness of the ruler and other patrons to allow experimentation with new architectural forms. The time of the Aḥmad Shāhī dynasty was an era of unparallel architectural activity. More than fifty mosques were erected in the new capital Aḥmadābād and few cities can boast of more or finer examples of monumental architecture. The skill of the artisans cannot be underestimated and it appears that the Gujarātīs were probably more resourceful and more creative than their counterparts elsewhere. The architectural style is elegant and polished on a scale never achieved even in temple construction. The indigenous influence continues to be felt both in decoration and in structural details, as for instance the arch which is used primarily as a symbol of the faith.

Finally, not to be underestimated was the influence of the Delhi Sultanate style. When Gujarat became independent the monuments of Delhi were at their best and the tradition transmitted was the most highly developed and refined then found in India. The northern style mixed freely with the beautiful Hindu-Jaina temple architecture found locally in Gujarat and there evolved a new convention, functionally Islamic but Hindu-Jaina in structure and ornament. The Hindu element may be noted in the ubiquitous use of the post-and-lintel system of construction in Gujarat.

Islamic architecture in Gujarat flourished for about 250 years, from the early fourteenth century, when the governors appointed by the Khaljī sultans of Delhi established themselves along the western seaboard, until the independent Sultanate of Gujarat was absorbed into the Mughal Empire in the late sixteenth century.

* * *

Islamic architecture in Gujarat is usually divided into three periods beginning in the first half of the fourteenth century, when the customary phase of demolition and reassembling took place. During the second period, with Aḥmadabād as the Aḥmad Shāhī capital, in the first half of the fifteenth century, architectural construction reached its zenith. The finest examples of the style as a whole were built during this period, such as the Jāmi' Mosque of Aḥmadābād. The final phase began during the latter part of the fifteenth century and lasted into the sixteenth, owing much to Sultan Maḥmūd I Begarha (1458-1511). During this last period an amazingly lavish style of architecture evolved, as may best be seen in the Champanīr Jāmi' Mosque.

Until recently it was believed that the earliest mosques and tombs in Gujarat were built at Patan and in the coastal towns of Broach and Cambay in the early fourteenth century. But a recent study[1] has shown that Gujarat was perhaps the only region in India with an established tradition of Islamic architecture in the twelfth century. The early Muslim monuments of the coastal town of Bhadreshwar, now in Kutch, still partially exist.

The extant Islamic monuments of Bhadreshwar[2] include the Shrine of Ibrāhīm (1159-60), perhaps the earliest Islamic structure in India, and two mosques, all three

[1]Mehrdad Shokoohy, "Muslim Architecture in Gujarat Prior to the Islamic Conquest," *Marg*, vol. XXXIX, no. 4, 1988, p. 75.

[2]Mehrdad Shokoohy, *Bhadresvar, the Oldest Islamic Monuments in India*, Leiden, 1988.

built of large blocks of stone in the post-and-lintel system. The three Bhadreshwar monuments each have an unusual feature not found elsewhere in India (with the exception of the Tomb of Sultan Gharī in Delhi), a colonnaded portico in front of the eastern entrance leading to the sanctuary. Curiously, the Khaljī occupation of Gujarat at the end of the thirteenth century, although producing a number of important mosques, resulted in no further monuments with a portico, a practice which had probably been adopted from temple architecture.

The Shrine of Ibrāhīm is square in plan, with a *miḥrāb* in the *qibla* wall and a finely carved corbelled dome. The now ruined Solah Khambhī Mosque (1223) is built in a hypostyle plan, with a courtyard, and one-aisled arcades on three sides and a two-aisled arcade on the *qibla* side. The portico is of seven bays divided by four aisles, taking up the entire width of the mosque. The smaller Chhotī Mosque, stylistically similar to the Shrine of Ibrāhīm, was probably also built in the mid-twelfth century. Here the colonnade is composed of two by four bays with another row of four in the sanctuary.

Despite the unsettled conditions of the thirteenth century, when Delhi was in Ghūrīd hands, Muslims apparently lived peacefully in Hindu Gujarat, where a brave ruler, Bhīmadeva, resisted all attacks from the capital until the end of the century. The Mosque of al-Iraji (1286-87) in Junāgadh was built during this time and has a sanctuary composed of three by three bays. The portico has two rows of four columns, with another four in the sanctuary.

The Mosque of al-Iraji was built about a century and a half after the Bhadreshwar monuments, and yet follows in plan and decoration its earlier prototypes. The monuments of Bhadreshwar appear to have become the established pattern in the coastal towns of Gujarat. With the conquest of Gujarat by 'Alā' al-Dīn Khaljī a change in the building style takes place and the portico is henceforth discarded for a more appropriate Islamic-type entrance.

Chronologically, the next mosques and tombs in Gujarat were built in Patan and in the coastal towns of Broach and Cambay. In the early capital of Patan the Tomb of Shaykh Farīd is one of the first Muslim buildings and over a thousand richly decorated pillars were assembled to form a now ruined Adina Mosque, of which only the foundations remain.

The earliest extant mosque in the coastal area is in the ancient seaport of Broach, one of the oldest cities in western India, where commerce with the Red Sea ports was carried out until it fell into Muslim hands during the raids of 'Alā' al-Dīn Khaljī in 1297. In the beginning of the fourteenth century a Jāmi' Mosque (1322) was built in a conventional design, a courtyard with gateways on three sides and a prayer hall on the fourth. From this time on the façades of Gujarātī mosques were of two types, either an open colonnade with the interior pillars exposed to view, or a screen of arches blocking the view of the *qibla*. The decision to use one or the other façade, open or closed, became a personal choice, since both forms were in use at the same time.

The Jāmi' Mosque of Broach (1322)[3] was constructed in the first of these styles, with an open prayer hall, built entirely in the pillar-and-lintel style, with a roof supported by carved temple pillars. The interior is divided into three pillared halls, actual temple *maṇḍapas*, removed in pieces and reassembled and reerected here.

[3]J.Burgess, *On the Muhammadan Architecture of Bharoch, Cambay, Dholka, Champanir and Mahmudabad in Gujarat* (Archaeological Survey of Western India, vol.VI), London, 1896, p. 22.

The three *miḥrābs* in the *qibla* wall are also copies of temple niches with a pointed Islamic arch filled with stone tracery introduced under the lintel. There were originally six perforated stone windows in this wall and two in each of the side walls. Beams support three large and ten small domes, and the ceilings are decorated with geometrical designs taken from temple decoration. In fact, the square sunk coffered ceilings originally found in temples continued to be used in mosques throughout the entire early Gujarat Islamic period. The designs were in no way contrary to Islam.

The outer walls of the mosque are plain with only narrow string courses as decoration and a series of carved buttresses indicating the interior *miḥrābs*. These walls are the earliest examples in Gujarat of original Islamic masonry, the stones often taken from temples, but recut and reconditioned to fit a mosque. The entire structure is crowned by three large and a number of small domes.

Shortly after the construction of the Broach Mosque, Muslim rule in Gujarat was administered from the flourishing ancient seaport of Cambay. In 1325, during the reign of Muḥammad Tughluq, the local builders were reinforced by a group of artisans recruited from Khaljī Delhi,[4] who were accustomed to working in the Islamic style of building as then practised and who became the supervisors of the project. Their influence can best be seen in the Cambay Jāmi' Mosque[Ill. 67] façade which consists of a three-arched opening, the central larger, although the interior is still in the pillar-and-lintel style. The closed-type of façade provided the model on which subsequent Gujarātī mosques would be constructed but side colonnades continued in the post-and-lintel style. In the Cambay Jāmi' Mosque the south side has a central double-storeyed dodecagonal rotunda with local temple pillars which originally supported a large corbelled dome. The pillared eastern entrance porch is entirely in local temple style. There are, however, other Khaljī features here such as the shape and position of the arches, the alternating broad and narrow masonry courses of the outer walls with their string courses and the architectural treatment of the building as a whole which resembles the style of Muhammad Khaljī II (1296-1316) as best seen in the Jamā'at Khāna Mosque in the Dargāh of Niẓām al-Dīn in Delhi. As in the Aḍhāī Din kā Jhoṃparā Mosque in Ajmer, two small pointed turrets are placed over the central arch of the sanctuary. This mosque is a first attempt by Gujarātī Hindu masons to build in the style of the conquerors, a step to be taken further in the next decade.

Two other mosques were constructed in the next half century. In Dholkā, 35 km southwest of Aḥmadābād, two mosques were built during the time when it was the residence of the governor of Delhi. The earlier Mosque of Hilāl Khān Qāẓī (1333), [Ill. 68] while small and relatively unimportant, introduced a pair of tall ornamental turrets flanking the central archway to the façade. A projecting cornice supported on carved brackets divides the fluted turrets into two unequal shafts, the upper narrower and surmounted by a finial. In construction and design the towers are Hindu, and it appears as if the builder had never seen a real minaret, which is here used as an attempt to introduce an important aspect of the new religion. These Hindu elements inserted into mosque turrets are significant as an early indication of the demand for a minaret, a feature to become an important factor in Gujarat mosque design.

In 1361, the Tanka Mosque was built in Dholkā[5] with an open prayer hall of about

[4]J. Burgess and H. Cousens, *A List of Antiquarian Remains in Bombay Presidency,* Bombay, 1885, pp. 267-68.
[5]Ibid., p. 33.

a hundred temple pillars. This structure is architecturally unimportant but it is one of the last buildings constructed in Gujarat in the fourteenth century, for the latter half of the century has left no monuments. The increased instability of the central power in Delhi had its ramifications in the provinces, where governors were more concerned with their own personal safety and in maintaining their own individual positions leaving little time for patronage of architecture.

After the Tanka Mosque there is a pause in the progress of the style. The second half of the century was a lull before the flowering of the new style of architecture under the rule of the inventive Aḥmad Shāh (1414-42) in the early years of the fifteenth century.

* * *

Although Muslim power increased until 1536, the rebellious spirit of the subject people was never subdued, nor were the majority of Gujarātīs converted to Islam. It is therefore not surprising that most of the monuments constructed in Gujarat were in and near the capitals, first Aḥmadābād and then Champanīr. Outside this area, people followed the old Hindu religion and built temples as before.

The earliest dated mosque in Aḥmadābād is the old Jāmi' known as Aḥmad Shāh's Mosque (1414) [Plan 9] abutting the south wall of the citadel. The sanctuary façade is composed of a screen of three arches, two on the sides and a larger central arch which frames two tall columns joined by a suspended Hindu cusped *toraṇa*, a feature soon incorporated into other Gujarātī mosques. The central arch is flanked by two large lightly decorated buttresses rising from the ground to the roof. The previously surmounting turrets were probably taken down or fell down in the 1819 earthquake. The question whether these buttresses were actual minarets for the call to prayer has not been satisfactorily answered but it appears unlikely, since the internal staircases actually lead to the roof. Whether or not these buttresses were functional, they are the earliest examples in Gujarat of gateway turrets brought down to the ground, and therefore, set an important precedent for all future paired gateway minarets, a feature soon to become enormously popular in Gujarat.

The interior has ten large domes divided into two rows with smaller domes between supported by one hundred and fifty two pillars. These are superimposed one upon another with blocks inserted to form a projecting hand, a feature to become common in later Gujarat mosques. Another innovation in this mosque is a type of clerestory created behind the raised central archway where a diffused light is admitted by carved stone screens. The galleries and stone screens are popular features in later mosque examples in Gujarat.

In the north-west corner twenty-five pillars are surrounded by perforated stone screens to form a *zanāna*. The enclosure for the sultan's harem was a feature of early Gujarātī mosques and appears only in royal mosques and not in those built by courtiers or private individuals. But even in the later royal mosques built in Gujarat this feature is omitted. An explanation of this might be found in the actual fabric of Gujarat Muslim society. Here, more than in any other part of Muslim India, there arose a mixed religious society developed by the many interreligious marriages arranged initially by Aḥmad Shāh, who himself married the daughter of a Rājpūt chief. It comes as no surprise, therefore, that as the Gujarātī mosque style evolves some of the functional Islamic adjuncts, such as the screened *zanāna* compartment, become obsolete.

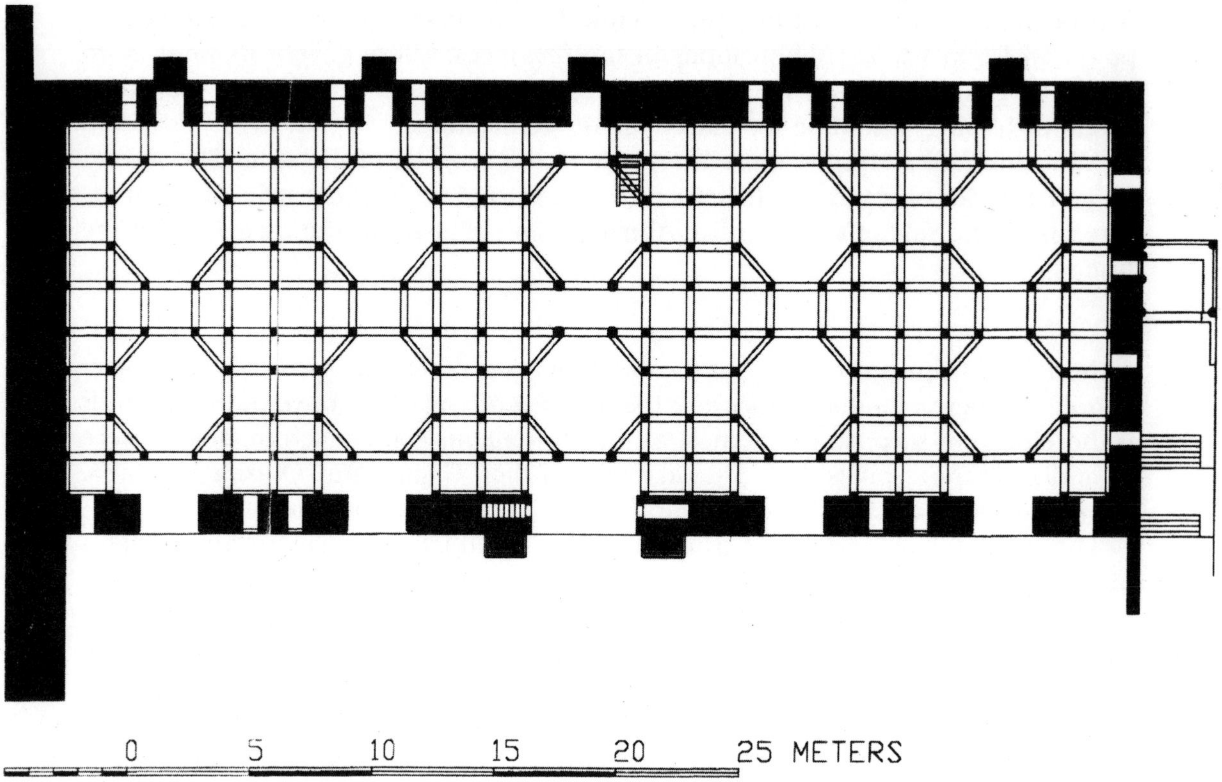

Plan 9. Aḥmadābād, Aḥmad Shāh's Mosque (after J. Burgess)

The Mosque of Haibat Khān, possibly a relative of Aḥmad Shāh, was probably built about the same time as the Mosque of Aḥmad Shāh in the citadel.[6] It belongs in style rather to the earlier mosques of Cambay and Dholkā. The slender unadorned round tapering towers over the central high arch of the screen are non-functional and in this respect resemble those on the Aḍhāī Din kā Jhoṃparā Mosque in Ajmer, the Jāmi' Mosque of Cambay and the Mosque of Hilāl Khān Qāzī in Dholkā. The only decoration on the towers is a carved ring-moulding which divides them into two sections. The thin tapering towers are surmounted by conical tops, a design probably derived from Jaina temples,[7] which makes its first appearance here and is to become a characteristic feature of the later minarets of Gujarat. Unusual also are the five rounded bastions on the exterior of the *qibla* wall. Both these engaged bastions and rounded turrets over the central archway suggest the influence of the Delhi style under Fīrūz Tughluq. If the dating of this mosque is correct and if it was built at the same time as the Jāmi' Mosque in the citadel, the question arises as to why the new type of buttresses extending from the ground to the roof, with surmounting pinnacles,

[6]J. Burgess, *The Muhammadan Architecture of Ahmadabad*, vol.1, London, 1900 (1905), p. 20.
[7]A.B.M. Husain, *The Manara in Indo-Muslim Architecture*, Dacca, 1970, p. 152.

were not used here also. It might be tempting to conclude that the innovation of ornate buttresses flanking a central archway starting from the ground rather than from the roof are first to be introduced into the royal Jāmi' Mosque in the citadel. For mosques not built with royal patronage, such as the Mosque of Haibat Khān, the cylindrical turrets set on the roof are still in use.

The Mosque of Sayyid Ālam stated to have been built in 1412[8] is apparently of somewhat later date, for stylistically it is an advance of the earlier mosques just considered. The central sanctuary chamber is screened by three arches, the higher central arch again flanked by a pair of highly decorated buttresses which run from the ground to the roof, and which were originally surmounted by the usual turrets. The flanking lower side wings of the sanctuary, however, are fronted by post-and-lintel porticos, which together with several other elements such as the projecting cornice and ornamental brackets, anticipate the next great monument, the Jāmi' Mosque. Most probably this mosque was erected in 1420,[9] although the inscription is difficult to read, since it is fragmentary. Many features are in a nascent stage on this monument, the work of an innovative architect perhaps not yet quite skilled enough to bring off the masterpiece soon to follow.

In 1407 Muzaffar declared his independence as Muzaffar Shāh, but ruled for only four years before his death, when he was succeeded by Shihāb al-Dīn Aḥmad Shāh (1411-42), his grandson. Aḥmad Shāh's rule of thirty-one years was a period of relentless warfare against Hūshang Shāh of Mālwā, the Rājpūt Rājā of Idar, and the Rājpūt chieftains of Champanīr, Dungarpur, Kota and Bundi, until eventually Gujarat consolidated all surrounding lands.

In the centre of the new city of Aḥmadābād Aḥmad Shāh started work on a great Jāmi' Mosque [Ill. 69] completed in 1424,[10] probably at that time the largest and grandest mosque in India. The mosque is in a hypostyle plan, the courtyard surrounded on the north, east and south sides by one-aisled pillared colonnades and on the west by a pillared prayer hall. In all there are two-hundred and sixty closely set Jaina temple pillars used to support fifteen domes, in three aisles, the central higher and larger than the others. The sanctuary is composed of three aisles divided into five domed bays each. There are five *miḥrābs* decorated in coloured marble.

An interesting feature of the interior first seen in Aḥmad's Mosque in the citadel in embryo form is the elevation of the central corridor to three storeys with the galleries supported on pillars and enclosed by perforated stone screens [Ill. 70]. The side aisles are double-storeyed and the remainder of the interior is built in one storey, except for the *zanāna* in the north-west corner, which, as usual, is on a second platform storey. The central elevation in particular is most attractive with its balconies overlooking the pillared loggia enclosed by stone screens which permit only a diffused light to penetrate.

The court façade of the sanctuary is a combination of two different styles. In the centre is a screen of three arches, the large central arch flanked by two richly carved buttresses the tops of which probably fell down in the 1819 earthquake. The lower part of the *manāras* is stepped square, but above they are five-sided and round, the

[8]J. Burgess, *The Muhammadan Architecture of Ahmadabad,* p. 22.

[9]John Burton-Page, "Medieval Ahmadabad," *Marg,* vol. XXXIX, no. 3,1988, p. 32.

[10]J. Burgess, *The Muhammadan Architecture of Ahmadabad,* p. 35; idem, *Report on the Antiquities of Kathiawad and Kachh,* London, 1876, p. 5.

entire surface heavily carved [Ill. 71]. The upper parts consisted of four carved storeys, separated by projecting cornices supported on brackets.[11] A flight of steps from the roof of the mosque led to the platform of the minarets, which were surmounted by a conical top and a finial. It seems probable that the minarets of the Jāmi' Mosque are the earliest example of a pair of gateway *ma'dhanas* in Gujarat[12] from which many later mosques were to draw inspiration. These towers were the famous shaking minarets of Aḥmadābād, whose sympathetic trembling remained a mystery. The central screen is linked by pillared porticos [Ill. 72] of post-and-beam construction to the façade of the south and north wings. Although this arrangement was first tried in the Sayyid Ālam Mosque a few years earlier, it is here in the Jāmi' Mosque that the juxtaposition of these different traditions is achieved most successfully. Behind the central arch are two tall pillars joined by a suspended cusped arch, a *toraṇa* modelled on Hindu design from temple gateways.

The Jāmi' Mosque is not part of the royal complex which also included a palace. The northern wall of the mosque extended along a royal processional way which led to the main palace gate. An area in front of the mosque is relegated to two further monuments, the Tomb of Aḥmad Shāh and the Tomb of the Queens, the royal ladies. The central feature of the processional route, connecting the palace and mosque, was a triple-arched triumphal arch, the Tīn Darwāza, the principal entrance to the Maidān Shāh, an outer court of the citadel, with a fountain and raised terrace in the centre. Over the beautifully pointed arches is a parapet in which there are three small projecting balconies on brackets such as are found at the contemporary Ādinātha Temple in Ranakpur and the Jaya Stambha in Chitorgarh. Interestingly, the latter monument was erected by Rāṇā Khumba to commemorate his victory over the Muslim ruler of Delhi.

The royal enclosure served as a meeting place for foreign diplomats who would, from here, approach the sultan seated on the terrace. From this elevated position the ruler reviewed his troops and held court beside the fountain. Maḥmūd Begarha sallied through the Tīn Darwāza at the age of fourteen to quell the rebellious nobles who disputed his succession. And even in the eighteenth century its beams were used by Maratha governors as targets, when they shot five arrows to predict the success or failure of an administrative law.[13]

The triple-arched gateway is a Roman Imperial conception first seen in the Arch of Augustus in the Roman Forum and the Arch of Tiberius in Orange, both of the first century. The design was then used frequently throughout the Imperial period until the reign of Constantine in the fourth century. But while the Romans used the Greek orders to frame and accent the larger central arch, the Aḥmad Shāhīs employed the usual decorated buttresses for the same purpose. But both the Romans and the Gujarātīs flanked the wider central arch with two narrower arches. In Roman times these strange monuments were connected with the idea of victory and a triumph was an honour approved by the Senate. This was celebrated by a special ritual procession where the troops marched before the people to exhibit the booty and prisoners of war to confirm the success of the army. It is an interesting aside that roofed balconies were added to the Tīn Darwāza, such as were found on the Tower

[11]Seen by James Forbes in 1781, as told by J. Burgess, *The Muhammadan Architecture of Ahmadabad,* p. 30.
[12]Husain, op. cit., p. 81.
[13]T.C. Hope, *Ahmadabad,* as told by J. Burgess, *The Muhammadan Architecture of Ahmadabad,* p. 25.

of Victory in nearby Chitorgarh, as well as on various contemporary Jaina temples. Architectually, the Roman triumphal arches became part of the medieval and Renaissance building tradition and thus changed the whole conception of European architecture. During the reigns of Aḥmad and his son Muḥammad the Aḥmad Shāhī dynasty was at its height, comparable in some ways to the great years of the Roman Empire in the first century of our era. Psychologically, the frame of mind of the Gujarātī rulers at this time might find a parallel in first century Rome. Although no Colosseum was built in Aḥmadābād, a comparison of the two realms adds interest and a little piquancy to an attempted understanding of the Gujarātī mind in the middle of the fifteenth century.

Aḥmad Shāh died in 1442 and the throne was occupied for the next sixteen years by two rulers, Aḥmad's son, Muḥammad Shāh (1442-51) and Quṭb al-Dīn (1451-58), both of whom continued architectural patronage and the building momentum started by Aḥmad Shāh. Muḥammad Shāh completed the tomb of his father, begun in the last reign in the enclosure reserved for it, near the eastern gate of the Jāmi' Mosque. The Tomb of Aḥmad Shāh is probably the earliest tomb in Gujarat and would serve as a prototype for the many mausolea to follow. It is a square domed monument, with projecting porticos on the sides, the one on the south serving as the entrance. The porticos are connecting to small domed corner rooms by enclosed verandahs. The plan of this square tomb is interesting. It is basically a tomb chamber surrounded by a pillared aisle and four square corner rooms. Of special note is the early use of perforated stone screens to join the pillars [Ill. 73]. In the middle chamber are three white marble tombs, in the centre that of Sultan Aḥmad Shāh, and on either side those of his son Muḥammad Shāh II and his grandson, Quṭb al-Dīn Shāh. Two other marble tombs are in the pillared halls on the west and east sides, the former probably belonging to a grandson of Ahmad Shāh,[14] the latter to Aḥmad Khān, the son of Maḥmūd Begarha.

In another adjacent enclosure are the Tombs of the Queens (Rānī-kā-Hujra) of Aḥmad Shāh, of similar design and probably built about the same time as the tomb of the sultan. Within an open court surrounded by an arcaded and pillared corridor is a central chamber with a platform on which are eight marble cenotaphs richly carved and inlaid with metal and mother-of-pearl. The central tomb is that of Mughalī Bībī, the wife of Muḥammad Shāh II, and the mother of Maḥmūd Begarha, who later married the Muslim Saint Shāh Ālam. Adjoining is another black marble tomb, once inlaid with mother-of-pearl, ascribed to Murkī Bībī, sister of Bībī Mughalī, the first wife of the saint, and a daughter of the Jām of Sind.[15] There is no mention of who the other ladies buried here might be.

The carving of the window screens and blind niches is of very superior workmanship with diversified designs and motifs. It is quite apparent that a group of expert stone carvers was employed by the court to decorate monuments built under royal patronage. These stone carvings would be surpassed in the next project at Sarkhej, where work was to be done in an even more difficult medium, metal.

The Gujarātī Muslim pillar was fully developed before the last years of Aḥmad Shāh's reign, having been used in the Jāmi' Mosque and in the Tomb of Aḥmad

[14] J. Burgess, *The Muhammadan Architecture of Ahmadabad*, p. 38.

[15] Bayley, *Gujarat*, pp.153-60 as told by J.Burgess, *The Muhammadan Architecture of Ahmadabad*, p. 40.

Shāh. It is again seen in this monument in the surrounding corridor. Three plinths are superimposed on which stands the real base composed of a square plinth and fillet divided by a thin torus. The capital has projecting brackets on each side and the abacus consists of two plinths of which the upper one is carved. There is also some carving on the neck of the shaft and on the two lower parts of the base. The shaft and base have thin flat somewhat narrow slabs applied to each face, a design generally found in temple construction and used here by the Hindu and Jaina masons.

* * *

Muḥammad Shāh II, Aḥmad's son and successor (1442-51) started another architectural project of considerable importance at Sarkej, soon to become the centre of further construction under Maḥmūd Begarha (1458-1511). A tomb and mosque were erected to the memory of Shaykh Aḥmad Khattrī, a famous Muslim saint, distantly related to Fīrūz Shāh Tughluq of Delhi. Known as Ganj Bakhsh in Gujarat where he settled in 1400, he became famous for his piety and soon found himself the adviser of Sultan Muzaffar and friend and guide of Aḥmad Shāh, his son. Although the saint helped to establish the city of Aḥmadābād in 1411, he refused all further rewards and settled as a recluse at Sarkej, where he died in 1446.

The tomb of the saint [Ill. 74] is the largest mausoleum in Gujarat, with a square central chamber surmounted by a large dome on twelve pillars with four concentric aisles on each side, roofed by smaller domes. The square formed by the inner row of pillars surrounding the central area around the tomb is divided from the rest of the interior by a screen connecting the pillars formed of perforated brass panels, fretted, chased and tooled into an infinite variety of patterns.

By the mid-fifteenth century the architectural style of Gujarat had become more Indian. The screen of arches was often omitted and only a row of columns supported by two minarets at each end replaced it. The huge Sarkej Mosque differs dramatically from the Jāmi' Mosque of Aḥmadābād. The screen of arches in front of the sanctuary is now totally gone, leaving the interior pillars exposed. There is in fact no formal facade at all, just a number of pillars massed together. Nor are there any minarets or flanking buttresses. Ten uniform corbelled domes arranged in two aisles complete the otherwise flat roof and are supported on pillars with the usual Jaina-type bracketed capitals.

It is difficult to believe that a Muslim population would have used this building as a place of worship. The feeling of the Sarkej monuments is entirely Indian and the construction so blatantly in the indigenous style perhaps indicates the personal predilection of the monarchs, since Sarkej was built as their private retreat. Maḥmūd Begarha who completed the project in 1451, afterwards added a tomb for himself on the east end of the north side near the tomb of the Shaykh with corbelled domes and pillars with Hindu bracket capitals, as well as another tomb for his wife, Bībī Rājābāī, on a nearby terrace. He also excavated a vast lake at the side of the mosque and added steps down to it. On the south side of the lake Maḥmūd built his palace entirely in the trabeate style, although his public projects in Aḥmadābād and in his new capital, Champanīr, are built in a totally different design.

With the palaces, tombs, gardens, pavilions and lakes built here, Sarkej became a great pilgrimage centre for later Gujarātī rulers and a royal burial ground. From these early Sarkej examples it might easily be concluded that the arch was never popular in Gujarat. It was certainly not a valuable structural component since Gujarātī minds continued to think in old indigenous terms.

One last remarkable monument might be added to the reign of Muḥammad Shāh, the mosque bearing the name of his son, Quṯb al-Dīn(1449)[Ill. 75], which adds no new architectural features to the style.[16] The sanctuary is roofed by five large and ten small domes and the façade is composed of five arched entrances, the central arch flanked by the usual ornate *mīnār* buttresses. These do not contain the stairs which run up straight in the walls to the roof. The carvings on existing buttresses is very Hindu in feeling[Ill. 76].

* * *

Quṯb al-Dīn's short rule of seven years (1451-58) produced not a single monument associated with him personally. There are, however, a mosque and tomb in the suburb of Rājpur [Ill. 77] whose patronage is uncertain. The inscription of the Bībījī Mosque ascribes the erection of the building to Sultan Quṯb al-Dīn.[17] But there is also some mention of Sayyid Buddha bin Sayyid Yāqūt and his wife, in whose memory it is said to have been built. A huge structure it has a triple-arched façade introduced in place of the open pillars in the wings. The monument is of special interest because the minarets which flank the central arched entrance are still standing, one actually intact. The tapering minaret is divided into four storeys by galleried balconies on carved brackets. The shaft is circular in the upper three sections, the lowest part above the buttresses octagonal. A conical dome caps the structure and an internal staircase winds upwards.

There is also the strange Mosque of Malik Sha'bān (1452) where a large central dome is surrounded by seven smaller domes, all with coffered Hindu-style ceilings. The central dome is supported by twelve pillars and the façade is open revealing a double row of pillars. But the interest in this mosque lies primarily in its unusual plan reminiscent of a Hindu *maṇḍapa,* which has led to speculation that it is a Hindu structure converted to a mosque.

Two other monuments were constructed during the reign of Quṯb al-Dīn Shāh but apparently by order of court officials. The Tomb of Daryā Khān and the Mosque of 'Alī Khān Bhukai in Dholkā differ in design and technique from other structures of the period, perhaps the result of an external influence. The two structures show stylistic similarities and are therefore of about the same date, the late reign of Quṯb al-Dīn or the early reign of Maḥmūd Shāh Begarha. Both are built not of stone as all other Gujarātī monuments of the time, but of brick, and both use no beams or pillars in their construction, only arches and solid brick piers.

Daryā Khān was a noble and a former minister at the court of Maḥmūd Shāh Begarha. The tomb where he is buried is an imposing square structure with a lofty central dome on a high drum and lower domed arched verandahs with pointed entrance arches on the sides opening on to the façade. The domes are all carried on brick squinches rather than on an indigenous beam-and-bracket support. The monument appears to have been intentionally built in the now popular arcuate style in this region where stone is not easily found. The monument was obviously built by

[16] J. Burgess and H. Cousens, *A Revised List of Antiquarian Remains in the Bombay Presidency,* vol. VIII, Bombay, 1897, p. 291; Burgess, *The Muhammadan Architecture of Ahmadabad,* p. 45.

[17] Burgess and Cousens, op. cit., p. 292.

men working in a foreign tradition with which they were familiar and which at this time appears to have found its way into Gujarat.

The Mosque of Alif Khān Bhukai, known as Khān-kī Mosque, has stylistic similarities to the Tomb of Daryā Khān and is therefore of about the same date, the reign of Quṭb al-Dīn or the early reign of Maḥmūd Shāh Begarha. Alif Khān Bhukai is known to have been one of the favourite companions of the young Mahmūd Begarha, who later bestowed the title Khān on him and made him commander of a large army.[18]

In plan the Mosque of Alif Khān is divided into three domed square halls by two walls perforated each by a large central and two smaller side arches, the surrounding walls pierced by windows, recesses and doors. The original facade of the mosque, now gone, was a screen with three arches, the central one flanked by two square solid towers in two receding storeys surmounted by a domed cupola. Stairs run up the ends of the mosque to parapet level and then into the towers, the upper storeys open on all four sides by pointed arches, the drum pierced with arched windows. At the top is a square domed canopy for the *mu'azzin.*

The towers of this mosque are most unusual, although not unique in Indian Islamic architecture. While square minarets are rare, the inspiration must have been closer at hand than eleventh century Egypt.[19] The square minaret was used, albeit briefly, to crown portals in fourteenth century Iran. In India in some of the earliest 'Ādil Shāhī mosques in Bījāpūr, dated to the early sixteenth century, square towers are found. For instance Ibrāhīm or 'Alī's Old Jāmi' Mosque has two three-storeyed brick minarets over the central piers of the façade, which are square on the lower courses and octagonal on the upper. At the centre of the roof of Ikhlās Khān's Mosque is a square minaret divided into two storeys by a cornice and two three-storeyed brick minarets, the lower stage of which is square over the central piers. While these mosques are of a somewhat later date, they must have had the same prototype as the Dholkā Mosque and, although reminiscent of western Islamic minarets, it is probable that the model on which these square minarets were based was closer to home.

The Mosque of Alif Khān is built of brick with two arches and solid brick piers, the only other monument of this material in Gujarat besides the Tomb of Daryā Khān. Stucco as ornament is also used. In India from earliest times there has been a preference for dressed stone in construction and decoration until well into the fourteenth century and it was not until the reign of Fīrūz Shāh Tughluq that rubble structures were finished by applying a layer of stucco. In the Deccan in Gulbarga, on the other hand, some exquisite stucco work may be found in the Dargāh of Mujārrad Kamāl[20] and on the Langar kī Mosque[21] but after the mid-fifteenth century, the art of stucco carving declined. Later stucco was not used in the same way in either Bīdar or Bījāpūr. It might be tempting to conclude that there were artisans trained in the art of stucco carving in Gulbarga during the first half of the fifteenth century, who seemed to understand the possibilities of stucco as a medium and used it in an imaginative way. Perhaps it might be suggested that these artisans were lured to Gujarat and to the grand Aḥmadābād court with its dependency of Dholkā.

* * *

[18]Burgess, *The Muhammadan Architecture of Ahmadabad,* p. 34.

[19]Husain, op. cit., p. 93.

[20]E. Schotten Merklinger, *Indian Islamic Architecture: The Deccan 1347-1686,* Warminster, 1981, p. 93.

[21]Ibid.

During the reign of Maḥmūd Begarha (1459-1511) Gujarat had its greatest days, when the building art reached its finest form. Although these were years filled with continual warfare and struggles with vassal states and neighbouring Muslim and Rājpūt powers, the conqueror's influence continued to increase. Much of the success and dynamism came from the ruler himself whose charismatic personality became a legend in Europe. Some say his beard descended to his waist, others that his moustache was long enough to be tied behind his head. Maḥmūd was a man with an insatiable appetite who immunized himself against possibly being poisoned by consuming miniscule quantities of the lethal brew so that "if a fly settled on his hand it fell dead." Europe was much aware of this great ruler and Samuel Butler dedicated the following lines to him:

"The Prince of Cambay's daily food
Is asp, a basilick and toad."

* * *

Most monuments surviving from the middle of the fifteenth century and later are mausolea with attached mosques, known as *rawzas*. Generally the mosques were open in plan and by this time had their minarets relegated to the corners of the façade, becoming even less important, slender non-functioning turrets.

The Mosque, and Tomb of Sayyid Usmān (1460) are two of the earliest monuments [Ill. 78] in Usmānpur near Aḥmadābād built in the reign of Maḥmūd Begarha. The mosque was built by the sultan in memory of the Saint Sayyid Usmān and the complex has become a shrine believed to be vested with miraculous powers of healing. The mosque façade has no screen of arches, just a range of pillars, and thus there is no place for the minarets except at each end of the pillared sanctuary. The tapering shafts of these turrets are divided into six storeys by projecting balconies supported on carved brackets. The lowest storey is stepped square to the roof, the next stage is octagonal, and the two top storeys are round. A winding staircase leads to the balconies.

In addition to being one of the earliest examples of a mosque with minarets placed at the front corners, another architectural innovation is introduced in the mosque. Balconied windows were to become one of the most distinguishing and delightful decorative devices of Gujarātī mosques at the end of the fifteenth century. They were first introduced, as here, attached to the sides of the mosque, but later were moved to the façade. In addition to the aesthetic appeal of the shallow balconies and prominent eaves, their perforated stone screens were a useful device for allowing extra light into the sanctuary.

The square domed structure has a central tomb chamber surrounded by two rows of pillars originally connected by now-missing stone screens. To support the large dome four additional pillars were introduced, and instead of eight supports, there are now twelve pillars on which the dome rests. A similar arrangement was first used a decade earlier in the Tomb of Shaykh Aḥmad Khattrī at Sarkej.

Two minor monuments of about the same time show a further development in mosque building. The Mosques of Miyān Khān Chishtī (1465), built by the minister Malik Maqsūd, and of Bībī Achuf Kiki (1462-72),commissioned by one of the chief ministers, Imād al-Mulk, for his wife, have a new type of façade. In both monuments a screen of three arches with ornate minarets rising up on each side of the central opening replaces the façade, originally seen in the Jāmi' Mosque, where an arched screen fronted the central part of the sanctuary, but where the wings retained a range of pillars. The interior of both is divided into three sections, each domed, the central corridor rising to an addition storey. The three structural domes show some further Islamic influence, as does the complete range of arches used here in a tentative fashion.

In the last quarter of the sixteenth century arches were used more frequently both in the capital and in the provinces. The arcuate system was becoming increasingly more popular in tomb construction, primarily because the square tomb design lent itself better to the use of the arch, whereas the pillared mosque interiors were more easily roofed by means of the beam-and-bracket system. While the use of arches in tombs may best be seen in the provinces, one example remains to be examined in Aḥmadābād.

The Tomb of Shāh Ālam, the Suhrawardī saint, was built by Tāj Khān Narpali, a noble at the court of Maḥmūd Begarha, about 1475. The Suhrawardī Ṣūfī Order was the second to appear in India and Shāh Ālam's ancestors were a long line of saints dating back to Sayyid Jalāl al-Dīn Surkh-posh (1199-1291) who settled in Uchh, Sind. From this line came Shāh Ālam's father, Burhān al-Dīn Quṭb-i Ālam (d.1453), who went to Gujarat and was buried at Vatva. The Tomb of Shāh Ālam was started some years before the tomb of his father, although the latter died in 1452, twenty-three years earlier. The location of Shāh Ālam's resting place is also superior, being just outside Aḥmadābād rather than at Vatva, a distance from the capital. It is obvious that Shāh Ālam had the ruler's protection and was involved in political matters, since his grave lies in such a choice spot in the capital while his spiritually more illustrious father was buried at a great distance from the capital. Shāh Ālam was a highly political figure, who, although remaining faithful to the tradition of his father, was active in the succession issue which broke out at Sultan Aḥmad's death in 1442, and who managed to eventually enthrone his protégé, the 13-year-old Fathe Khān soon to become the greatest ruler of Gujarat under the name of Maḥmūd Begarha in 1459.

The Tomb of Shāh Ālam [Ill. 79] occupies the central position of a group of buildings that were built over the next ten years. The square monument stands on a low platform and has three concentric squares of pillars encircling the domed tomb chamber, while the exterior screen still consists of a range of pillars, the spaces between are filled with an arcade of pointed arches fitted with perforated screens. Although the arches were not soundly built, for they have all fallen, the fact that they were used at all at this time in the capital is significant and shows that the architects of Aḥmadābād were finally beginning to revert to the arcuate system generally used in other Islamic countries. Tombs outside Aḥmadābād made even more use of the arcuate system. This can best be seen in the groups of tombs at Vatva and Maḥmūdābād, which appear to be more experimental in the use of arches.

The earlier monument is the Tomb of Sayyid Burhān al-Dīn Quṭb-i Ālam, the grandson of the famous Suhrawardī saint of Uchh, Sayyid Jalāl Bukhārī (1308-84). Quṭb-i Ālam migrated to Gujarat in 1400, founded an order there, and counted Sultan Aḥmad Shāh among his disciples. The sultan, in fact, built his new capital at the very place where his patron saint had settled.

The Tomb of Quṭb-i Ālam is an enormous square structure built in two storeys, the upper domed chamber with three arches on each side. The ground floor has broad inner arches around the tomb chamber and an outer narrower arcade also built with arches. The arcades have all collapsed indicating that the builders were not yet accustomed to working with the arch form successfully. The plan is in the same concentric system as in pillared tombs, a double arcade forming the interior, inside which is a corridor of arches, with the tomb in the centre. The monument is remarkable since all parts are either arched or vaulted. By this time some buildings appear to have accepted the arcuate system, believing that their works could now be more flexible while remaining structurally sound. Unfortunately, the Indian masons were not yet experienced in the construction of arches and the trial effort ended ingloriously with the collapse of the arcades. But out of the ruins of this monument arose another tomb a few years later where the defects were remedied.

The full potential of the use of the arch is next seen on a monument in Maḥmūdābād, a town which takes its name from Sultan Maḥmūd Begarha who founded and fortified it about 1479. Among the small group of tombs here dated to about the end of the fifteenth century is the important Tomb of Mubārak Sayyid (1484), one of Maḥmūd Begarha's ministers, standing on a platform with a protruding porch on the east side. In plan the tomb is square with the usual concentric rows of ranged pillars, here in massive form consisting of four square pillars grouped together. The innermost twelve piers support the central dome and are joined by perforated screens. Outside these, enclosing the tomb proper, is a double corridor supported on 36 piers, with arches between each pier and roofed by small domes of various internal patterns. The outer arches are open with no screens, these only being found around the central tomb chamber, inside the innermost colonnade. The tall drum of the dome has pointed aches filled with perforated screens.

Apparently Gujarātī builders now understood the potential of the arch and have used it structurally here. Perhaps an outside influence was at work, for at this time craftsmen were being attracted to Gujarat and the influence of a master mason from Lodhī Delhi might be detected in the construction of the piers, as well as in the dome, cupolas and *chhatris* over the clerestory. Open arches constructed in this particular way were not used anywhere else in the fifteenth century and some scholars have ascribed the tomb on this stylistic evidence to about a hundred years later (1588). However, because most later mosques and tombs are larger in scale and have lost much of the virility and beauty of the earlier monuments, I believe the Tomb of Mubārak Sayyid was constructed in the late fifteenth century and probably in 1484. The simplicity of the monument and its elegant and appropriate details have rarely been surpassed in India. The Tomb of Mubārak Sayyid, therefore, belongs to the Aḥmad Shāhī style its most virilent and elegant stage, to the reign of Maḥmūd Begarha in the late fifteenth century.

About this same time, Maḥmūd built a new capital at Champanīr but construction continued in the old style in the old wealthy capital and more and more adorned mosques were built during the last thirty years of the reign of the sultan. The Mosque of Muhāfiz Khān (1485-92), built by Jāmi' al-Dīn Muhāfiz Khān, governor of Aḥmadābād under Maḥmūd Begarha, although small in size, is one of the most richly carved monuments and has been called an "architectural gem of refinement." The façade is pierced by three high arched entrances and the roof is supported on eight columns dividing the sanctuary into five rows of three bays. The *mīnārs* of the mosque are among the best preserved in Gujarat and are at the ends of the façade, stepping square until roof level, then divided into three tapering octagonal storeys by carved brackets and topped by conical cupolas. Spiral staircases inside the *ma'dhanas* ascend to the roof and two highly decorated oriel windows project from the sides of the sanctuary.

During the first quarter of the sixteenth century several mosques were built with similar internal features. A typical example is the Rānī Rūpavatī Mosque [Ill. 80] built towards the end of the reign of Maḥmūd Begarha and named after two ladies of the royal household who were buried in the adjoining *rawza.*

In this monument both the arcuate and trabeate style of construction are used. The façade screen is pierced by three arched entrances and hides three large domes. The wider central arched entrance opposite the higher central dome is flanked by minaret buttresses and smaller arched entrances opposite the other two side domes. The façade is completed by balconied windows on each side and lattice windows near the ends of the façade. In front of and behind the three larger domes and at the ends of the mosque are smaller domes, the rest of the spaces roofed by flat stones.

The central part of the façade is raised above the general roof level making room for the great central arched entrance and screening off the clerestory. It is flanked by richly adorned minaret buttresses [Ill. 81]. The three large domes each stand on twelve pillars, so arranged that the central part is raised to admit light into the interior. The pillars which support the central dome are twice as high as those of the side domes, and two rows of short columns stand on the roof to make up the height. In front of these, internally, is a richly carved balustrade. Reflected light is admitted into the mosque from the roof into the dome, giving a pleasing effect without glare. A screen of perforated stonework was introduced between the shorter and outer columns which produces an especially beautiful effect.

These early sixteenth century mosques were an attempt to combine the two systems of construction. The tomb on the north-west side has a surrounding corridor supported on twenty pillars with a small dome over each corner, similar to the later Tomb of Rānī Sipari, but in this early example the base of the dome has been lowered to bring it into harmony. There are two white marble graves in the interior, the central one of which belongs to Rūpavatī. In all probability the tomb is contemporary with the mosque.

Some very fine buildings continued to be produced in the subsequent reigns of Muzaffar II, Bahādur and Maḥmūd III, but the vigour which had characterized the earlier monuments seemed to be diminishing. The Mosque and Tomb of Rānī Sipari (1514) [Ill. 82] are among the most notable of the later structures and the mosque in particular has been called "one of the most exquisite buildings in the world" and the "gem of Aḥmadābād." The mosque was commissioned by one of the wives of Maḥmūd Begarha, mother of his son Abū Bakr Khān, whose name was Rānī Sipari.[22]

The small mosque is only two bays deep and of the open-fronted type, with a row of paired pillars in the front and six domes over the three large areas in both aisles. The usual clerestory is missing and attention is drawn to the tall slender turrets at the ends of the facade. Having no internal stairs, the soild minarets extend the entire height. From this time on open mosques have their minarets relegated to the ends of the façade. But even in closed mosques, where minarets had always projected from the centre flanking the central arch, they are gradually diminishing in

[22]J. Burgess, *The Muhammadan Architecture of Ahmadabad*, p. 84.

importance, becoming ever more slender, and eventually turning into mere ornamental turrets. The tall slender finials at the ends of the Rānī Sipari façade have assumed the final form of the minaret, now transformed from a functional tower with a winding stairway into a solid and ornamental accessory, a symbolic appendage at the expense of utility.[23]

In fifteenth century Gujarat minarets are used in many ways to emphasize, balance, or decorate the west façades. The prime importance was not apparently in the functional use of the minaret but in its most correct and aesthetically pleasing position on a monument. By the sixteenth century, the Hindu element, which has always remained strong in Gujarat, finally appears to have attained the upper hand again, relegating one of the most important Islamic functional elements to the façade sides as decoration. It is tempting to conclude that Muslim society in sixteenth century, Gujarat appears to have had no urgent need to retain a functional minaret.

Standing in the north-east corner of the royal enclosure of Aḥmadābād, the Mosque of Siddi Sayyid [Plan 10] has been attributed to a slave of Aḥmad Shāh I, but the architectural style suggests a much later date, certainly to the end of the reign of Maḥmūd Begarha or to the reign of a distinguished noble of the time of Sultan Mufzaffar III (1561-72). The mosque is open in the front with four piers supporting five arches. Eight pillars support arcades of arches over which is a flat roof. This arrangement is another departure from the more conventional mosque design as seen in Gujarat. The ceiling is supported by various methods, brackets, diagonal beams and squinches, the latter showing how slowly this method of dome transition, so common in northern India, was being accepted by Gujarātī builders, who for centuries had followed a different structural method. The unfinished octagonal *mīnārs* which have not been carried above the roof are attached to the front corners of the mosque and are considerably less ornately carved than the usual minarets of the city.[24] They contain spiral staircases which rise to the roof and are thus real *ma'dhanas.*

The mosque is famous for its ten carved semicircular tympani windows of exquisite tracery in the form of tree stems and branches. Two of the four in the *qibla* wall are considered to be the finest example of carved stone tracery in India, surpassing even those of Āgrā and Delhi. There are three other windows in the south end of the building and three empty spaces in the north end for similar windows, which were never inserted.[25]

The tympani windows are cut in the usual Gujarātī sandstone and are not mere imitations of nature, the pattern being spread over the whole surface. The screens are used here as a finely meshed surface on which the artist could express himself. One of the windows is composed of a series of palms alternating with flowering trees, the tendrils and leaves filling the background[Ill. 83]. The second window has a single central tree entwined around a palm, with branches snaking outwards to cover the field of the composition[Ill. 84]. Called "palm and parasite" motif it is rendered in a sensitive and original way. Although frequently ascribed to the influence of Hindu aesthetics and artists, it has recently been interpreted as a tree of life motif which in Islamic times dates back to the Umayyad period where it appeared in the eighth century Qasr al-Hayr complex and three centuries later in the blind window grills of

[23]Ibid.

[24]"Siddi Sayyid's Mosque, Aḥmadābād," *Archaeological Survey of India, Annual Report, 1902-3,* Calcutta, 1904, p. 30

[25]Ibid.

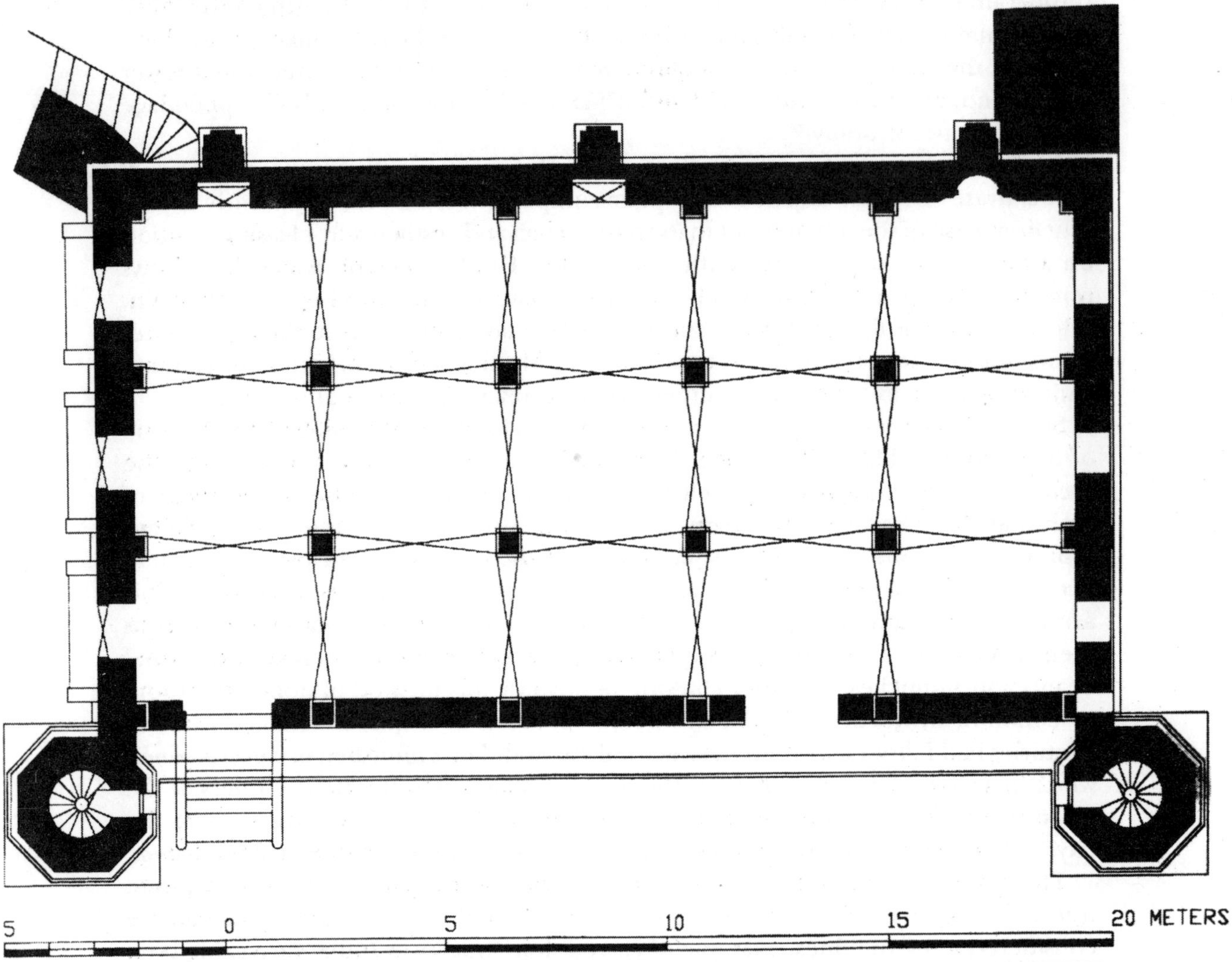

Plan 10. Aḥmadābād, Siddi Saiyyid's Mosque (after J. Burgess)

al-Hakīm Mosque minaret in Cairo. The Siddi Sayyid windows thus represent an eastern extension of a well established Islamic tradition.[26] But the technique has also been found in a pair of heraldic peacocks disposed around a tree in a Chalukyan temple at Pattadkal.[27]

If the windows are of Hindu inspiration, the animals are probably omitted in the Muslim context since the windows appear in the prayer hall walls. Perhaps we ought to conclude that the splendid tympani grills of the Siddi Sayyid Mosque belong to both the Hindu and Islamic tradition and are on amalgam of two differing aesthetic systems. As is often the case in cross-breeding, they have a strength and a sensitivity far exceeding the result of either system alone, for they symbolize the best and most fruitful union of the Hindu and the Muslim.

[26]F.B. Flood, "The Tree of Life as a Decorative Device in Islamic Window-Fillings: The Mobility of a Leitmotif," *Oriental Art*, vol. XXXVII, no. 4, Winter 1991/2, pp. 209-22.

[27]Ibid., p. 215.

The Mosque of Sīddī Sayyid is the last monument to show any originality, to demonstrate that art was still alive. While other mosques were produced along the same lines for some further years they were mere repetitions of structures erected during the time when Gujarātī architecture was at its prime.

Sultan Maḥmūd Begarha began building a new capital at Champanīr in 1485, after the capture of the fort from the Hindu chief Jaysingh Patai Rawal in 1484. It is believed to have taken twenty-three years to build the new site which was occupied for only a quarter of a century before being finally abandoned to the jungle. Yet in those two decades Champanīr was the political capital of Gujarat and the favourite residence of the sultans. In 1536, often the death of Bahādur Shāh, the court was moved back to Aḥmadābād and the decline of Champanīr began.

The majority of monuments which have survived here are mosques and tombs, since these were not dismantled and plundered. The Jāmi' Mosque[Ill. 85], the finest building in Champanīr, was built in a hypostyle plan, with a courtyard surrounded on three sides by one-aisled open arcades, while the sanctuary is eleven aisles deep divided by pillars into twenty-three bays. The containing walls are unusually ornate, for in addition to three imposing entrance chambers, there are openings with perforated screens. The prayer hall has three rows of domes, four in the front and back rows and three in the middle, opposite the spaces separating the domes in the other rows.

The sanctuary facade is fronted by a screen with five pointed arched entrances, the central one double the width of the others, with two slender minarets flanking the central opening. Only the minaret bases are adorned, the upper five stages are left with no decoration. Three balconied windows relieve the otherwise austere façade, one over the central arch and two others on each side of the minarets. The pillared prayer hall has a central corridor in three storeys rising from the middle bay [Ill. 86] and a mezzanine gallery for the *zanāna* at the northern end. In principal this scheme follows that of the Aḥmadābād Jāmi' Mosque, yet here the Hindu influence is even more evident.

The carved decoration in some cases shows signs of becoming mannered and mechanical and the craftsmanship is less vigorous than in early examples, indicating that the art has passed its prime. Nevertheless, the carving of the balcony brackets remains superb.

An unique feature is the rich ornamental treatment of the exterior, with traceried openings and fine entrance pavilions [Ill. 87]. The sanctuary façade contains five pointed archways with two slender minarets flanking the central opening, enriched with prominent balconied windows, a typical Gujarātī vernacular device. The Champanīr Mosque is modelled on the Jāmi' Mosque of Aḥmadābād built seventy-five years earlier, but with certain subtle refinements. Around the upper balconies are stone seats for meditation, set above and apart from the worshippers of the main hall below.

Other surviving buildings in Champanīr also have unusual characteristics not found elsewhere perhaps due to the isolated position of the new capital. They include the Nagīna Mosque (mid-sixteenth century), another variation on the theme of the Jāmi' Mosque and the Borah Mosque (mid-sixteenth century). Numerous tombs also dot the area. All are square with a domed central chamber surrounded by arcades crowned with smaller domes and a portico on one side. All have a carved arch, which imparts exceptional vigour and elegance.

* * *

The Gujarat architectural style penetrated into the surrounding territory and its influence can be seen in several buildings in western India. Among these are three mosques now located in the state of Jodhpur in Rajasthan, one in the town of Nagaur, and the others in Jalor. In Nagaur is the Shams Mosque [Ill. 88], believed to have been founded by the governor Shams Khān in the thirteenth century, although it may have had minarets restored by Fīrūz Shāh Tughluq in the following century. But the façade with its tall narrow arches and in the interior the clerestory gallery under the central dome point to fifteenth century Gujarat influence. The other two mosques in Jalor, the Fort and Topkhāna[Ill. 89] Mosques, were probably both built in the first half of the sixteenth century. The Fort Mosque follows the Aḥmadābād style quite closely, but the Topkhāna Mosque arches are filled with stone lattice screens. It was generally the decorative treatment of the Gujarātī façades that affected the styles with which Gujarat came into contact. Foremost now among this architectural ornament is the minaret, a once-functional but now purely decorative adjunct.

CHAPTER 9

Sind (1398-1592) and the Punjab (1150-1325)

The history of Sind from the period of Arab conquest early in the eighth century to independence is obscure. From the first conquest in 712 to 1010, when conquered by Maḥmūd of Ghaznī, Sind was ruled by hereditary governors appointed by the Abbāsid Caliph of Baghdād. From the early eighth century until the reign of Farukhzād in 1053, Sind was at least nominally a province of the empire of Ghaznī. In that year the Sumras, a native Rājpūt tribe of lower Sind, established themselves but failed to extend their authority over Upper Sind and Multān. Sind was then conquered by Mu'izz al-Dīn Muḥammad Ghūrī, and governed by his lieutenant, Naṣīr al-Dīn Qabacha, who attempted after his master's death, to assert his own independence until he in turn was defeated by Shams al-Dīn Iltutmish.

Very little is known of the nature and extent of the authority the later Slave dynasty had over Sind. Probably the degree varied with the personality of both the Delhi sultan and of the ruler of Sind. The Khaljīs and Tughluqs (especially Ghiyāth al-Dīn) defended Sind and kept it from being overrun by the Mongols. Yet, in spite of the power of the Delhi government, the Sumras retained almost complete autonomy, even during the reign of Muḥammad Tughluq, when nearly all of the rest of the subcontinent was ruled from Delhi. No central power, therefore, came to their rescue, when in 1336 another Rājpūt tribe, the Sammas of Kutch and lower Sind, usurped the throne. The new rulers, who had been converted to Islam in the eighth century, chose the title of Jam. During this period Sind came into direct contact with the Sultanate of Delhi and Persian rather than Arabic was made the official language of government. This period also saw the beginning of Sindī Ṣūfī movements and the popularization of their teachings.

By a payment of tribute, the first three rulers of the Samma line acknowledged the supremacy of Muḥammad Tughluq. The next ruler, however, renounced his allegiance to Delhi but during the following reign was compelled by Fīrūz Shāh to return to the Tughluq fold.

The disintegration of Muḥammad Tughluq's great empire after the death of Fīrūz Shāh, and the contraction of the Delhi Sultanate after the invasion of Tīmūr, absolved the Jams of Sind from any further allegiance to a central authority. They ruled Sind as independent sovereigns until the reign of Jam Niẓām al-Dīn (Jam Nindo), in the second half of the fifteenth century. The Arghun tribe now became more powerful in lower Sind and the ruling Sammas sought the help of the ruler of Gujarat. The alliance, however, was not able to stop the Arghun drive and in 1521 Shāh Beg conquered Sind and expelled the last Samma ruler, Jam Fīrūz, who fled to Gujarat.

Shāh Beg was the first of a long line of Arghun rulers and upon his death in 1524, the succession passed to his son, Shāh Husayn who in 1528 conquered Multān for a short time. During the reign of Shāh Husayn, the Mughal Sultan Humāyūn fled from Lahore and took refuge in Sind before setting off a year later to Persia. During this flight, Humāyūn's son, Akbar, was born in Umarkot in 1542.

Shāh Husayn Arghun was soon deserted by his nobles, who turned to Mīrzā Muḥammad 'Īsā Tarkhān, a member of the elder branch of the tribe, and elected him as their leader. During his life Shāh Husayn ceded a large part of Sind to 'Īsā, the rest of the province falling into his possession on Husayn's death in 1555, when the elder branch of the Arghun dynasty ended. Muḥammad 'Īsā Tarkhān died in 1567 and was succeeded by his son, Mīrzā Muḥammad Baqi Tarkhān, who reigned peacefully until 1585, when the throne passed to Mīrzā Jānī Beg Tarkhān, the grandson of Muḥammad Baqi.

At this time Sind was the home of many interesting people including Shāh Abdul Karīm of Bhurai, the poet saint of Sind, and grandfather of Shāh Abdul Latīf Bhital. Another personality was Makhdūm Nooh of Halla, who first translated the *Qur'ān* into Persian on the subcontinent.

On the death of Mīrzā Shāh Husayn, Sind was divided into the Sultanate of Thatta under Mīrzā 'Īsā Tarkhān and the Sultanate of Bakhar under Maḥmūd Khān. The two rulers never cooperated with each other and this allowed the continual Portuguese incursions into Sind which eventually resulted in the dreadful attack on Thatta in 1557, when the city was burnt and the population massacred. Hostilities increased between the sons of Mīrzā 'Īsā Tarkhān and peace returned to Sind only in the reign of Mīrzā Jānī Beg. In the end, however, the Mughals marched victoriously into Sind and forced Mīrzā Jānī Beg to surrender.

Although conquered by Akbar, Sind was still administered independently as a province by Mīrzā Jānī Beg and his son, Mīrzā Ghāzī Beg. But after the latter's death, the province passed under the direct control of the Mughal emperor, who appointed the future governors of Sind from 1592 to 1773.

* * *

The ancient town of Thatta was a flourishing centre of trade and industry with over one-hundred thousand inhabitants. About 6 km away, on the plateau of the Makhli Hill Range are the ruins of over a million graves. The entire area, it is believed, was for centuries regarded as a great necropolis. Standing within this sacred cemetery are the large mausolea of many of the former Samma, Arghun and Tarkhān rulers of the fourteenth to the sixteenth centuries. The entire area is virtually covered with graves and tombs, from some very elaborate memorials to the simple white-washed structures of modern times. It is not known when Makhli Hill was first used as a cemetery but evidently from a very early time it was invested with a sacred nature which accumulated as one Sayyid after another was buried here. The Samma Jams had their capital, Samui, just below the north end of the hill and according to one popular tradition, Jam Tamachi and the fisherman's daughter he made his queen, are laid in two old tombs at the north end.

With Jam Niẓām al-Dīn we come into history. There is no doubt about the identity of his tomb built in 1508. The Arghuns, who expelled his son, lived at Sukkur and were interred at Mecca, but under the Tarkhāns who followed, Thatta again becomes the capital of lower Sind, when an era of architectural magnificence sets in. Legend states that Makhli Hill was given its name by the occupant of one of the earliest tombs, a woman called Makhli.

The architecture of lower Sind is derived more from Persian and Gujarātī sources than from north India. Sind, from its position, has always been considered outside India, and Sindī architecture has some affinity with Persia and countries lying west of the Indus. The Sindī architectural style represents an independent development which started before the Mughals and lasted for some time after as a continuous tradition, and includes some of the most vigorous stone carvings and finely glazed tile work on the subcontinent.

The tomb structures of lower Sind differ from others in South Asia. The larger memorial structures fall into two distinct types. The monuments belonging to the first category are constructed of cut stone and covered in carved stone designs, obviously influenced by such contemporary Mughal architecture as Akbar's capital of Fatepūr Sikrī near Āgrā. Most of the early tombs, the Tombs of Jam Niẓām al-Dīn, Mubārak Khān, Jam Bābā, Mīrzā Khān I and his son, Baqi Beg Tarkhān, fall into this category. These buildings have a trabeate form of construction, the domes are corbelled and the arches treated merely as decorative devices. While the structural system is unsophisticated, the stone carving is excellent. Stone monuments continued to be built well into the seventeenth century and the most imposing mausoleum on Makhli Hill, the Tomb of Mīrzā Khān Tarkhān II (1644), belongs to this group.

The plan of all stone monuments is very simple. They are canopied tombs standing on pillars built over the grave arranged on a platform. On Makhli Hill are dozens of such pavilions, large and small, on eight or twelve pillars surmounted by a Hindu *chhatri*. The domes of these monuments are flat in shape and made of carved corbels surmounted by finials and supported on small pillars with stone corbels below the eaves.

The second type of memorial structure is built entirely of brick, the plinth alone made of stone. It is covered almost completely with coloured tiles, which, unfortunately, have now virtually all disappeared. From what has survived, however, it is possible to tell that the colours used were chiefly two transparent blues, a rich cobalt and a light turquoise, and white. A buff unglazed tile is also frequently found. Sindī tiles, unlike those of Multān and of other sites in the Punjab, were always laid in a flat surface with cement as binding agent.[1] The transparent colours of the Sindī tiles differ from Mughal work, where the colours are more opaque.[2] Possibly the Sindī tiles are a regional invention produced in Halla, about 35 km north of Thatta, a well-known and productive pottery centre during medieval times. The brick structures appear to be modelled on Persian and other western Islamic prototypes.

* * *

Various problems remain unsolved in the study of the monuments of Makhli Hill. The appearance on one site of two distinct building traditions, clearly influenced by two differing sources, is a puzzle. The problem is further complicated, since not all stone memorials are pre-Mughal nor all brick structures of the Mughal period. There appears no clear time demarkation, monuments of both types were built in the sixteenth and seventeenth centuries.

One of the earliest extant memorials of Makhli Hill is the Tomb of Mubārak Khān (d.1490), the distinguished general of Jam Niẓām al-Dīn. Built on a high plinth and enclosed by stone walls, the square monument has very little decoration on its two

[1]H. Cousens, *The Antiquities of Sind*, Karachi, 1975, p. 113.
[2]Ibid.

gateways. The stone carving consists of arabesques and other floral patterns indicating that an independent building tradition existed in lower Sind as early as the end of the fifteenth century.

The Tomb of the learned and wise Samma ruler, Jam Niẓām al-Dīn [Ill. 90], provides a vivid illustration of Hindu and Gujarātī influence in lower Sind. Jam Niẓām al-Dīn built the new town of Thatta and reigned there for nearly fifty years (1462-1509). His young son and successor, Fīrūz, apparently constructed his father's mausoleum about 1509, but Daryā Khān, the famous minister, might also have been involved in this amazing project, a mixture of Gujarātī, Hindu, Islamic and Sindī styles.

A stone enclosure wall surrounds the unfinished square sepulchral chamber, the work having stopped when the walls reached the springing point. The corners of the chamber are spanned by pointed arches springing from above the lintel height of the door. Higher up the corners of the octagon are also spanned to make a sixteen-sided drum which is obviously intended to support a dome [Ill. 91]. The pointed arches used in the zone of transition are corbelled and not true arches, as in several other stone monuments in lower Sind.[3] The wall surfaces are decorated by narrow carved bands alternating with broader courses of plain stone [Ill. 92]. The carved motifs include sunflowers, pointed arches, calligraphy, lotuses and geese which are sacred in Hindu lore. Although many of the motifs are taken from Hindu art it is not at all certain that material from any earlier Hindu temple was used in the construction of the tomb.

At both corners are miniature temple spires (*śikharas*) decorated with intricate detailed carvings. As on other tombs in lower Sind, there is no separate mosque attached, a *miḥrāb* in the *qibla* wall serving this purpose [Ill. 93]. The *miḥrāb* in this monument is delicately carved and probably of Hindu workmanship. The highlight of the decoration is the richly carved projection of the *miḥrāb* on the exterior. The base consists of classical Hindu mouldings over which is a row of shallow niches with pointed arches. Above these is an array of deeply carved miniature *śikharas*, columns, serpentine brackets and rosettes, mingled with pointed arches springing from projected brackets. This ensemble is topped by a projecting balcony with a free-standing arcade on several columns. About half the monument has miniature *śikharas* at the corners, a favourite form of ornament on Hindu temples, but foreign to Muslims, who preferred domes.

Small balconies [Ill. 94] add a delightful and original touch to the exterior walls. No great blocks of ashlar are used in the construction of the tomb. Instead, thin slabs of stone are set on edge and the interior walls filled with rubble, with no bonding between the two shells.

The first Tarkhān ruler of lower Sind, Mīrzā 'Īsā Khān, the Elder, was buried in a stone tomb (1572) standing with several smaller tombs in a large square courtyard. All the memorials are built of carved stone with perforated stone slabs introduced occasionally.

The stone Tomb of Jam Bābā (1608) [Ill. 95], a square structure standing south of the much larger tomb of his son, Mīrzā Khān II, was originally covered by three domes of which only the central one survives. The *miḥrāb* and the walls are carved with geometrical and arabesque designs [Ill. 96] including the sunflower and swastika motifs asymmetrically combined to produce a lace-like effect. The twelve-pillared verandah on the south side, at the main entrance, is a later addition.

[3]Ibid., p. 115.

The Tomb of Mīrzā 'Īsā Khān II (1644)[Ill. 97], governor of Thatta under the Mughals, is the most impressive and largest stone monument on Makhli Hill. Construction started in 1627 in the beginning of the reign of Shāh Jahān, when Nawāb Amīr Khān, son of Nawāb Kāsim Khān, was governor of Sind. It was completed in 1644 before 'Īsā Khān's death. The square tomb stands on a raised platform in the centre of a courtyard and is built of large carved buff-coloured sandstone blocks. A stone dome crowns the roof of the main structure.

Around the tomb is a double-storeyed gallery[Ill. 98] composed of one-hundred and twenty-eight massive square carved stone pillars rising the entire height of the dome. Each pillar is cut from a single piece of stone between the base and the capital [Ill. 99]. In the centre of each side are three narrow cusped arches surmounted by a wide parapet. The roof of the gallery and of the upper storey consist of carved stone beams and slabs.

On a raised platform inside the domed structure are eleven graves, each bearing an Arabic inscription. Two flights of stone stairs on the east side lead to the roof. The pillars of the interior are made of a single piece of stone and are carved, as are the walls. The highlight of the decoration is the richly carved *miḥrāb* [Ill. 100]. At first glance the carving appears to be a modified copy of the local tile work, a plastic reproduction of the more colourful tile method. But on closer examination it resembles the work found at Akbar's capital of Fatehpūr Sīkrī. The carving, both in relief and incised, is some of the finest on Makhli Hill. It is interesting that the influence of Mughal architecture extended so far west to the distant province of Sind. Outside, within an enclosure of their own, are the graves of the ladies of the family which are distinguished by their flat tops.

The earliest brick monument on Makhli Hill is the Tomb of Nawāb Khalīl Khān (1572-84), who governed lower Sind during the reign of Mīrzā Maḥmūd Baqi Khān. In plan it is a solid octagonal structure with a pointed brick dome set on a very high drum. The eight sides of the tomb have deeply arched recesses, those on the north and south much larger than the others and pierced with doorways leading into the sepulchral chamber. Internally the octagonal plan becomes a square. Originally probably the entire structure was covered with turquoise coloured tiles, since traces are still seen.

Four graves lie in the interior. It is commonly believed that they are the remains of holy men. The Nawāb apparently left instructions for his own body to be buried outside the mausoleum and the grave in its own enclosure to the north-west of the tomb probably contains his remains. The structure is a pure Iranian design, a most unusual monument for South Asia.

In 1572, on the death of Mīrzā 'Īsā Khān Tarkhān, his son, Mīrzā Muḥammad Baqi Khān, assumed the government of lower Sind. His tomb (1586)stands in the centre of a large courtyard and has a stone foundation and plinth and a superstructure of glazed bricks. Stone slabs over the doorways bear Arabic inscriptions.

Mīrzā Jānī Beg, the last independent Tarkhān ruler of Thatta, lost Sind to one of Akbar's generals. For the last years of the Sindī ruler's life (d.1599), he owed allegiance to the Mughal emperor but in return, he received a title and had the province restored to him. His son, Mīrzā Ghāzī Beg, succeeded to the throne and was simultanenously appointed governor of the province of Qandahār. He was murdered in 1612 and the remains of both Jānī Beg and his son were interred in this tomb in 1613.

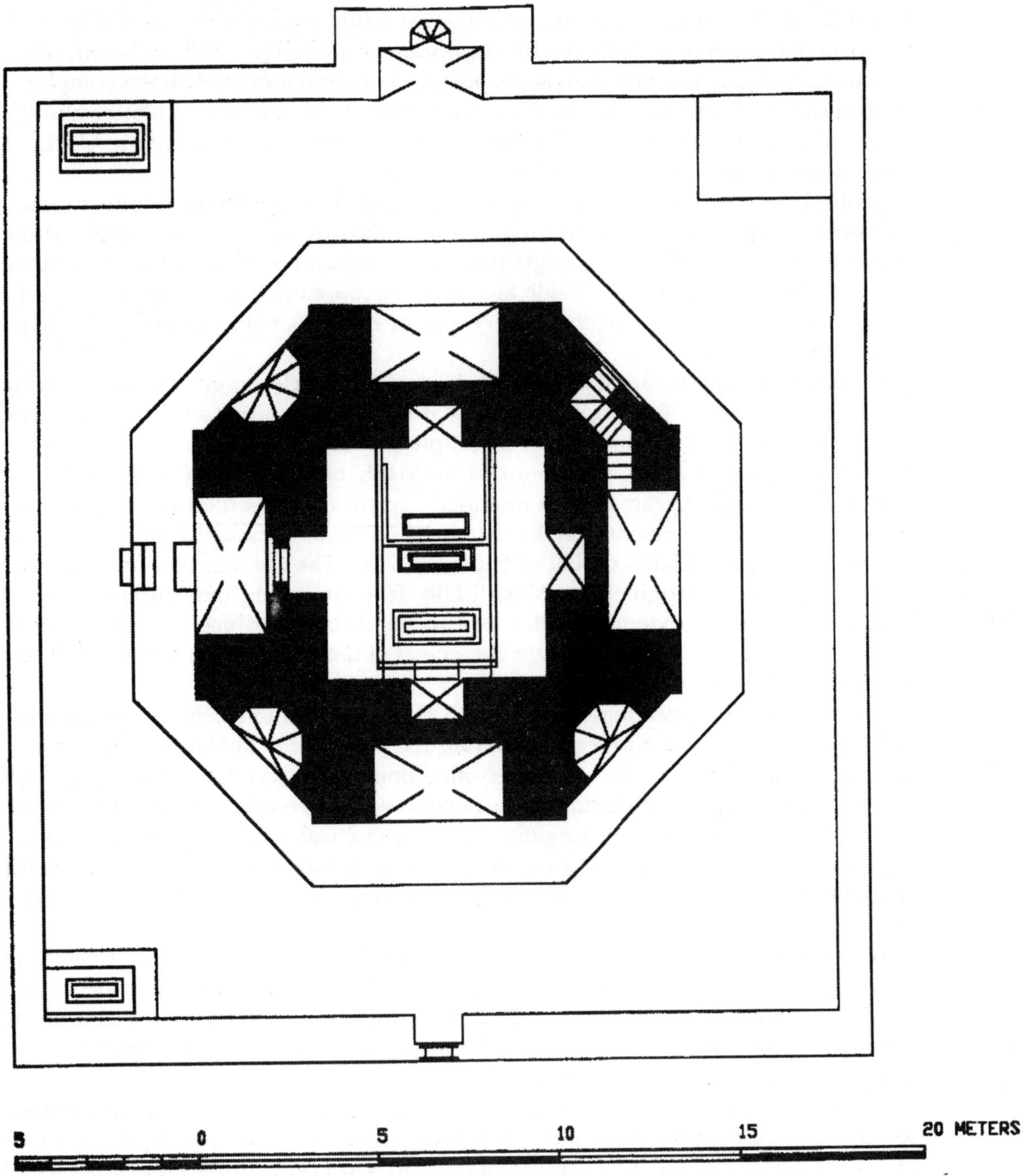

Plan 11. Makhli Hill, Tomb of Mīrzā Jānī Beg (after H. Cousens)

The octagonal domed Tomb of Mīrzā Jānī Beg [Plan 11] stands on a high plinth in a courtyard. The plinth is stone but the entire superstructure is brick, a line of glazed blue alternating with unglazed red. This quaint striped pattern is unusual and unknown elsewhere in Sind. There is a carved *miḥrāb* in the western wall and half-domed recesses and arched door-frames carved in geometric patterns on the four sides. Above the doorways are panels with Arabic inscriptions in white and dark blue tiles. The interior of the monument is covered with some of the finest tiles in Sind. There are three graves, two of marble and one of stone in the interior.

The Tomb of Dīwān Shurfa Khān (1638)[Ill. 101][Plan 12] and the adjoining mosque (1642) are the best preserved and most colourful of the brick monuments of Makhli Hill. Standing on a platform in a large courtyard, the square tomb was originally covered with light blue tiles. At the corners heavy round towers, each with an enclosed staircase, lead to the roof. The Persian-style dome was also originally covered in light blue tiles. The red brick walls have light blue tiles in the joints. The colour scheme is carried further on the inside, where bands of tiles have been set near the springing line of the dome. The interior of the dome is decorated with a radiating design of glazed bricks in chevron pattern[Ill. 102]. The central gravestone is elaborately carved in geometric patterns and calligraphy. The *miḥrāb* set into the western wall[Ill. 103] of the enclosure is also decorated with tiles, as is the central part of the mosque.

The Makhli Hill necropolis contains the largest concentration of structures representative of the period in lower Sind. Other examples are in the adjacent town of Thatta and in the numerous graveyards in the region, especially the finely carved sandstone canopy tombs of Chawkhaṇḍī[Ill. 104].

* * *

The Arabs conquered Multān three times in the eighth and ninth centuries and considered it the principal city of Upper Sind. In fact, Multān was the capital of a region which was often closely connected with Sind, but was regarded as a province of the Delhi Sultanate, to which it was finally annexed by Shams al-Dīn Iltutmish when he defeated Muḥammad Ghurī's governor. The authority of the Delhi Sultan was nominally retained until the disruption of the Delhi Sultanate after the invasion of Tīmūr. But the next Delhi dynasty, the Sayyids, who began their rule in 1414, could not extend their authority further than the immediate neighbourhood of Delhi. Muḥammad Sayyid, the third of the line, did not even nominate the governor of Multān and the people, therefore, turned their devotion to the line of a local saint, Bābā al-Dīn Zakariya, who had died in Multān in 1267. In 1438 they chose as their ruler Shaykh Yūsuf Quraishī, the guardian of the saint's shrine.

The Shaykh had the merits and defects of one who has chosen a life of seclusion and devotion. Although his rule was mild and beneficent, he was ill-equipped to fight any political enemies. It was therefore not difficult for an Afghan chief, Sahra Langah of Sibi, to ingratiate himself, profess devotion, and give his daughter in marriage to the saint. Paternal affection was not the only reason the Afghan visited Multān so often and in 1440 he succeeded in penetrating the Shaykh's citadel with his troops. The ruler was deposed and banished to Delhi. Sahra was thus free to assume the title of Sultan Quṭb al-Dīn and to found the Langah dynasty, which endured almost as long as Multān remained independent from Delhi. The sultan died in 1456 after a reign of sixteen years and was succeeded by his son, Husayn I, who ruled until 1502.

In 1527 Mīrzā Shāh Husayn Arghun of Sind invaded the much reduced realm of Multān at the instigation of Bābur. During the skirmishes, Shāh Maḥmūd, Husayn's unpopular grandson, was poisoned by the commander of his own troops, Langar

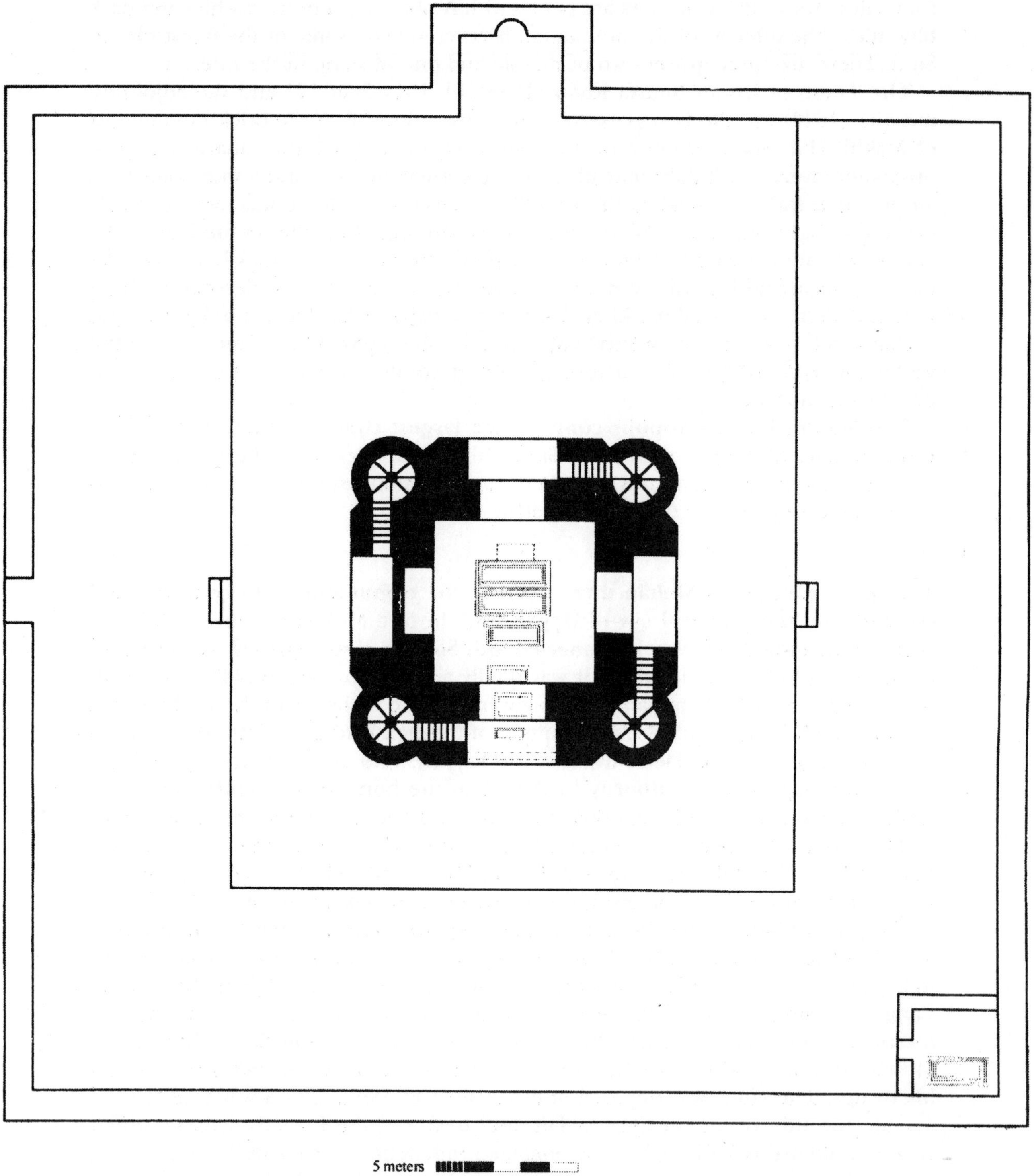

Plan 12. Makhli Hill, Tomb of Dīwān Shurfa Khān (after H. Cousens)

Khān, who then himself deserted to the enemy. The city fell in 1528, after a year's resistance, and Husayn II, son of Maḥmūd, was deposed. The Sultanate of the Punjab, with Multān as capital, was for a short time annexed to Sind but, thereafter, Kāmrān Mīrzā, brother of the Mughal Emperor Humāyūn of Delhi and governor of the Punjab, became its ruler. At last, Multān was reunited with Delhi from which it had been severed for more than a century.

* * *

The earliest provincial style of architecture of which today nothing survives was in the Punjab, since the first contacts with Islam were made in the cities of Multān and Lahore. Islam penetrated this area at different times and by separate routes. Multān first came under Islamic influence from the early Arab invasions of Sind in the eighth century and in the ninth century was made the capital of an independent Arab state. From then on contacts were continued with southern Persia to which there was easy access by sea, river and road. The Punjab, and Multān in particular, had always been more Iranian than Indian, as its architectural remains testify. In the tenth century Maḥmūd of Ghaznī wrested Lahore from Hindū rule and brought it into his realm. When the Ghūrīds destroyed Ghaznī, Lahore became the actual capital of a reduced Ghaznavīd empire and in the early twelfth century royal palaces were constructed. None of these is extant and there is no information available because the invading Ghūrīd forces in the mid-twelfth century destroyed everything in their wake. Most probably the Lahore palaces were similar to those in the parent city of Ghaznī, of which again there are only fragmentary remains. At one time a wooden-type of architecture was favoured here which must have resembled some twelfth century Seljuq work. Probably the architectural style of Lahore, although of different origin, had much in common with the monuments of Multān.Generally, the vanished monuments of Lahore and those extant in Multān are regarded as the Punjab style.

The architecture of the Punjab was constructed mainly of brick, since stone was not readily available. Thin broad bricks were used and for additional strength they were set upright. The bricks were reinforced by wooden beams inserted in the walls. The post-and-beam system rather than arches was used. For greater stability, the brick and timber walls were built at an incline, perhaps a survival of an ancient mud-brick tradition. Sloping walls later found their way to Delhi and were used frequently during Tughluq times. Doorways, windows, alcoves and overhanging balconies were in wood. Painted plaster and panels of coloured glazed tiles made up the decoration.

* * *

In Multān there are some tombs built between the middle of the twelfth to the beginning of the fourteenth century which best illustrate the Punjab style. Each of the mausolea has been heavily restored in later centuries, but the original plan has been preserved. A saint associated with the history of Multān is buried in each.

The Tomb of Shāh Rukn-i Ālam (1320-24) [Ill. 105], the last of the series, perhaps best illustrates the style. The monument was originally erected by Ghiyāth al-Dīn Tughluq for his own use but when he ascended the throne, he constructed another tomb for himself at Delhi and presented the Multān structure to his spiritual guide, Shāh Rukn-i Ālam, a man with much religious and political influence on the Tughluq sultans.

The tomb is octagonal in plan with sloping walls for better stability and sloping tapering buttresses becoming domed turrets above the parapet. The stilted dome and domed turrets have ornamental finials. These features were to influence the development of later Islamic architecture in Delhi.

The tomb is constructed of sand-coloured fired bricks bonded at intervals with courses of carved *shīsham* wood, following an indigenous form of construction dating back to the prehistoric Indus Valley civilization. The walls are ornamented with panels and string-courses of carved brickwork, glazed tiles with and without raised patterns in white, dark, light and turquoise blue, adding both shadow and colour to the sumptuous composition[Ill. 106].

The Tomb of Shāh Rukn-i Ālam expresses in architectural terms the underlying ideology of its builder. The sloping walls and inclined buttresses at the outer angles were obviously built for stability and permanence. The tomb was intended to dominate the surrounding terrain and to add an interesting dimension to an otherwise flat piece of land. The thick defensive walls successfully kept out the scorching sun and the only permitted light came diffused through perforated screens. The wonderfully coloured tiles must have helped to enormously lift the jaded sun-drenched spirit, a technique well understood in equally arid Iran.

CHAPTER 10

Mālwā(1405-1559), Chanderī(1425-1562) and Khāndesh(1398-1601)

Mālwā situated at the cross-roads between Delhi, the Deccan and Gujarat, has always been of strategic and commercial importance. In the thirteenth century Sultan Iltutmish of Delhi was sufficiently attracted to the benefits of establishing a southern province that he invaded and attempted to annex Ujjain, the old Mālwā capital. Nothing came of this early raid, Mālwā becoming a province of the Delhi Sultanate only in 1305, when 'Alā' al-Dīn Khaljī sent the formidable general Ā'īn al-Mulk to attempt a final conquest. For a century Mālwā was a province of Delhi, but, in 1401-2 the Afghan governor of Dhār, Dilāwar Khān, declared his independence during the confusion following Tīmūr's invasion of north India. Dilāwar Khān never assumed the title of royalty, but in 1406 Alp Khān, his son, impatient with events, poisoned his father, ascended the throne under the title Hūshang Shāh, and made Māṇḍū the capital of the Ghūrīd Dynasty of Mālwā.

Hūshang's reputation rests on his military achievements for he consolidated the territories of the new Gujarat sultanate and extended the borders wherever possible, northwards to Kalpī and southwards to Kerala. He concentrated on maintaining peace by successfully resolving the conflicting interests of Delhi, Jaunpūr, the Deccan and Gujarat. To solidify his position, the new ruler even attempted to attract Hindus to his prosperous lands.

On his death in 1435 Hūshang was succeeded by his son Muḥammad, who ruled for only one year and was deposed and poisoned by Hūshang's minister and brother-in-law, Maḥmūd Khaljī. Maḥmūd ascended the throne in 1436 to reign for a glorious thirty-three years which proved to be the highwater mark of Mālwā medieval history. He managed to end conflicts with Gujarat, the Bahmānī sultans, Jaunpūr, and the Rāṇā of Chitor and succeeded in extending Mālwā's borders on all sides. The sultan also founded schools and hospitals for his subjects.

On Maḥmūd's death in 1469, he was succeeded by his son, Ghiyāth al-Dīn, who ruled peacefully for the next thirty years. But in 1500, another son, Naṣīr al-Dīn, forced the abdication of Ghiyāth al-Dīn, ascending the throne himself to usher in ten years of cruelty which ended only with his own death in 1510.

The glory of Mālwā and its capital, Māṇḍū, now appeared to be over. The Mālwā Sultanate fell into confusion and the next ruler, Maḥmūd II, changed the policies of the government by dismissing the powerful Rājpūt minister, Medinī Rai, the faithful servant of his predecessors. The new sultan came into further dispute with the Rāṇā of Chitor and Bahādur Shāh of Gujarat, who finally invaded Mālwā and captured Māṇḍū in 1531. Maḥmūd II and his son were executed and Mālwā was incorporated into the Sultanate of Gujarat. The Mughal emperor, Humāyūn next invaded Gujarat and defeated Bahādur Shāh in 1535. The capture of Māṇḍū was avoided by the speedy withdrawal of Mughal troops, when a more important threat appeared on the horizon in the form of Shīr Shāh of Bengal. The son of an officer of Maḥmūd II, Bahādur Shāh, who next ascended the Mālwā throne, once again declared his independence and ushered in the last and final stage of Mālwā Sultanate history.

In the magical landscape of Māṇḍū, among the spurs of the Vindhya mountain range, a drama now enfolded between Bāz Bahādur and his beloved dancing girl, Rūpamatī, immortalized in verse and prose. However, the story of the "City of Joy" and of the sultan who devoted himself to music and to the "Lady of the Lotus" is now forgotten. The remains of the buildings of the grand city are in ruins.

In 1561, Akbar's army under Adham Khān defeated Bāz Bahādur's troops. The sultan escaped but his beloved, Rūpamatī poisoned herself rather than submit to another. The story, however, does not quite end here, for Bāz Bahādur once again returned to Māṇḍū to rule for yet another short time. But in 1562 another Mughal army invaded Mālwā and forced the Sultan's final withdrawal to Chitor, where he remained in exile until 1570 before surrendering to Akbar. This proved the end of the independent Sultanate of Mālwā but not of Bāz Bahādur, who eventually became a musician at Akbar's court.

Mālwā Islamic architecture is seen at its best in Māṇḍū, the capital of the Ghūrī sultans during most of the fifteenth century. But before Māṇḍū, in 1305, 'Alā' al-Dīn Khaljī's general, Ā'īn al-Mulk, conquered the smaller city of Dhār from the Paramāra Rājā Mahlakdeva. Here overlooking the Narbadā valley in the Vindhya range, the Delhi-appointed rulers of Mālwā remained until 1408, when the provincial capital was transferred to Māṇḍū.

Two early mosques in Dhār are examples of the initial phase of the architectural style of Mālwā. The Mosque of Kamāl al-Dīn Maulā, a disciple of Niẓām al-Dīn Chishtī of Delhi, built around 1400, is the earliest Islamic structure in Dhār. The second monument is the Lāl(Jāmi') Mosque, with an inscription bearing the date 1404/5 on the east and north entrances,[1] built by the Tughluq governor, Dilāwar Khān, at the time he declared himself independent. The Lāl Mosque as other early mosques is built with a flat roof supported on sixty-four reused Hindu temple pillars and three corbelled interior domes. Innovative pointed arches are placed between the pillars on the central portico and although of no structural use, they add an element of Islamic ornament by the pierced patterns of the arch spandrels. Once introduced, this scheme was repeated a half century later in Malik Mughīs' Mosque in Māṇḍū.

* * *

The history of Māṇḍū actually begins in the year 1401, when Dilāwar Khān, sensing the helpless and vulnerable position of the Delhi Sultanate, after the invasion of Tīmūr, declared his independence. In 1405, he built the Mosque of Dilāwar Khān (1405),[2] the earliest Muslim structure in Māṇḍu. The Mosque of Dilāwar Khān is attached by an enclosed passage to a royal palace known as the Hindola Mahal. What is not quite clear is whether the mosque was actually used only by the ruling family, since the steps approaching it are found at the end of the enclosed passage. The plan of the mosque is a simple hypostyle courtyard with a prayer hall of four pillared aisles and arcades of one aisle on the north, south and east sides. The *qibla* wall has a central *miḥrāb* surrounded by bands of carving. The court façade of the prayer area has thirteen openings and above them is a frieze of trefoils. The main door, decorated

[1] *Epigraphia Indo-Moslemica, 1909-10,* p. 12.
[2] Ibid.

with scrolls and medallions, is on the east side, with subsidiary entrances on the north and south sides.

The best example of the earliest phase of Mālwā Islamic architecture is the Mosque of Malik Mughīs (1432)[Ill. 107], father of Maḥmūd Khaljī.[3] The structure is particularly interesting for introducing some original constructional ideas. Except for the much less distinguished earlier monuments, this typical Mālwā structure is built on a high square plinth with arched cells in the ground storey and two *mīnārs* resembling Tughluq prototypes at the front corners. A flight of steps on the east side leads to a projected arcaded entrance porch.

The plan of the interior is a simple hypostyle, a square court surrounded on the north, south and east by one-aisled pillared arcades. The four-aisled prayer hall combines the arch and the pillar-and-beam in one structure. At three points in the prayer hall the pillars are arranged to form shallow-domed open spaces[Ill. 108], in fact, bisecting the hall with an axial nave leading to the *miḥrāb* and two aisles. The spaces are filled with pointed arches springing from the eight surrounding pillars. The *qibla* wall has fifteen niches, with blue tilework and some carved scrolls in the *miḥrāb*. Above the open façade are three pointed domes supported on octagonal drums and encircled with a parapet of merlons.

* * *

The middle phase of Mālwā Islamic architecture was initiated by the next Sultan, Hūshang Khān, who succeeded his father, Dilāwar, in 1406 and ruled for about twenty years. Hūshang's greatest claim in history is his fine taste in architecture, which was subsequently to make Māṇḍū one of the great cities of India. So magnificent were the structures of this reign that later art historians have called the style classical.

The largest and most important monument of the age is the Jāmi' Mosque started by Sultan Hūshang and later finished by his successor, Maḥmūd I, sometime between 1440 and 1454.[4] A projecting domed entrance porch on the east façade [Ill. 109] is the main entrance to the large structure built on a high plinth and approached by a steep flight of steps. The ground storey arcaded cells were used as a *sarā'ī*. The entrance porch has traces of coloured tile work on the sides of the doorway and pierced masonry screens to admit light. There are two subsidiary entrances on the north side probably intended for the *zanāna* and the priests.

The square interior court is surrounded on each side by eleven arched openings [Ill.110], the north and south arcades three aisles deep, the east side two, and the prayer hall five. The sanctuary façade is crowned by three domes and eighty-five cylindrical cupolas, each a roof over the interior bays.

The interior walls of the columned prayer hall and the pillars are faced with the pinkish-red Māṇḍū sandstone and ornament is restricted to the *miḥrāb*, the middle niche of the seventeen in the *qibla* wall, which is framed by several bands of carving. Crenellations crown the niches and the pillared black stone jambs flanking their sides are carved in Hindu designs. The *mimbar*, which is also carved with the same ornament, is supported by four arches and is crowned by a marble dome[Ill. 111].

The Jāmi' Mosque has a very interesting arrangement of arches and pillars. Many of the arches are double, yet detached from each other, thus giving extra support where most needed, under the three large domes and the domical roofs of the

[3]Ibid.

[4]Ibid., pp. 22-23; Ghulam Yazdani, *Mandu, The City of Joy*, Oxford, 1929, pp. 50-51.

sanctuary and along the façades of the four arcades facing the court. The line of double arches continues from the court into the prayer hall, forming the outer support of the end domes. By this plan the three large domes have a double row of arches on all four sides of their base, and a cluster of four pillars at the corners.

At each end of the sanctuary, below the large side domes, is a screened area supported by nine short columns, from the top of which arches spring diagonally, intersecting each other at the apex of the vaulted ceiling. These secluded rooms were probably intended for the *zanāna* on the north side, and for royal visitors on the other.

The Tomb of Sultan Hūshang is another important monument of the classical period, started by the sultan himself and finished, by his son, Maḥmūd Khaljī, about 1439. The tomb [Ills. 112-13]stands on a square decorated plinth in the centre of a small enclosed area and is contiguous to the western wall of the Jāmi' Mosque. The main entrance to the enclosed area is a domed porch on the north side. On the west end of the enclosure is a pillared arcade which may have served as the prayer area or as the *dharmaśālā* referred to by earlier writers. The pillars of this western arcade were apparently newly cut for their use here.

The mausoleum is covered with white marble and surmounted by a marble-faced double dome and by four conically shaped smaller cupolas at each corner. The central dome has an unusual finial composed of a pedestal, a censer-shaped stand, two pots, an orb and a crescent, a rather foreign scheme. The exterior is finished with a wide *chhajja* supported on serpentine brackets [Ill. 114] and a band of ornamental miniature arches carved in relief. The entrance is the central opening on the south side and there are triple-arched openings on two other sides. The other openings are filled with pierced masonry screens. There is no ornament on the rest of the exterior walls.

The square interior has an arch thrown across each corner to support the weight of the dome, which is transformed first into an octagon and then into a sixteen-sided figure. Along the dome rim are some bands of mouldings composed of ornamental arches set in blue tilework.

The casket-shaped sarcophagus of Hūshang, on a low marble plinth, has a carved *miḥrāb* on top and tesserae of small squares of black and yellow stone. There are five other sarcophagi, three in marble, one finished in stucco and the last in pink sandstone. It appears from an inscription that the mausoleum of Hūshang remained a pilgrimage site well into Mughal times[5] and that in 1658 four architects from Shāh Jahān's court came to Māṇḍū to worshop at the shrine of its master builder.

There are some other similar but smaller tombs in Māṇḍū all of an apparently later date. They are certainly copied from the Tomb of Hūshang, which served as the prototype. Of the later tombs, that of Daryā Khān, an official employed at the court of Māṇḍū during the reign of Maḥmūd II (1510-26), is probably the largest. In plan it follows the earlier model and is a square tomb situated on a square plinth with an arched entrance on the north side and arched windows fitted with pierced masonry screens on the other sides. But instead of the white marble facing of the earlier tomb, to be copied in later times by the Mughals, the Tomb of Daryā Khān is faced with red sandstone and decorated with three bands of mouldings. Traces also remain of coloured tilework in various shades of green, yellow, blue and white.

The tomb has one large dome and four small ones at the corners, each on an

[5]Yazdani, op. cit., p. 48.

octagonal drum. The interior has no decoration except a band of miniature arches with traces of deep blue tilework. There are three sarcophagi in the middle, one similar to that of Maḥmūd Khaljī.

This style of tomb continued to be built until the annexation of Mālwā by the Mughals, as can be seen in the plan of those tombs now known as the Dāī kā Maḥal and the Chhappan Maḥal, dated probably to the reign of Naṣīr al-Dīn.

Early in the fifteenth century, when Māṇḍū became the new capital, crenellated city walls with fortified entrances to the city were built. The first of these, the Ālamgīr Gate was later rebuilt by the Mughal Emperor Aurangzīb. It is an arched entrance with two square bastions at each end of the wall which leads to a second entrance, the Bhaṅgī Darwāza, built in a pillar-and-beam style. From here the principal entrance on the north side of the fort, the Delhi Darwāza (1405-6) [Ill. 115] is reached. This is a large gateway composed of a series of arched entrances decorated with a "spear-head"[6] fringe.

A seven-storeyed tower and a *madrasa* were constructed opposite the Jāmi' Mosque by Sultan Maḥmūd Khaljī[7] after his victory over the Rājā of Chitor in 1443. At a later time the *madrasa* and tower were both used as a frame to construct the Tomb of Maḥmūd. The weakened foundations apparently could not support such a massive structure and required extensive repairs one hundred and fifty years after its completion. This would also account for its collapse along with the once famous *haft manzil* glorified by all writers who saw it.

The *madrasa*, known as the Ashrafī Maḥal, was situated in the centre of a large plinth, and was built as an adjunct to the Jāmi' Mosque of Hūshang. About 1450 Maḥmūd Khaljī blocked the façade and quadrangle for the basement of a tomb and expanded the corner bastion into the Tower of Victory. The base of the tower is of red sandstone and the upper storeys were probably of the same material and must have been girdled with marble string courses inlaid with *miḥrāb*-and-diamond-shaped marble pieces.

The plinth of the *madrasa* was formerly a court surrounded on the north, south and east by double arcades, the outer wider than the inner, each with nineteen bays. The west side was contiguous to the Jāmi' Mosque.

A ramp led up to the projecting square sandstone entrance porch of the Ashrafī Maḥal. At each corner of the plinth were round towers the base of the one on the north-west side being considerably larger than the other. A flight of steps inside the tower is now in complete ruin above plinth level.

What remains of the later Tomb of Maḥmūd Khaljī shows that although constructed of sandstone the monument must have been lined inside and out with marble and have had its doorways, windows and cornices sumptuously carved and inlaid with jasper, marble and cornelian.

There are nine sarcophagi in the interior, which has led to the conclusion that here might be the tomb of the entire Khaljī dynasty rather than that of only Maḥmūd Khaljī. The central main sarcophagus, made of one solid block of white marble, probably belongs to Maḥmud Khaljī, the others of various coloured marble, to Malik

[6]John Burton-Page in "Indo-Islamic Architecture: A Commentary on Some False Assumptions," *AAARP*, 1974, p.15, refers to the unfortunate general use of the term "spearhead fringe" of arches, when it seems evident that this characteristic decoration is due to a series of conventionalised lotus buds rather than being a symbol of martial intent.

[7]Jahangir refers to the tower in his *Memoirs*. See A. Rogers (translation) and H. Beveridge (editor), London, 1909, pp. 381-83.

Mughīs and his successors Ghiyāth al-Dīn and Naṣīr al-Dīn Khaljī.

The Hindola Maḥal was built by Hūshang about 1425 to serve as an assembly or *durbār* hall. In appearance almost like a castle keep with heavy sloping walls, this structure is an unusual example of the middle classical style of Mālwā architecture. The slope of the walls is so pronounced that the monument creates the impression of actually swaying, hence its name is Hindola or Swinging Palace.

The structure is T-shaped, the main upright stem serving as the Audience Hall, the transverse section having been added later as a guard-house. The east and west sides are pierced by six tall deeply recessed arched openings containing a doorway and an upper window each. The south side has three similar arches, the main entrance leading through the middle arch.

The northern transverse section is double-storeyed with domed balconied oriel windows filled with pierced masonry screens on the west side[Ill.116]. These were used for the enjoyment of the *zanāna*, to watch the passing cavalcades near the hall.

The interior of the Hindola Maḥal is one large hall with five high pointed arches thrown across the width[Ill. 117] to act as structural support for the flat roof which once covered the structure. The transverse section has passages, store rooms, a stairway and a broad ramp leading to a separate compartment on the second storey. The upper storey is one long hall divided into three aisles by two rows of pillars. It overlooks the main hall through arched openings. The main passage of approach on the north side is a flight of sloping stages called the Hathi Charhan. Here ladies were carried up by palanquin or pony although it is doubtful, as its name implies, that the stages were wide enough to allow access to an elephant.

The middle phase of Mālwā architecture ends on a lighter note. The slim double-storeyed palace known as the Jahāz Maḥal(Ship Palace) extends along the edge of two small lakes[Ill. 118], the Kaphur and Munja Talao, and in shape actually suggests a ship. Stylistically, its rather light and bright surfaces and airy superstructure point to a monument built during the age of Ghiyāth al-Dīn (1469-1500). Numerous traces of water channels attest to its former use as a true water palace. The long eastern facade has a central marble-faced arched entrance framed by fluted bands and supported by piers flanked by thin octagonal marble colonnades. The entire surface is relieved by a projecting cornice on brackets and horizontal bands of red sandstone. The ground storey is a continuous arcade while the upper storey is covered in plaster and relieved by small false arches and a quincefoil floral ornament. Over each corner of the façade is a domed pavilion.

The interior of the ground floor is a long columned rectangular hall divided by nine large arches springing from thick columns. A projecting domed pavilion at the west end of the back wall bears traces of blue and yellow tilework. On both sides of this hall there are corridors and subsidiary chambers, the one on the south side with traces of water channels and an aquaduct. The space at the north end has a door, which leads to a colonnade built around an octagonal cistern, probably the royal bath with steps at the west end leading up to the roof terrace. On this upper open space are various open pavilions, kiosks and projecting balconies, all reflected on the lake below. In the centre of the western side, immediately above the projecting pavilion of the ground floor, is another interesting pavilion with traces of coloured tilework both on the exterior and interior and on the crenellations. On the east side, opposite the projecting pavilion is a pyramid-domed rectangular *chhatri* with three beam-and-lintel openings on each side. The rest of the terrace is filled with water channels, a water-lift, and an open bath at the northern end equipped with broad steps and landings, which might be used to rest on the ascent.

In style the Jahāz Maḥal does not really fit into the simple vigorous middle period of Mālwā Islamic architecture. Its lightly fanciful mood is more characteristic of the final phase of this period when the early Muslim form has been blended with an indigenous Hindu style.

* * *

The third and final phase of Mālwā Muslim architecture dominated the end of the fifteenth and first half of the sixteenth centuries. The sultan enriched his capital to provide sumptuous retreats where music might be played and poetry read, and these recreational *venues* were not merely adjuncts of court life but their *raison d'être.* Palaces, pavilions and summer villas were built, the ground floor generally with living areas grouped around the pools and fountains of the court. Domed open galleries allowed splendid views from above. The two most interesting examples of the final phase of Māṇḍū architecture are the Palace of Bāz Bahādur and the Pavilion of Rūpamatī, where unfolded one of the most poignant love stories of the time, the love of Bāz Bahādur for the beautiful dancer, Rūpamatī.

An inscription over the door of Bāz Bahādur's Palace indicates that the structure was first built by Naṣīr al-Dīn in 1508 and that Bāz Bahādur added extensions when he later came to live here.[8]

Built on the slope of the hill to the east of the Riwa lake, the arched entrance of the palace is approached from the lake by a flight of steps. A porch passes to a rectangular outer court from where a passage leads to a square inner court surrounded by halls on all four sides. On the north side nine arched entrances open onto apartments arranged as a colonnade with rooms on both ends. An octagonal pavilion projects from the back wall and overlooks the garden below.

The eastern side of the court has square rooms at both ends and an open space between. In the western side is the entrance to the palace, with a square room at both ends. The south side is a slim vaulted hall flanked by a pair of rooms at each end and divided into three bays by low arches.

An opening in the back wall leads to another but smaller square court, perhaps intended for palace attendants. The eastern side of this court has a narrow rectangular hall with three arched openings; the south side also has three arched openings but is a double row of apartments. The western side contains the entrance and two additional rooms. Between the two inner courts a flight of steps leads to the terrace which has two *bārādarīs* in the north-east and north-west corners.

Rūpamatī's Palace, situated on a hill beyond the Palace of Bāz Bahādur, was originally probably constructed as an observation post, an ideal place to watch the movements of the enemy from the north. The main hall appears to be from a very early date, perhaps constructed during the reign of Dilāwar Khān or Hūshang, but the pavilions and basement are dated later to the reign of Maḥmūd Khaljī or Ghiyāth al-Dīn. The walls have a slope which is reminiscent of earlier Tughluq structures.

The original building consisted of a hall with five arched openings in the centre and a room at each end with one arched opening. The basement was added later to house the extra guards necessary to protect the palace. Due to the slope of the hill on which it is built, the basement has a curious shape, in various places its roof acting

[8]Yazdani, op. cit., p. 93.

as a terrace floor for the palace above. On the east side there is an exterior corridor with eleven arched openings towards the north. Arches thrown across the hall support the roof. On the west is an extension of the basement with eleven arched openings towards the north, which contains a large cistern in which monsoon water was caught to fill the reservoir below.

Rūpamatī's name, however, is associated with the square roof pavilions[Ill. 119]. These delightful additions are crowned with fluted hemispherical domes and have three unequal arched openings on each side. It is in this wonderful setting, overlooking the Nimar Valley, that the famous dancing girl spent her quiet moments; here was her retreat for prayers.

* * *

The architectural remains of Chanderī also belongs to the reigns of the sultans of Mālwā. The town lies in a valley surrounded by the Vindhya Range on the old high road to the Deccan. In the eleventh century, it was mentioned by al-Biruni and in the thirteenth century it was invaded by the young Balban of Delhi. By the fourteenth century, during the reign of 'Alā' al-Dīn Khaljī, it ranked among the most important cities in Hindustan and was called the "Gate of Mālwā" in Muslim chronicles. Even the famous Moorish traveller, Ibn Battūta, visited it on this way south to Mālābār.

The most brilliant period of Chanderī, however, is linked with the Ghūrī and Khaljī Sultanates of Māṇḍū in the fifteenth and sixteenth centuries, when as a dependency of Māṇḍu, patronage of art and architecture flourished. For a relatively peaceful short period of slightly over a century, the Mālwā sultans gave special patronage to architecture and have left here, a fair distance from the capital, an extremely interesting group of monuments.

The medieval town of Chanderī was built by the Ghūrīd Sultans of Mālwā in the early fifteenth century. During the next century Chanderī was to remain an important outpost of the Māṇḍū sultans, an observatory from where the movements of the Delhi sultans could be noted. In 1438 Chanderī was wrestled by the new Khaljī rulers of Māṇḍū and held by them until 1513 when the governor of Chanderī, Bahdjat Khān, sought the support of Sikandar Lodī. The Lodī ruler duly replied and for two years the troops remained until they were ousted by the Rāṇā of Chitor, who captured the fort of Chanderī and set up his own governor, Medinī Rai.

From then on Chanderī was a coveted prize changing hands frequently, and in 1528 passed next to the Mughal ruler, Bābur, who later returned it for a short time to Māṇḍū. It was lost again to Purbiyā Rājpūt Pūran Mal, but the new Delhi ruler, Shīr Shāh Sūr finally attached it again to the Delhi Sultanate for a short time. For the next three years Chanderī passed between the Rājpūts and Shīr Shāh, who finally retook it in 1543. And because the fate of Chanderī was tied to that of Māṇḍū, it had some final years of freedom during the short reign of Bāz Bahādur (1555-62) in Māṇḍū and in 1562, along with Māṇḍū, was annexed to the Mughal Empire under Akbar.

A large number of fifteenth century mosques were built in Chanderī, but the Jāmi' Mosque [Plan 13] is the only one which remains in its original medieval form. Stylistically, it is similar to the Jāmi' Mosque of Māṇḍū, and probably dates from about the same time, from the late reign of Hūshang or early reign of Maḥmūd.

A projecting entrance porch on the east façade leads to a square court surrounded on all sides by arcades, although the one on the east side is no longer extant. The

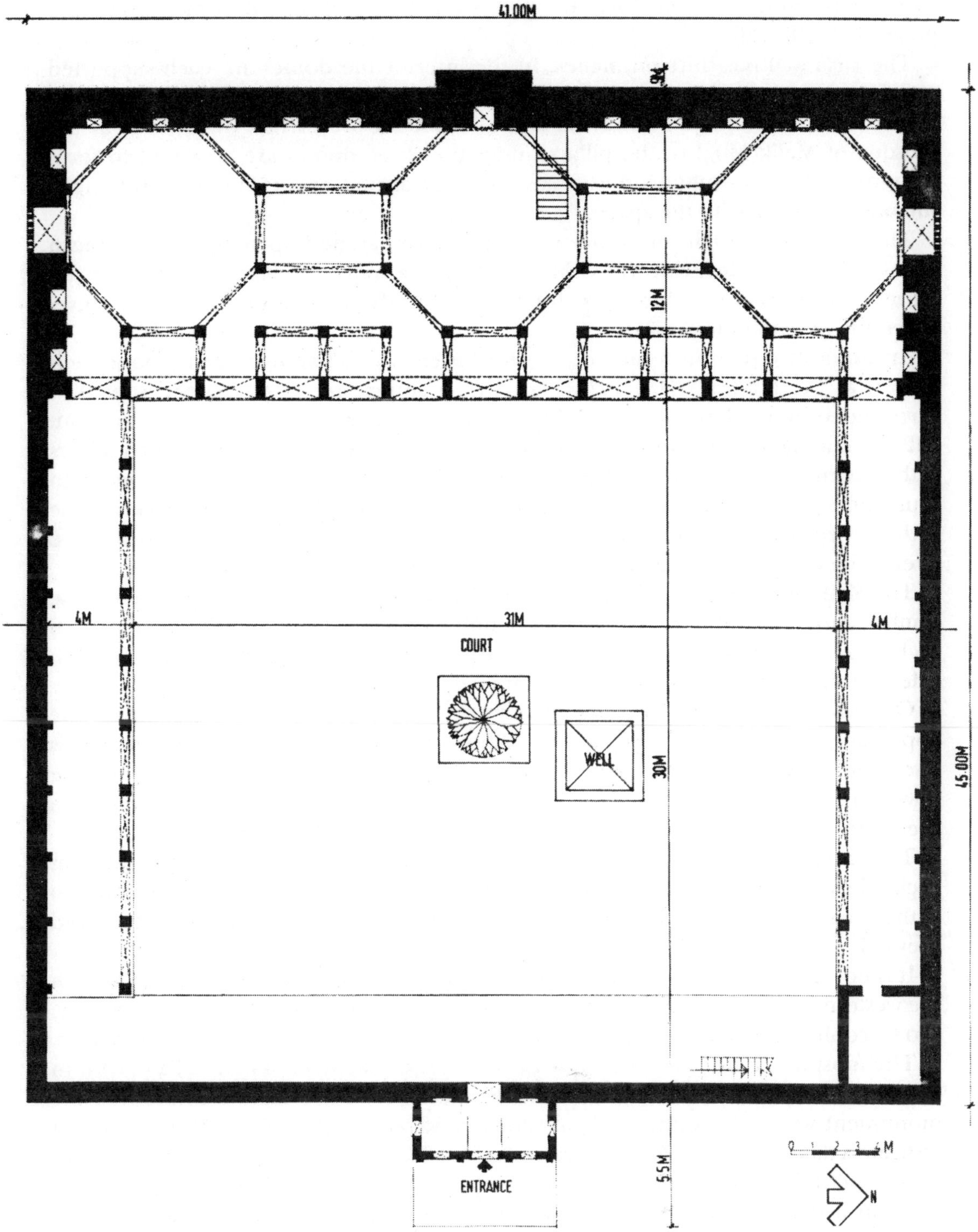

Plan 13. Chanderī, Jāmi' Mosque

north and south arcades are one bay deep, the prayer hall three bays deep with a corridor running between the court and the hall. Three stilted domes crown the prayer hall [Ill. 120].

The *qibla* wall has thirteen niches. In the interior the domes are each supported on eight piers and the central dome is flanked by two barrel vaulted halls which project as pyramid-shaped roofs. As in earlier Mālwā prayer hall plans, such as the Mosque of Malik Mughīs, the pillars under the three domes are arranged to form octagonal shallow-domed open areas. Pointed arches springing from the eight surrounding pillars fill the spaces.

The prayer hall opens onto the court with eleven arched openings, the northern and southern arcades with nine. Surrounding the walls are *chhajjas* supported on Hindu-type convoluted brackets, for which the Mughals later found good use, especially at Fatehpūr Sīkrī.

An innovative plan in tomb construction is seen in Chanderī in the monument known as the Madrasa [Ill. 121][Plan 14], a square formerly domed structure surrounded by a pillared arcade of five pointed arches on each side, dated to about 1425.[9] An arched verandah forms the otherwise plain exterior. Four engaged towers with battlemented friezes are at the corners and these formerly were crowned with four domes. The square interior is enclosed on all but the northern entrance side with arched openings filled with pierced masonry screens [Ill. 122], such as were later to be used by the Mughals.

The Shāhzādī-kā Rawza [Ill. 123] was built about fifty years later. The grey sandstone tomb is square and on the exterior has a double-storeyed façade, with five ogee-shaped arched openings filled with pierced masonry screens flanked by five pillars on each side. On the north side is an arched entrance.

One of the most unusual characteristics of Chanderī Muslim architecture is the appearance of a double *chhajja*, as on this monument, where the entire structure is encircled by two *chhajjas*, the upper on massive brackets for decoration only, and the lower to serve a structural need. Six serpentine brackets on each side spring from the shafts of the pillars.

The interior of the monument has three ornamental arches on two storeys on each side, with unusually large squinches in the phase of transition. The only decoration is the lotus medallions of the arch spandels and the ornamental frieze of coloured tilework.

It is not clear whether the Shāhzādī-kā Rawza is a tomb, since there is no *miḥrāb* on the western wall and since the main entrance is on the south side. There are, however, two sarcophagi in the interior, although it is not known who actually lies buried here.

The most important monument in Chanderī is the Kūshak Maḥāl at Fathabād, in a suburb of Chanderī. Four inscriptions to the right of the stairs indicate that the monument was built during the governorship of Malik Mallū Sultānī, which would indicate a date of about 1432 for its construction. However, it is questionable whether these inscriptions are *in situ* for there also appears evidence of an inscription now fixed in a stepwell called the Āliyā Bāolī situated near the Kūshak Maḥal, which mentions the construction of a palace in 1499.[10]

In plan the Kūshak Maḥal [Plan 15] is square with arched entrance gateways on each side. Just within each of the four gateways are two flights of steps which ascend

[9]R. Nath, *The Art of Chanderi,* Delhi, 1979, p. 23.

[10]*Epigraphia Indo-Moslemica, Arabic and Persian Supplement 1964*; Nath, op. cit., p. 14.

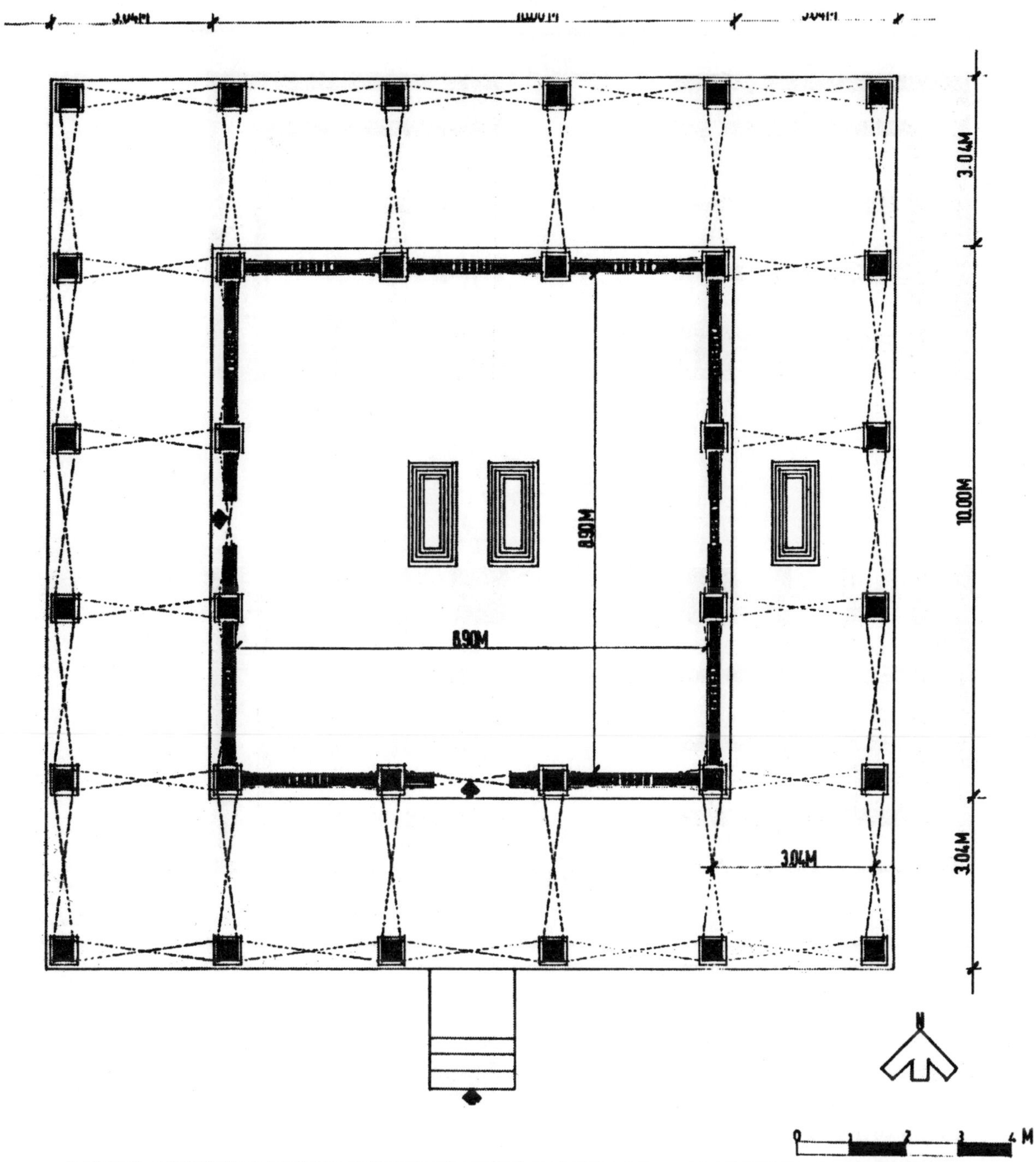

Plan 14. Chanderī, Madrasa.

to the upper storeys. Balconied windows relieve the otherwise plain walls.

The interior is divided into four squares by intersecting vaults[Ill. 124], crossing at right angles. The plan is cruciform, the open passages in the middle of each side bisecting each other at right angles and forming four three-storeyed quadrants at the four corners. The quadrants are four separate palaces at equal distances from

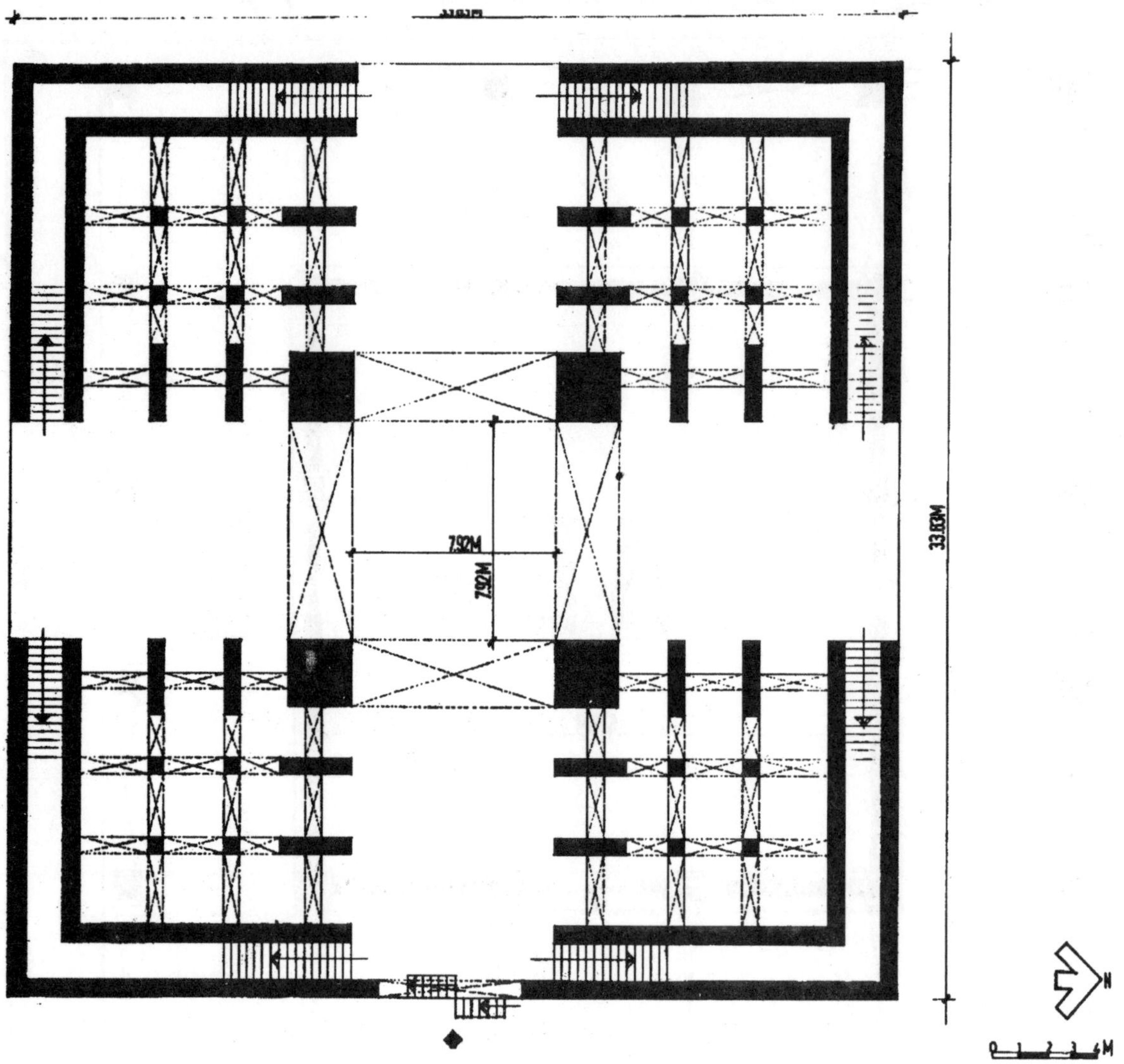

Plan 15. Chanderī, Kushak Maḥal

each other, connected and separated by cruciform passages. The remains of a fourth storey exist and it is not clear whether this is the fabled seven-storeyed palace Maḥmūd Khaljī ordered to be built in 1445 in Fathabād, when sultan passed here on his way to Jaunpūr.

'Īdgāhs or wall mosques, used primarily for the two 'Īd festivals, have no enclosed courtyard. The *'īdgāh* of Chanderī is composed of a wall with seven *miḥrābs* and two round end towers.

A final monument in Chanderī is the double-storeyed seventeenth century Badal Maḥal Darwāza [Ill. 125], apparently a triumphal gateway, not being attached to another structure, with its two tapering engaged turrets reminiscent of Tughluq Delhi. The strength and vigour of early Māṇḍū and Chanderī monuments are now gone and what remains is a feeble attempt to display functional elements as ornament.

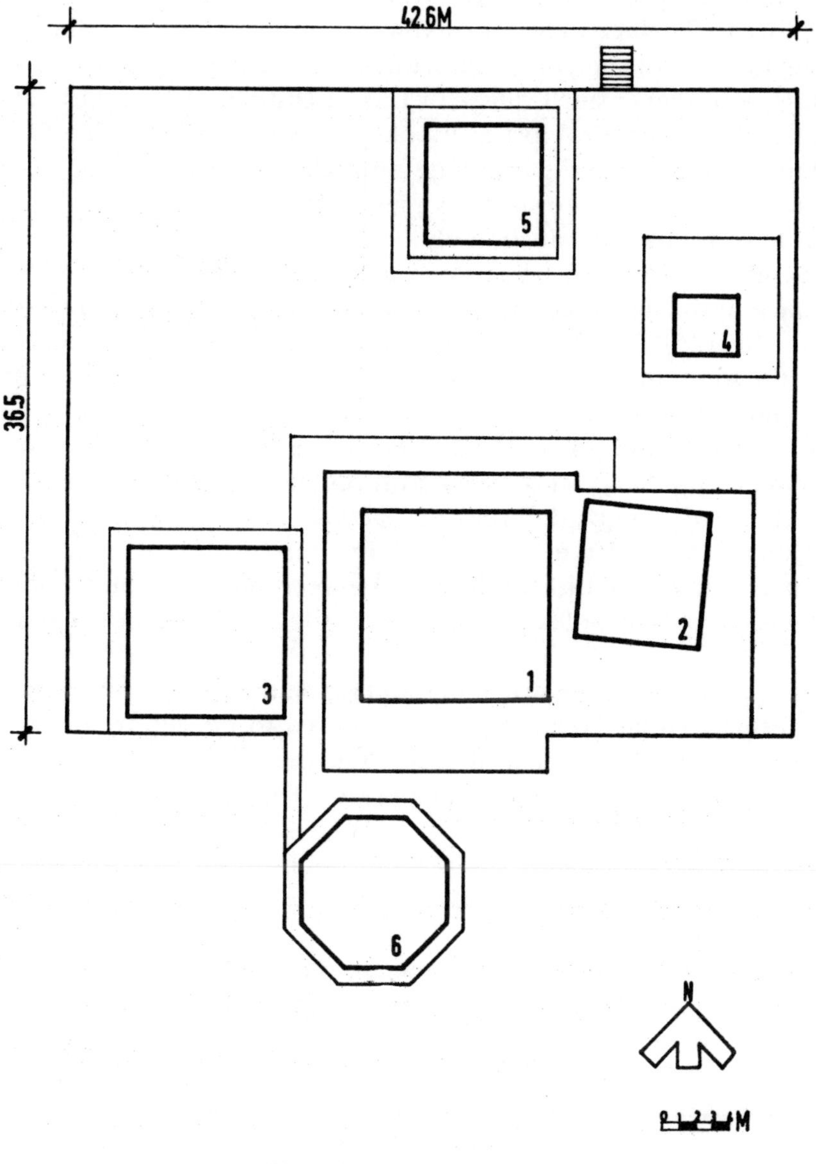

Plan 16. Thalner, Five Tombs

Possibly at this time a regional school of architecture in Gwalior, itself a composite of the Delhi, Mālwā, Rajasthan and Gujarat styles, influenced the Chanderī workmen and caused them to construct this odd monument.[11]

* * *

Khāndesh is not really in Mālwā, but more to the north-west between the Deccan and Mālwā. Although small in area, in the fifteenth and sixteenth centuries the independent rulers of Khāndesh produced a number of quite original monuments. The geographical position of this small state wedged between its powerful neighbours of the Deccan, Gujarat and Mālwā, naturally made it especially vulnerable to external

[11]Percy Brown, *Indian Architecture: The Islamic Period,* Bombay, 1968, p. 65.

influence. Under the patronage of the Fārūqī dynasty (1382-1600), the local capitals of Burhānpūr and Thalner were adorned with a number of interesting structures.

Belonging to about the end of the fifteenth century is a group of tombs in Thalner, now nothing more than a small village in Dhulia District, Maharashtra, but once an important site with a powerful fort overlooking the Tapti River[12] The Fārūqī Khāns built their tombs here generally in groups on a plinth.

The Thalner tombs were not mere copies of Māṇḍū monuments. The principal innovations here are the introduction of openings on each side of a central doorway and the raising of the dome by means of a tall octagonal drum.

Five square and one octagonal tomb make up the main group of Thalner monuments [Ill. 126][Plan 16]. The brick and plaster octagonal Tomb no. 6 [Ill. 127] lies to the south of the others and supposedly belongs to a brother of Mubārak Khān. The plinth on which it stands has collapsed, as has the dome and the west and north-west wall above plinth level. Arched entrances to the tomb were on four main sides, with arched openings set in recessed rectangular panels on alternating sides. Complicated carved designs different on each side cover the structure [Ill. 128]. The only other octagonal tombs found at this time in this area are the Tomb of Dilāwar Khān in Holkondā in the Deccan between Gulbarga and Bīdar, and the Tomb of Jamshīd Qulī in Golkondā. No similar tomb is found in Gujarat, Mālwā or Khāndesh.

Tomb no. 2 is a small square structure standing on the east side of a plinth and is of lighter stone than Tomb 1[Plan 17]. It is believed to be the Tomb of Alktatmish Khān and is crowned by one central dome. On each side are three masonry-filled arched panels springing from Hindu-style pillars. The only entrance today is in the south wall.

There are windows on the north and south walls on the interior, the east wall is plain, while the west wall has three *miḥrābs*. There is an inscription over the window of the centre of the north wall.

Tomb 1 is the most impressive of these six mausolea, resembling the Tomb of Hūshang in nearby Māṇḍū. The tomb carries an inscription which states that Miran Mubārak Khān (d.1457) is buried here. The tall central dome was originally surrounded by four corner domes. Each side consists of a large central arched panel with a "spearhead" fringe flanked by engaged octagonal pilasters which continue above the cornice level. The tympanum of the south entrance door was formerly filled with pierced masonry screens.

The interior of the tomb is an octagon and each wall is a tall arch which has within it smaller arches, surrounded by irregularly sized niches. The internal arches and corner rooms stand on a plinth surrounding the inner floor. At the centre of each wall are rectangular chambers, the one on the south wall forming an entrance porch. The interior of the dome is ribbed and decorated with bands of carving.

The square Tomb no. 3 [Ill. 129]stands at the western end of the plinth and is believed to be the Tomb of 'Ādil Khān Fārūqī. On the south façade are four blind niches each surmounted by a number of merlons and an entrance, the other door being on the north side. The east and west walls are unadorned except for the *chhajja*

[12]John Burton-Page, "Survey of the Tombs of the Faruqi Dynasty: Thalner," an unpublished paper read at the Centre of South Asian Studies, School of Oriental and African Studies, University of London, in 1973 based on preliminary work done by the speaker, Garry Martin and George Michell. It was thanks to this research that my attention was first drawn to Thalner. The classification of monuments was also done with the help of this initial research.

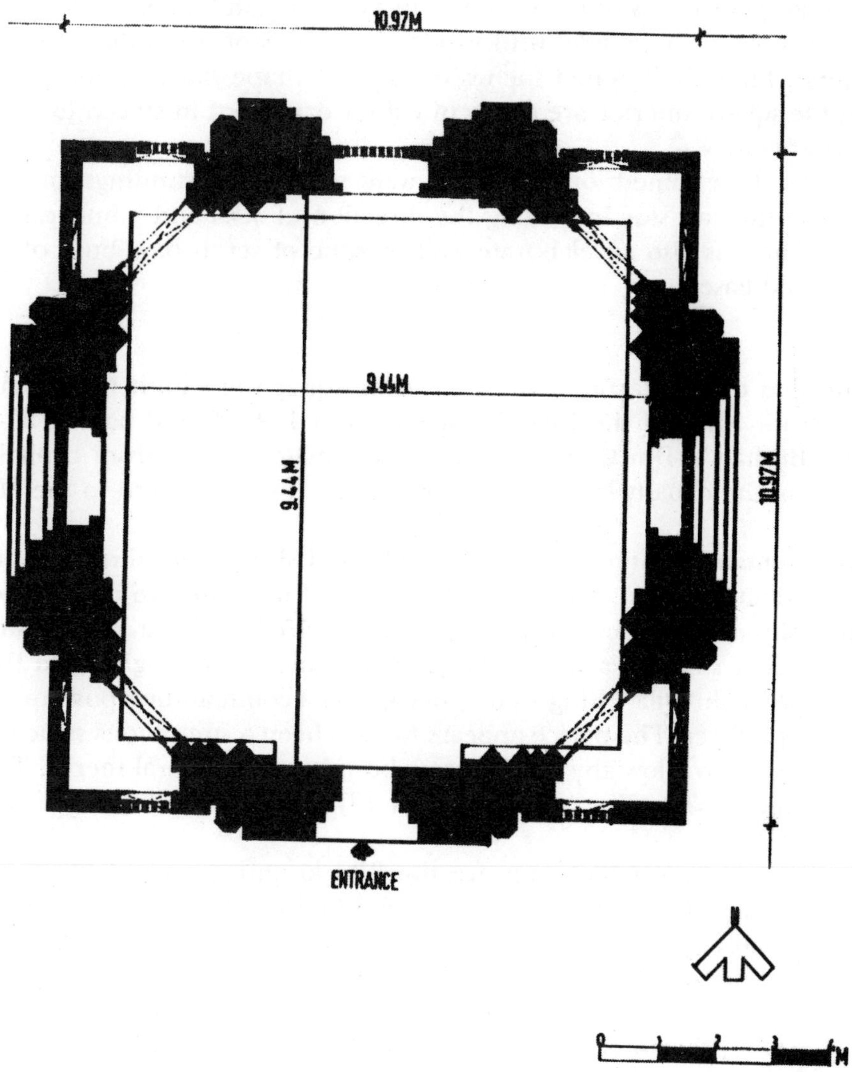

Plan 17. Thalner, Tomb no. 1

carried on carved stone brackets. The structure is crowned by a main dome and four smaller corner domes, the drums of which are of brick and were once plastered. Tomb no. 5 is a small square structure with one tall stilted dome and four simple corner *guldastas.*

Tomb no. 7 is another small square heavily whitewashed structure with a single fine marble cenotaph said to be that of Haẓrat Shāh Rājā, a disciple of Ā'īn al-Mulk of Delhi. It is topped by an almost hemispherical dome with an *amalaka*-and-*kalaśa* finial. There is a row of blind merlons at the top instead of the usual *chhajja.*

Tomb no. 8 is a ruined structure said to belong to *wazīr* al-'Āzam Muhi al-Dīn. Tomb no. 9 is a small structure attributed to Amīn al-Dīn, with a doorway on the south side and window openings on the other three sides, with no *miḥrāb.*

Tomb no.10 is said to belong to Bībī Areza and stands remote from the main group on a high plinth. It is of brick with a stucco facing and a tall dome. As usual, the doorway is on the south side, with window openings on the other three sides, with no *miḥrāb.* Engrailed arched niches of Mughal shape flank openings on the exterior. In the square interior are traces of colour ornament in stucco to the dado and in the roof arches.

There are also four ruined open mosque walls in Thalner, running north-south, with a niche on the east side indicating the direction of *qibla* and a buttress on the western side. There is also an elaborate wall mosque of seven bays built of reused Hindu pillars and bases.

* * *

Towards the end of the Fārūqī Dynasty, two mosques were built in Burhānpūr. Founded by Naṣīr Khān of the Fārūqī dynasty about 1398-99 and named after the Deccan saint Burhān al-Dīn Gharīb, Burhānpūr remained the Fārūqī capital until the overthrow of the dynasty by Akbar in 1601, when it was annexed to the Mughal Empire.

Burhānpūr contains a large number of tombs and shrines of saints and mystics, many from Sind and Gujarat. Among the buildings of note the two most important are the Jāmi‘ Mosque, built by ‘Ādil Shāh Fārūqī in 1588 and the Bībī kī Mosque. Some of the earlier structures are the large citadel and palace high up in the fort known as the Bādshāhī Qila‘ (King's Fort) occupying a commanding position on the banks of the Tapti River. The palace appears to have been a sumptuous structure but it is now too ruined to allow any conjectures about its architectural merits. There is also a tomb known as the King's Tomb [Plan 18] and the small Mosque of Shāh Mansūr.

The two most important buildings are the Bībī kī and the Jāmi‘ Mosques, the latter built by ‘Ādil Shāh Fārūqī in 1588 and finished by the Mughals. The Bībī kī Mosque was probably constructed by the wife of Sultan ‘Ādil Shāh Fārūqī II sometime during the nine years after her husband's death in 1520, when she retained authority during the succeeding reigns of her two sons, Miran Muḥammad and Mubārak. ‘Ādil Shāh Fārūqī apparently moved his capital from Thalner to Burhānpūr and it seems only natural that a mosque should have been one of the first works erected for the adornment of the new capital.

In plan the Bībī kī Mosque [Plan 19] is of the closed variety, as found in Gujarat and consists of a prayer hall which is four by fifteen aisles. Four middle pillars are omitted at the north and south ends, the open spaces instead covered by large domes springing from an octagon. The larger space has an additional row of three arches springing from the four square piers which support the dome. There are five façade arches, the central archway wider than those on the sides. Massive square minarets, some of the best preserved *ma'dhana* to find their way from Gujarat to Khāndesh, flank the façade. The towers resemble Gujarātī minarets, but they differ by having four oriel windows with balconies on the highest storey instead of the plain arch openings leading to the gallery of the top storey. The minarets are crowned with conical caps similar to Gujarātī towers and are surmounted by a dome.

The two *mīnārs* which flank the middle arches are five storeys in height, the two lower storeys of stone, the upper three of brick, apparently later additions which match the brick work of the whole front wall of the mosque. The three large domes

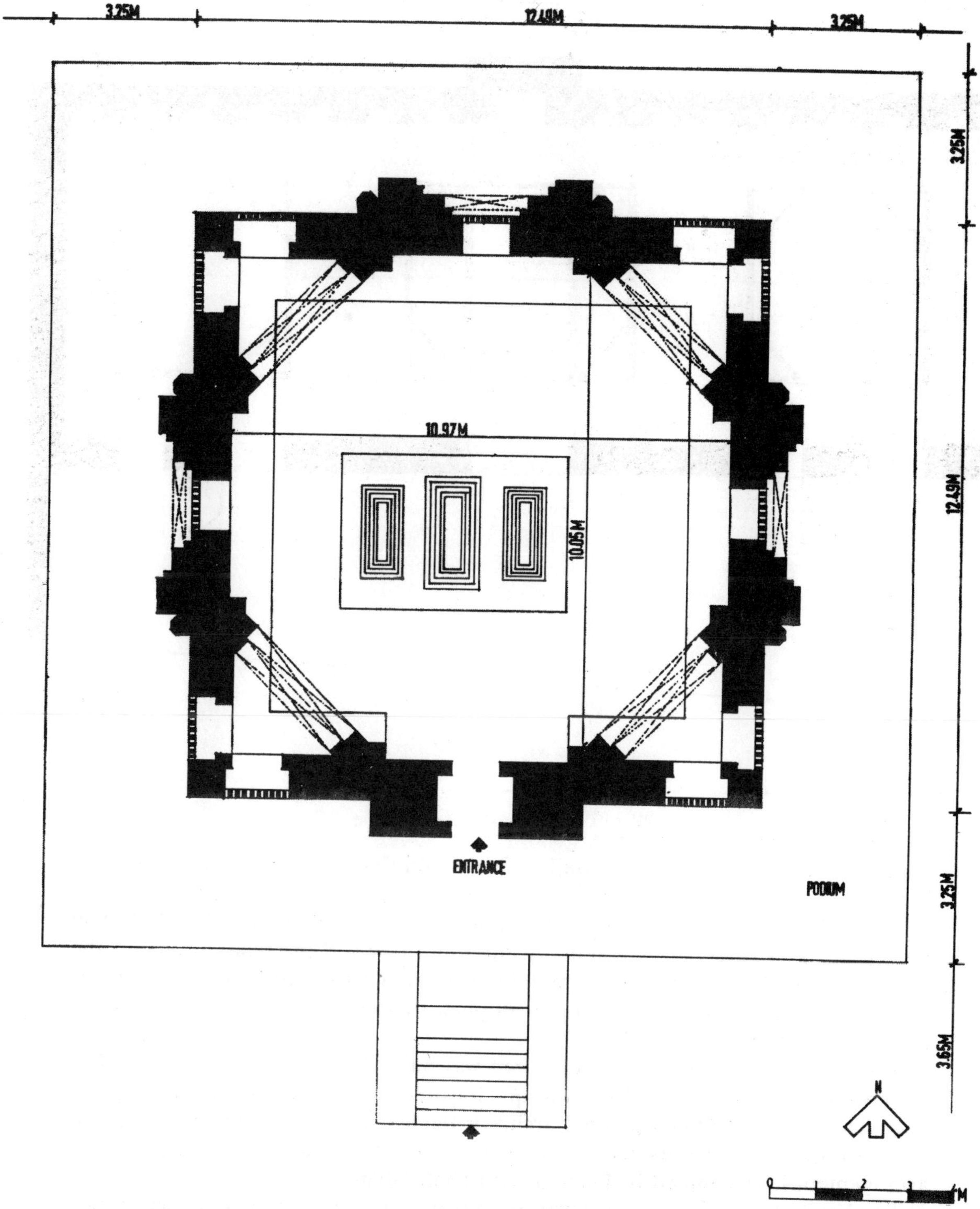

Plan 18. Burhānpūr, King's Tomb

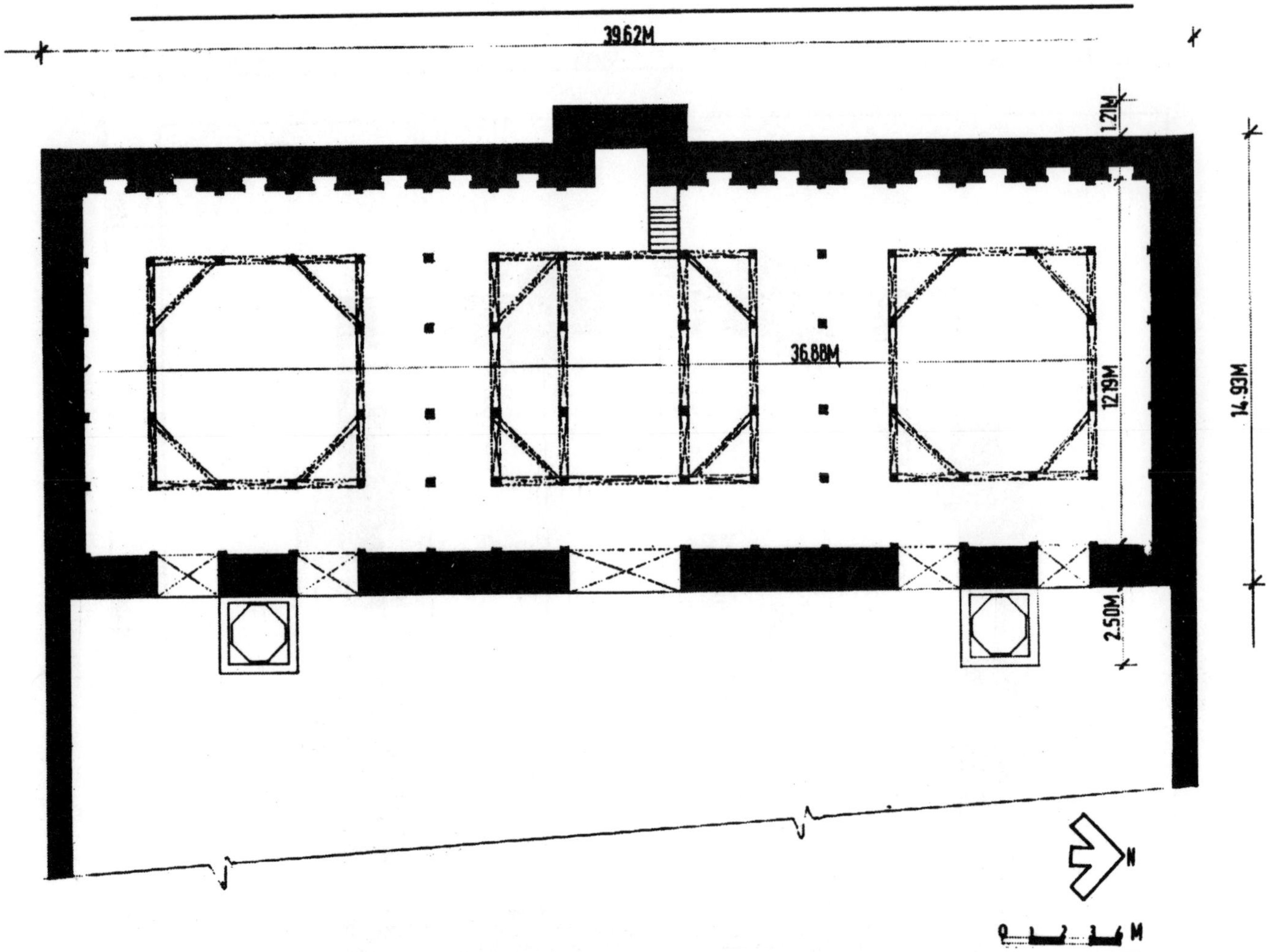

Plan 19. Burhānpūr, Bībī kī Mosque

are hidden by the thick brick wall built as a later addition on top of the original stone battlement.

The walls of the courtyard are in ruins and the entrance gateway is closed. Not all piers have been indented, only those in the south row and the pilasters against the back wall, along with one in the middle octagon. This unfinished state probably indicates that work on the mosque was stopped suddenly, perhaps by the death of the queen who commissioned it.

The Jāmi' Mosque of Burhānpūr(1588) was built by 'Ādil Shāh Fārūqī IV. The plan is similar to that of the Bībī kī Mosque for there is a prayer hall of five by fifteen bays. The façade of fifteen pointed arches is flanked by two tall minarets, the earliest examples of minarets actually attached to the two quoins of a structure, an arrangement later adopted by Jahāngīr and Shāh Jahān.

The Jāmi' Mosque has little exterior ornament, only a floriated battlement which runs around the walls. In the interior the pilasters of the seventeen *miḥrāb* niches in the back wall are elaborately carved and there is a great contrast between these and the other plain piers and walls. It seems likely that work was suddenly stopped by Akbar's conquest of Khāndesh eleven years after the inscription, in 1589. Further repairs were made by Akbar and Aurangzīb.

In Burhānpūr there is another series of tombs of the Fārūqī sultans, Mubārak Shāh, 'Ādil Shāh and Naṣīr Khān (1399-1437), which show a marked affinity to the more famous Tomb of Hūshang at Māṇḍū.

When Khāndesh fell to the Mughals in 1601, building did not stop. The Tomb of Shāh Nawāz Khān brings together features from Gujarat, Tughluq and Lodī Delhi, and Bījāpūr. But it is apparent that the earlier originality is now gone and that this is the last architectural attempt in Khāndesh before its total eclipse.

Chapter 11

Jaunpūr (1376-1479)

Among the dynasties founded by the Tughluq-appointed governors and their successors, a short-lived but brilliant line was that of the Sharqīs of Jaunpūr. The Sultanate of Jaunpūr was founded by Malik Sarwar, who had risen to power in the confusion following Fīrūz Shāh Tughluq's death in 1388. The new Delhi ruler, Fīrūz's youngest son, Muḥammad Shāh (1390-93), conferred the title of Sharqī sultan (Ruler of the Eastern Kingdom) upon Malik Sarwar, making him first ruler and then governor of Jaunpūr, the newly founded city on the Gumptī River. The clever new ruler of Jaunpūr soon enlarged his territory to include Kanauj, Oudh and Bihar, and continuously crushed uprisings by the Hindu chiefs in other areas, until he was finally acknowledged as their ruler. When Tīmūr left Delhi, Sarwar proclaimed himself the independent ruler of Jaunpūr. Thus began the short-lived but distinguished Sharqī dynasty which managed to endure just somewhat over a century. At the end of the fourteenth century, in its heyday, the Sultanate of Jaunpūr stretched along the plain from Kanauj to Bihar, and from the Ganges to the Himalayan Tarai, occupying most of northern India corresponding roughly to the later Sultanate of Oudh between Delhi and Bengal.

Jaunpūr was the first Muslim stronghold planted in the very midst of the most Hindu part of northern India. Maḥmūd of Ghaznī never penetrated this far but legend records the triumphant march of his nephew, the youthful and heroic Sālār Mas'ūd, who ravaged the lands up to the gates of Benares, destroying the temples of Ratangarh, laying a claim to the lands which later became the Muslim stronghold of Zafarābād. Because he died defending his faith on the battlefield, Sālār Mas'ūd has for centuries been revered by Muslims who visit his grave at Bahraich, where the martyred prince is believed to have appeared to the aged Fīrūz Tughluq to warn him of his impending end.[1]

Jaunpūr was established in 1358 by Fīrūz Shāh Tughluq on an ancient Hindu pilgrimage site, the temple where Rāmachandra slew the giant demon Kavalavīra. Fīrūz constructed a fort soon to become the capital of the later Sharqī sultans. Malik Sarwar's successors descended from his adopted sons, Malik Mubārak Qaranfal (1399-1401) and his younger brother, Ibrāhīm Shāh Sharqī (1401-40), children of a slave water-bearer of Fīrūz's court. During the latter reign, Jaunpūr became a powerful state, a seat of learning and a refuge for men of letters in the days of anarchy following Tīmūr's devastation of Delhi.

Despite many handicaps, the Sultanate of Jaunpūr was a focal point in the history of medieval India for over a century. During this relatively short time six rulers occupied the throne. Malik Sarwar and Mubārak governed for only a brief period, but Ibrāhīm, Maḥmūd and Husayn held the reigns of power from 1401 to 1495, and

[1]A. Fuhrer and E. Smith, *The Sharqi Architecture of Jaunpur*, Archaeological Survey of India, New Imperial Series, vol. XI, Calcutta, 1869, p. 16.

during this period Jaunpūr rose to its preeminent position in northern India. Hemmed in on all sides by the hostile powers of Delhi, Mālwā and Orissa, the Sharqī rulers increased their military strength, amassing possibly the largest army in fifteenth century India.

Despite this continual military activity, the Sharqī sultans found time for many cultural and educational pursuits. They were great patrons of all the arts and music, encouraged education, and drew scholars and saints into their realm. Jaunpūr became the site of many splendid monuments of which, unfortunately, not much remains due to the ruthless destruction of the city, when in 1495 upon the defeat of Husayn Shāh, it became part of the lands of Sikandar Lodī. The surviving monuments are mainly mosques, their destruction considered sacrilegious by the zealous Muslims. An occasional surviving wall of a palace or fort is all that remains of what must have been some splendid secular monuments. It is also obvious from remains of bridges, canals, wells and gardens that the Sharqī sultans were concerned with improving the welfare of their subjects.

Jaunpūr became one of the most renowned seats of Muslim learning in the East. Eminent scholars flocked to it from all of India but especially from Delhi to escape political events. Builders and masons were driven from the ruined capital by the Mongol invaders. They enriched the life of Jaunpūr and produced some great academic works to be used later throughout the entire country. In the seventeenth century Shāh Jahān called Jaunpūr the Shīrāz of India.

At this time Jaunpūr overshadowed Delhi in size, prestige and architectural achievements. Some of the most important mystic orders and movements of the period were in Jaunpūr. Shāh Madār, who migrated from Syria and founded the Madāriya Order at Mākanpur, belongs to the Sharqī period. Some of the leaders of the Hindu Bhaktī movements, such as Kabīr, lived in the area ruled by the Sharqī sultans. Sayyid Muḥammad, the founder of the Mahdawi movement, to become a force in subsequent years, and the founder of the Shattari movement, Shāh Abdullāh, made Jaunpūr their headquarters.

The origin of the Sharqī architectural style may be found in the village of Zafarābād, a suburb of Jaunpūr.[2] Zafar Khān, governor appointed by Fīrūz Shāh Tughluq, is said to have founded a city here and to have called it Shahr Anwār, but some walls of the old fort are all that remain of this endeavour. The Mosque of Shaykh Barban (1311) is an early rather crude improvisation using materials taken from Jaina temples in the vicinity. The hypostyle hall has a flat roof carried by over sixty pillars, but the massive front displays a rudimentary pylon, an enormous *īwān* form, to become one of the hallmarks of the architecture of this region.

The fort of Jaunpūr, built by Fīrūz Shāh Tughluq, overlooks the north of the Gumptī River. It is surrounded by a stone wall around an earthen mound which uses earlier masonry inscribed with Hindu motifs. Most of the fort's towers were blown up after the 1857 Mutiny but the entrance gate constructed by Munim Khān survives. Remnants of its original ornament of blue and yellow glazed brick are still visible.

According to an inscription[3] the oldest monument in Jaunpūr is the Fort Mosque built in 1377 by Ibrāhīm Naib Barbek, the brother of Fīrūz Shāh Tughluq. The *mīnār* is probably in its original state. The mosque is divided into three chambers by two

[2]Ibid., pp. 64-66.

[3]*Proceedings of the Asiatic Society of Bengal*, 1875, p.14; A. Fuhrer and E. Smith, op. cit., p. 26.

internal vaults. The central chamber has low plastered domes and the wings are divided into five double bays. Pilasters of the Tughluq type project from the back and two side enclosing walls. Between the mosque and the river wall is a round magazine tower with the *hammām* (baths) (1420) of Ibrāhīm on the left side.

Ibrāhīm Shāh, who reigned from 1401 to 1440, was the most distinguished Sharqī ruler. He not only repelled the military and diplomatic advances of Maḥmūd, the sultan of Delhi, but even invaded the capital himself in 1413 during the confusion following Maḥmūd's death. Only Khizr Khān's appearance on the scene made the brave Sharqī ruler retreat. The Sayyids, who eventually wrested power in Delhi, finally concluded peace with Ibrāhīm in 1427, arranging to cement the bond by the marriage of Bībī, daughter of Mubārak Khān, to the crown prince of Jaunpūr. The last decade of Ibrāhīm's life was peaceful, the sultan now devoting his time to his beloved people, to education and the arts. Ibrāhīm also finished the Atālā Mosque which Fīrūz had started in 1376.[4]

This monument is the first in a series of three mosques built by the Sharqīs on a plan similar to that of the Begampūrī Mosque, Muḥammad Tughluq's Jāmi' Mosque, in Delhi. But instead of using rubble, the Jaunpūr masons built their monuments in fine grey sandstone and granite, either taken directly from pre-existing temples or dressed especially by masons whose marks may still be seen on parts of the structure.

The Atālā Mosque [Ill. 130] is situated north-east of the fort on the site of an old Hindu temple dedicated to Atālā Devī. The plan is a traditional hypostyle, a square open courtyard surrounded on all sides by arches [Ill. 131], the western side serving as a sanctuary. The triple-aisled north, south and east arcades are double-storeyed with a row of rooms on the outer side fronted by a pillared verandah facing the street. Probably this addition provided accommodation for travellers and merchants. In the middle of these outer façades is an entrance gateway, each with staircases to the upper storey. The gateways on the north and south sides are distinguished by leading to octagonal domed rooms on the courtyard side. The third entrance on the east side is larger and in design akin to the massive entrance *īwān* of the prayer hall.

The triple-aisled prayer hall is the most striking part of the mosque. It is divided into five compartments, a central corridor flanked by pillared single-storeyed wings with two low double-storeyed rooms at both ends, originally closed off by perforated stone screens. On the *qibla* wall are three *miḥrābs* [Ill. 132] and a *mimbar* in the central aisle, seven *miḥrābs* in each of the wings and three in each of the *zanāna* rooms. A large hemispherical dome is supported on an arcaded drum in the central corridor, and each of the lateral wings has an hemispherical dome resting on beams forming hexagons and octagons. The central dome is constructed of circular courses of stone, the inner ribbed, the outer covered in cement to give it the desired shape.

In the centre of the courtyard side of the arcade, instead of minarets, rises a tall entrance *īwān* with staircases on both sides leading to the top. The arched recess is flanked by two enormous battered towers divided into six storeys and decorated with string courses and recessed arches. The central pylon-like *īwān* marks the principal and subsidiary façades of the prayer hall. The upper portion of the arched fringed recess is divided from the lower by a lintel above which are pierced openings originally probably closed with screenwork. Fronting the wings are similar smaller entrance *īwān* leading to the domed chambers within.

[4]A. Fuhrer and E. Smith, op. cit., pp. 38-40.

The rear wall of the sanctuary is relieved by three projecting surfaces, one corresponding to each of the principal compartments of the interior and thus to the domes above. Each quoin of these projections, as well as the two main corners of the building, has a tapering turret, recalling the architectural style of Fīrūz Shāh Tughluq.

Many features of the Atālā Mosque resemble work in Tughluq Delhi. For instance the battered walls of the tower flanking the three entrance *īwān*, the tapering of the corner bastions, the post-and-lintel galleries, fringed arches and domed pinnacles recall Delhi work under Muḥammad Tughluq and Fīrūz Shāh Tughluq. It was after the sack of Delhi by Tīmūr, under the Sharqī rulers, that Hindu and Muslim builders trained in Tughluq Delhi fled to Jaunpūr and started to build for their new patron. They reproduced some of the works earlier constructed in the capital. Taking Muḥammad Tughluq's Jāmi' (Begampūr) Mosque as their departure, they introduced a new and exciting concept in this earliest of Jaunpūr Mosques, a great entrance portal in the centre of the courtyard side of the western arcade, with two smaller portals in the wings. Unfortunately, they had not the time or the experience to work out a final solution in the relationship between the arcade and the entrance portal, which hides the dome from the front. The dome is, in fact, sometimes visible below the upper level of the clerestory windows. But in general the great bulk of the entrance towers overpower and obscure the domes, which are only visible from the side and the back. These magnified portals competed for the attention generally given to domes. Whatever their origin, these Jaunpūr *īwān* are clearly the precursors of some of the great Mughal gateways, such as the Buland Darwāza at Fatehpūr Sīkrī. But the massive scale of the entrance *īwān* hides the fact that the Pathan architects of Jaunpūr were the first in India to make domes and their adjuncts an imposing part of a range of building.[5] The Atālā Mosque furnished the model for all subsequent mosques of Jaunpūr, by none of which, in design, it was ever excelled.

The Khaljīs Mukhlis and the Jhāngīrī Mosques were also built in Jaunpūr in 1430. The former was commissioned by two of Ibrāhīm Sharqī's nobles, Malik Khaljīs and Malik Mukhlis for the Persian saint Shaykh Usmān Jaunpūr.[6] Originally from Shīrāz, the Shaykh migrated to Delhi and in the political chaos of the late fourteenth century gravitated to Jaunpūr, where he was received by Ibrāhīm Sharqī. Among the Shaykh's devotees were the two nobles who gave the mosque its name. In addition to this structure, the two patrons also built a monastery and a shrine for the saint near which his descendants still live.[7] The mosque was constructed on the site of the Hindu temple of Vijaya Chandra and is a plain austere edifice modelled on the Atālā Mosque, with a domed central corridor and flanking wings.

The Jahāngīrī Mosque of which only the central arch of the screen survives, lies outside the city of Jaunpūr next to the royal residence. It was built by order of Sultan Ibrāhīm Shāh in honour of his teacher, Sayyid Sadr Jahān Ajmal, on the site of the famous Hindu temple of Jayachandra. Since the saint died in 1405, it appears likely that the mosque was constructed in the early part of the reign of Ibrāhīm. Sayyid Ajmal was a renowned scholar who was held in great esteem by all. It is recorded that one night the Sayyid saw the Prophet in a dream and, upon rising, found Muḥammad's

[5]Ibid., pp. 29-30.

[6]*Tajalli-i Nur*, pp. 45-46 as told by M.M. Saeed, *The Sharqi Sultanate of Jaunpūr: A Political and Cultural History*, Karachi, 1972, p. 255.

[7]Ibid.

footprints where he had seen him standing in the dream. The site was later marked by the construction of a mosque known as the Qadam Rasūl. An indication of the devotion of the entire royal family to this saint may be seen in the spot chosen for his burial royal near the Tomb of Shāhzādah, a son of Ibrāhīm Sharqī, who was one of his devotees.

Sultan Ibrāhīm was succeeded on the throne by his son Maḥmūd(1440-57), who together with his queen, Bībī, a princess of the ruling Sayyid family of Delhi, was much interested in cultural and religious matters. Much of the sultan's time, however, was spent in fighting neighbouring Hindu principalities and during his time of absence the queen ruled the country and continued the construction of mosques and schools for her subjects.

The Lāl Darwāza Mosque is the only remaining monument built during the reign of Maḥmūd. Finished in 1447 and apparently dedicated to 'Alī-Dā'ūd, a celebrated saint of Jaunpūr, the Lāl Darwāza Mosque resembles on a smaller scale both the earlier Atālā and the later Jāmi' Mosques. It is believed that the architect or head mason was a Hindu named Kamau, and this could prove that Hindu masons were used in its construction.[8] Perhaps for this reason the Lāl Darwāza Mosque has a lighter more Hindu feeling than either of the other two great mosques in Jaunpūr.

The smallest of the Jaunpūr mosques, the Lāl Darwāza[Ill. 133], apparently was a private chapel entered by a "high gate painted with vermilion" which belonged to a palace complex built by Bībī Rājā, wife of Sultan Maḥmūd (1440-57). The mosque has arcades on three sides each only two bays in depth, with no verandah on the street side. The sanctuary is divided into three parts, a central chamber and flanking rectangular wings, each of four aisles. The central chamber is square in plan with an unusual entrance hall of three bays leading into the courtyard. A single dome crowns the monument. Another variation in this one-storeyed mosque is the position on an upper level to the right and left of the domed central chamber of two screened rooms used for the ladies of the court. Similar screened areas are at both ends of the sanctuary in the Atālā Mosque, but here they have been moved to a more central position, next to the domed chamber. It might not be too fanciful to suggest that this preferential treatment to the ladies was probably given by the patron of the mosque, Bībī Rājā, who herself had experienced some of the deprivations accorded her sex.

The next ruler, Husayn Shāh (1458-79), in 1478 completed the largest and most ambitious of the Jaunpūr mosques, the Jāmi' [Ill.134]. The foundation of this monument had been laid during the last years of the reign of Ibrāhīm, and subsequently construction was started by Maḥmūd. Husayn extended his realm by successfully conquering Etawa, Sambhal and Badaon, finally even making the Rājā of Gwalior his vassal. But Bahlol Lodī was too strong for him and, in the end, at the fatal battle of Kanauj in 1477 the victorious Delhi ruler deprived Husayn of all his possessions. For a further few years the last Jaunpūr ruler was allowed to live in his capital, but eventually had to flee to Bihar, while Bahlol Lodī's son, Sikandar, destroyed the glorious Sharqī capital including the once splendid palaces and royal tombs. With great difficulty, the mighty Lodī conqueror was prevented from demolishing the mosques of Jaunpūr. But the Jāmi' Mosque lost its splendid inscribed gate. Sikandar Lodī appears to have also torn down the royal residential quarters adjacent to it, as well as a

[8]A. Fuhrer and E. Smith, op. cit., p. 51 state that the inscription probably refers to the date of erection of the cloisters.

college and some of the arcades of the mosques. Maulānā Safī Jaunpūrī, heading a number of protesting *'ulamā*, restrained the Lodī ruler from blowing up the Jaunpur mosques by gunpowder. Once again the tide had turned and the lands of the Delhi Sultanate touched the frontiers of Bengal.

The plan of the Jāmi' Mosque follows the model of the Atālā Mosque on a larger scale. Unlike the earlier monument, it stands on a raised platform, approached by a flight of steps. Small shops and a verandah on the north, south and east sides form a basement storey, above which are the arcades surrounding the courtyard of the mosque. In the middle of the façades are large domed gateways, the one of the east side having been destroyed by Sikandar Lodī.

The sanctuary is divided into five sections, a domed central chamber with pillared wings surrounded by the second storey *zanāna* rooms, at the north and south end by vast barrel vaulted halls[Ill. 135]. The vaults are roofed in stone and the vault is so constructed that its upper surface forms the external roof of the building.

The dome of the central chamber of the sanctuary is possibly a double dome, two thin domes with an empty space between.[9] However, this is not substantiated and has been refuted by some scholars.[10]

The central *īwān* of the Atālā and Jāmi' Mosques are the highest in India. Never less than 3.4 m. thick, the recess has a small entrance arch within the larger one, each with a beam across it, surmounted by three rows of arched clerestory windows. These sanctuary screen entrances are one of the most striking and original inventions of Muslim buildings in India. Perhaps the pylon with its great archway may have a derivation of its own and represents the last phase of a psychology closely connected with the progressive history of Islam. It is similar to the gateway of a fortress and Islam, a militant movement, had to provide shelter for its followers. Fortresses with their defensive walls became rallying points in Islam and their gates are vitally important. The fortified gateway, therefore, became a symbol, its shape, although not its intention, finally passing gradually into Islamic religious architecture to form the central feature of the mosque façade.

[9]A. Cunningham, *Archaeological Reports*, vol. XI, p. 115.
[10]A. Fuhrer and E. Smith, op. cit., p. 54.

Chapter 12

The Deccan: The Bahmānī Dynasty (1347-1518)

Muslim armies first appeared in the Deccan in 1294, when, by a daring raid, 'Alā' al-Dīn Khaljī, nephew of the Sultan of Delhi, successfully attacked and captured Deogir, the northern most Deccan Hindu kingdom.

After his return to Delhi in 1296, 'Alā' al-Dīn, now the new sultan, continually invaded the Deccan, until in 1318 he finally successfully annexed Deogir. During the first quarter of the fourteenth century other Hindu powers were subdued until much of the Deccan came under the sway of the Delhi Sultanate.

Disorder followed the death of 'Alā' al-Dīn Khaljī in 1316, and peace returned only in 1321 with the accession of Muḥammad, the second sultan of the Tughluq dynasty. The new ruler appeared to have everything in his favour and yet, at the end of his reign in 1351, the vast Tughluq Sultanate was considerably reduced. The people, the nobility and the clergy all looked with longing for a change of regime.

One of the chief causes of the decline of the Tughluq empire was Muḥammad's decision to move his capital from Delhi to a more southern administrative centre. Deogir, renamed Daulatābād, became the focus of these new plans in 1327 and nobles and the army alike were impelled to emigrate and settle there.

The following ten years the sultan shuttled back and forth between the two capitals and during this decade the Sultanate appeared to be stable and prosperous. This was the opinion of Ibn Battūta, the Moorish traveller, when he came to India in 1333. The calm, however, was only a superficial lull before the storm. Sensing the unrest of his subjects, the sultan suddenly ordered the return of the nobility and the administration to the old capital. But it was too late to save the tottering empire.

The ferocious tyranny of Muhammad drove his subjects to rebellion in all quarters of the land. In 1347 the large unwieldy Tughluq Sultanate finally disintegrated, the amīrs of the Deccan successfully revolting against the central authority of the sultan.

Daulatābād is the most famous and the most impregnable fortress in the Deccan. An old Hindu stronghold and capital of the Hindu Yādava dynasty, it was first captured in 1294 by 'Alā' al-Dīn Khaljī, who forced the Hindu ruler to pay a large tribute. In 1308 Deogir became a part of the Delhi Tughluq Sultanate and was renamed Daulatābād.

The sultans of the Bahmānī dynasty strengthened the walls of the fort and built stone battlements and round bastions. There are also a series of heavily-built ramparts and the entire fort is encircled by a moat. The only entrance is an iron gate on the base of the steps, which could be made impassable at times of siege by the placing of an iron brazier in the entrance passage, the heat from the fire would kindle it and prevent all intrusions.[1]

[1]John Burton-Page, "Daulatabad," *Marg*, vol. XXXVII, no. 3, p. 20

'Alā' al-Dīn Hasan, the first Bahmānī ruler, established his capital at Gulbarga and left Daulatābād as the most powerful stronghold in the north-west of his possessions; it subsequently became the headquarters of the northern Bahmānī province.

When the Bahmānī Sultanate disintegrated into five successor states, Daulatābād passed to the Niẓām Shāhī dynasty. During the wars of Shāh Jahān the site was taken by the Mughals in 1633 and disappears from history except for an addenda—the last Quṯb Shāhī sultan of Hyderabad was imprisoned here until the breakup of the Mughal empire in 1757.

Among the ruins of Daulatābād is the Jāmi' Mosque outside the fort, which bears an inscription of 1318, recording its erection during the reign of Quṯb al-Dīn Mubārak Khaljī. The mosque is a square structure with a prayer hall of twenty-five aisles divided into five bays by pillars which support a flat roof. At the corners of the *qibla* wall are tapering fluted turrets resembling the Quṯb Mīnār in Delhi. The enclosure walls have an entrance gate on each side, the one on the east side supporting a tall dome.

A short distance to the north of the Jāmi' Mosque stands a separate tower, the Chānd Mīnār[Ill. 136]. Its position indicates that it had other than religious purposes, since it apparently was also used in the defense of the citadel. The *mīnār* is built in four circular storeys, one section being fluted. Except for the Hindu-type brackets supporting the balconies, the design is purely Islamic. The ornament consists of string courses, blind parapets, blind arches and traces of coloured tiles.

The *mīnār* stands by a small mosque known today as the Ek Mīnār kī Mosque, which bears an inscription stating that the tower was erected in 1445 by order of Parwīz, son of Qarandal[2] during the reign of 'Alā' al-Dīn Aḥmad Bahmānī.

* * *

Gulbarga became the seat of the Bahmānī sultans of the Deccan and remained the capital until 1424, when the sultan, court and army moved to Bīdar. The first ruler of Gulbarga was Hasan Bahmān Shāh, a young Persian adventurer, who claimed descent from the legendary Persian King Isfandiyār, one of the key figures in Firdawsī's *Shāhnāma.* An able administrator and a zealous leader, he expanded the newly founded Bahmānī Sultanate and divided it into four provinces, Gulbarga, Daulatābād, Berār and Bīdar, assigning a governor to each. The provinces were governed quite independently of the central government and even maintained their own armies, which could, however, be requisitioned by the sultan in time of need.

When Hasan Bahmān died in 1358 he was succeeded by Muḥammad I, who managed to keep peace for about a decade. Having no worries in his foreign relations, the new sultan turned to reorganising his administration, the army and the provincial governments. A man fond of learning and poetry, Muḥammad spent much of his time enticing men of letters to his court. Most of his architectural energies were directed to increasing the number of fortresses within the Sultanate, partly as a response to the rising power of the neighbouring Hindu state of Vijayanagar. Gulbarga was probably strongly fortified during this time, and at least three important religious monuments were initiated—the Shāh Bāzār Mosque, the celebrated Jāmi' Mosque in the fort, and the sultan's own mausoleum.

Muḥammad died in 1375, bequeathing to his son and successor, Mujāhid, a strongly united country. But internal peace did not last long, and for about the next twenty years there followed a period of short reigns, notably those of Muḥammad II and

[2] *Epigraphia Indo-Moslemica, 1907-8,* pp. 21-22; *1964,* pp. 36-37.

Dā'ūd II. During these decades the Bahmānī sultans were taken up with wars with the Hindu kingdom of Vijayanagar and with internal conflicts. The influx of foreign *āfāqīs* from Persia and other central Islamic lands caused problems with the original colonists from the north, who had settled in the Deccan, and the *habshīs* or Abyssinians.

North India's strong cultural influence on the Deccan now began to weaken and the political and cultural authority from the north, which had played so important a role during the Khaljī and Tughluq periods, no longer directly affected the south. Nor did the power of Delhi again increase until the advent of the Mughals in the seventeenth century.

Muḥammad II, Ḥasan Bahmān's youngest son, was elevated to the throne in 1378. The nineteen years of his reign brought peace at last to the exhausted Bahmānī state. The new sultan, himself a scholar of Arabic and Persian, attracted to the Deccan numerous foreign writers and even attempted to bring the famous Persian poet, Hafīz, to the Gulbarga court.

For a long time Muḥammad had no successors, since his heir and son was born only in old age. The sultan, therefore, virtually adopted his nephew Fīrūz and Aḥmad, giving them the best possible education, and considered Fīrūz, the elder, as heir and successor to the throne. When Fīrūz finally did begin his long reign in 1397, he saw his task as that of unifier and he steered a middle course to coalesce the many dividing factions into an homogeneous state. To set about a reconciliation with the Hindu sections of the population, he elevated Hindus to prominent government posts, and even himself married the daughter of Devarāya, the Vijayanagar ruler. This synthesis of Hindu and Muslim cultures, stressed by several historians,[3] also had its impact upon the various monuments erected during Fīrūz's reign. The monumental tomb of the sultan and the little-known palace city of Fīrūzābād south of the capital are testaments to the genius of this enlightened monarch.

In 1422 after the death of Fīrūz, his brother, Aḥmad, the last Bahmānī sultan to rule from Gulbarga, was raised to the throne. During the reign the *āfāqī* influx reached its height, and it was accompanied by an increase in the popularity of the Shī'ā doctrine. Despite this, the fusion of cultures that had been characteristic of the reign of Fīrūz continued as, for instance, in the use of the Hindu calendar. The struggle with Vijayanagar resulted in victories for Aḥmad's armies, but military difficulties arose in Gujarat and Tilangana. The reason for the shift of capital from Gulbarga to Bīdar in 1424 is not entirely clear, but the powerful emerging *āfāqī* nobles and their demands made such a move imperative. Also important was the location of Gulbarga, since it was so close to the border of Vijayanagar. In 1436 Aḥmad died in Bīdar, and the future monuments of the Bahmānī dynasty continued to be erected in the new capital.

During the fifteenth and sixteenth centuries, Gulbarga remained an important provincial city under the Bahmānī successors, the Barīdīs. At the end of the sixteenth century, Gulbarga was absorbed into the Sultanate of Bījāpūr and several monuments constructed by governors and generals of the 'Ādil Shāhī rulers date from this period.

* * *

Gulbarga is dominated by a heavily defended citadel that once gave protection to the Bahmānī rulers. The fort is contained within double tapering stone walls,

[3]For instance, see H.K. Sherwani, "Tajud-Din Firoz and the Synthesis of Bahmani Culture," *New Indian Antiquary*, vol. VI, no. 4 (1943-44), pp. 75-89.

frequently pierced by semi-circular bastions and surrounded by a wide moat. The principal gateways on the east and west sides consist of pointed arched openings flanked by bastions and approached by a bridge across the moat. The strongly fortified western gateway faced the open countryside, the town itself being to the east.

North of the Gulbarga fort is the late fourteenth-century Shāh Bāzār Mosque, which dates to the reign of Muḥammad I (1358-75). This first mosque built in Gulbarga establishes the model for all subsequent mosque construction in the Deccan.

From the mid-fourteenth century onwards two types of mosque plans evolved in Gulbarga. Congregational mosques were built in a simple hypostyle plan, an open court surrounded on four sides by arcades, the prayer chamber on the western side deeper than the other three. Mosques which were not congregational mosques generally had no court and had smaller prayer chambers consisting of between three and six bays.

The Shāh Bāzār Mosque was apparently built as a congregational mosque and has a square plan formed by the prayer hall, the court and enclosing walls. The gateway in the middle of the eastern wall is a domed chamber, with an arched opening in the middle of each side, a parapet of merlons with fluted corner finials, and a flat dome. The gateway resembles contemporary tomb structures. The prayer hall is divided into fifteen aisles by six domed bays on plain masonry piers. No arcades surround the court, only vestiges of small openings, mere decoration along the north, south and east sides.

Not all congregational mosques were built in the orthodox hypostyle plan. One notable exception is the Jāmi' Mosque[Ill. 137], which dominates the strongly defended Gulbarga fort and now stands in isolation, once probably surrounded by royal and military structures. In addition to being the largest monument in the city it also marks a turning point in the history of Deccan mosque construction. According to an inscription placed in the wall near the northern entrance, this monument was built by Rafī, son of Shams, the son of Mansūr of Qazvīn, in 1367.[4] However, at least one recent scholar has doubted the validity of this date, suggesting that the building is more likely to have been completed during the reign of Fīrūz in the fifteenth century.[5] There certainly is evidence of later restorations, and the immense scale of the monument and the elaboration of some of its parts might well suggest a somewhat later date.

The plan of the Jāmi' Mosque is unique in India and is the only example of a completely covered mosque with no courtyard. The scheme is a subtle combination of differently sized bays, roofed with domes and pointed vaults [Ill. 138]. The sixty-three bays of the interior (nine by seven domed bays) are covered by small domes supported on pendentives, four domes are at the corners, and a large dome on a square clerestory is placed over the central *miḥrāb.* The side arcades are roofed by pointed vaults. In the prayer chamber two series of six domed bays flank the dome chamber in front of the *miḥrāb,* which has arched niches and squinches of an ornate trefoil shape [Ill. 139]. The *miḥrāb* niche [Ill. 140] and the friezes of merlons at the base of the dome are also trefoil. Surrounding the bays on the north, east and south are single aisles of wide bays, with "squat" arches springing from low piers [Ill. 141],

[4] *Epigraphia Indo-Moslemica, 1907-8,* pp.1-2; *1909-10,* p. 90.

[5] Z.A. Desai, "Architecture: The Bahmanis," *History of the Medieval Deccan,* edited by H.K. Sherwani and P.M. Joshi, Hyderabad, 1974, vol. II, pp. 240-43.

an unexpected contrast to the slim arches of the central aisles, which spring from high piers and have narrow spans [Ill. 142]. The wide arch with low imposts was destined to become popular not only in Gulbarga but later in 'Ādil Shāhī monuments.

The exterior walls of the mosque are pierced with a series of open archways filled with geometric screens of perforated masonry, to allow light into the enclosed building. The arched entrance portal on the north side is probably a later addition. Rising over the western end and above the prayer chamber is the dome on a square platform. The merlon parapet and corner finials are characteristic of the early Bahmānī style.

Accommodating up to five thousand worshippers, the Jāmi' Mosque is obviously a major monument and a striking innovation in terms of its plan, whose origin might be sought outside India, even direct influence from Spain having been suggested by some authorities[6] seems unlikely. More probably this foreign concept was transplanted and reworked in the south Indian context. Significantly, the completely roofed mosque had no successor in India, the scheme having been abandoned perhaps due to the difficulty of draining so extensive a flat roof during the rains.[7] It also did not confirm to the traditional model of a mosque.[8] In actual fact, the covered mosque may simply have been unsuitable for the mild winters and extremely hot summers, since a roof restricts the circulation of air. Whatever the reason, the Gulbarga Mosque is an example of a foreign idea which does not meet the needs of the local people and for practical purposes is therefore soon abandoned.

It is also curious that there is no *mimbar* in the mosque. Since every mosque is equipped with this adjunct, one of the prime requisites of Islam from where the *imām* leads the congregation in prayer, it is not clear why it was omitted from the Jāmi' Mosque. Also missing is a cistern to be used for the equally necessary task of cleansing before prayer. It has even been noted[9] that on important ceremonial occasions most of the worshippers in the mosque were obstructed from seeing the central praying area at all.

In the Gulbarga Fort there is no building extant which could have been used for public audiences. Nor is there any epigraphical evidence, to my knowledge, that any ever existed. Might there be reason to believe that the fort mosque was used for civil matters? It is rare to find new features introduced into religious structures and if the Jāmi' Mosque was rather a multi-purpose monument, then the architect might more easily have slipped in some foreign ideas. There must have been some reason why all innovations appeared in the Jāmi' Mosque and none in the contemporary Shāh Bāzār Mosque. Religious architecture changes very slowly. If the Jāmi' Mosque had been intended as a public audience hall, the conservative *'ulamā* would have been more tolerant of innovations than if the monument were intended for strictly religious matters.

Another explanation might be that the newly converted Hindus felt more comfortable praying in a covered area, with little light and air and thick walls, like Hindu temples. Even Fīrūz Tughluq's pavilion in Delhi appears, from literary sources, to have been a massive stepped building, more like a pyramid, with small interior chambers. Little is known about secular buildings built in north India before the

[6]James Fergusson, *History of Indian and Eastern Architecture*, vol. II, London, 1910, p. 266.
[7]See G. Yazdani, "The Great Mosque of Gulbarga," *Islamic Culture*, vol. II, 1928, p. 18.
[8]John Marshall, "The Monuments of Muslim India," *Cambridge History of India*, vol. III, New Delhi, 1965, p. 635.
[9]Ibid.

sixteenth century, and it is therefore difficult to know whether any of the palaces Fīrūz Tughluq had built was a prototype for the Gulbarga Mosque. Whatever its original function, and despite the fact that its plan was soon discarded, many of the innovations of the Gulbarga mosque remain in the repertoire of the religious monuments of the later Bahmānī rulers in Bīdar and the 'Ādil Shāhī rulers in Bījāpūr.

Just north of the Jāmi' Mosque is the Langar kī Mosque and accompanying tomb, probably dating to the early fifteenth century. The prayer chamber of this mosque is distinguished by its pointed vault in the construction of which wooden ribbing was used in imitation of timber supports [Ill. 143], a clear indication of the impact of indigenous Indian building systems on Islamic architecture at this period. Of interest also are the three entrance arches, each provided with trefoil contours on the exterior. Rising over the parapet above the central bay is a small arcaded projection.

Stucco was used to decorate external and interior parts of monuments in the Deccan before this date. But in the Langar kī Mosque the decoration is more refined and used more extensively. The entire tympanum over the *miḥrāb* is filled with exquisite stucco detail[Ill. 144].

Stucco is not used as decoration on the interior of monuments during the reign of the Bahmānī dynasty in Bīdar and when next found, on the Tomb of 'Alī Barīd in Bīdar, the motifs appear lifeless copies of earlier designs, perhaps indicating that few Indians craftsmen now understood how to work stucco and were thus not able to recognize its potential as decoration. The natural inclination of the local craftsmen in a land so rich in stone was to work the stone and not to cover it, in other words, to carve the stone as if it were stucco.

But in fifteenth century Gulbarga there appears to have lived a group of carvers trained to work in stucco who understood the potential of the medium and used it to express the repetitious designs so often found in Islamic art.[10] Three monuments including the Langar kī Mosque, all different, yet all displaying stucco decoration of a superior imaginative manner, all in Gulbarga, testify that men skilled in the art of stucco carving lived and worked in Gulbarga after the capital had been moved and the political supremacy had passed to Bīdar.[11]

In Gulbarga there are two groups of royal tombs belonging to the Bahmānī rulers. Just beyond the fortified western gate of the citadel are the earlier mausolea, of which the Tombs of Ḥasan Bahmān (d.1358) and Muḥammad I (d.1375) are typical examples. They are simple undecorated square chambers, with slightly sloping walls, low domes and fluted corner finials. The only elements of interest are the tall narrow archways in the middle of each side. Even the later Tomb of Muḥammad II (d.1397) follows this simple scheme, which is clearly derived from the somewhat more ornate Tughluq prototypes.

Found also in this area is an interesting anonymous mausoleum probably dating from the middle of the fifteenth century, which is exceptional for two reasons. Here is the first fluted dome to be found in the Deccan with unusually rich interior stucco decoration, not unlike the ornament found in the Langar kī Mosque of about the same date.

The later Bahmānī sultans were buried in the second group of royal tombs in a necropolis east of the city known as the "Seven Domes" or *haft gumbad.* The earliest of these, the Tomb of Mujāhid (d.1378) differs very little from the monuments of the

[10]Carr Stephen, *Archaeology and Monumental Remains of Delhi,* Allahabad, 1964, p. 125.

[11]E. Schotten Merklinger, *Indian Islamic Architecture: The Deccan 1347-1686,* Warminster, 1981, p. 95.

first group. The sloping walls without decoration, the flat dome and the fluted corner finials are still present. Within are graves three of which are said to be those of the sultan, his wife and his sister. The tomb of the next sultan, Dā'ūd (d.1378) introduces an unusual variation of this form, since it contains two domed chambers linked by a narrow interior corridor to create a double mausoleum.

The Tomb of Fīrūz (d.1422) [Ill. 145], however, is the masterpiece of this series. Not only is it the largest and best decorated but it also shows the fully evolved Bahmānī style, no longer dependent on the earlier Delhi models of the Tughlūq period. The tomb demonstrates the successful inclusion of Hindu details, and shows in architectural terms the spirit of synthesis that characterised the reign of Fīrūz.

The Tomb of Fīrūz, as that of Dā'ūd, is also a double structure, the two domes rising above the parapet of trefoil merlons with fluted corner finials. It shows, however, some important innovations. The walls are no longer plain and tapering, and the façade is double-storeyed, divided into a number of recesses framed by arches with angular contours in two or three planes. The niches on the upper storeys are filled with pierced masonry screens in geometrical patterns. Above the entrances, eaves appear supported on Hindu temple-like brackets. Bands of lotus decoration and arabesques, as well as roundels of geometric designs, all executed in finely cut plaster, cover the exterior.

The interior is richly ornamented with stucco and painted panels, bands and roundels. The *miḥrāb* [Ill. 146] is the most embellished part of the entire structure. Only the barest traces of the magnificently painted decoration on the domes survive, but parts of the richly worked stucco, fluted bands and medallions, may still be seen.

When Muḥammad Tughluq decided to make Daulatābād his second capital in 1325, ṣūfī mystics along with government officials left Delhi for the south. There appears to have been little choice regarding the actual migration, because the sultan forced all government employees, the *'ulamā* and shaykhs of Delhi to follow. The new setting, however, proved more fruitful and enjoyable than expected and many holy men decided to stay, spreading to the south the tradition of organized ṣūfī movements in the north.

The first Bahmānī ruler, Ḥasan Gangu, sought the help of ṣūfī saints to consolidate and strengthen his newly-won power, and his successors did likewise. A ruler was virtually powerless without the support of these holy men, to whom large endowments were willed in exchange for the spiritual moral support deemed so important. Shaykhs helped at accessions and in time of war, exercising enormous influence in all aspects of life. Rulers had not always relied on shaykhs and their goodwill, for the earlier tradition kept ṣūfī mystics away from politics. Once a shaykh accepted royal patronage, he lost his own moral freedom. Eventually, the shaykh even lost his most sacred right to choose his spiritual successor, and hereditary succession became the rule.

In 1401 the famous Saint Ḥaẓrat Gīsū Darāz arrived in Gulbarga and settled in a monastery near the Jāmi' Mosque in the fort. Fīrūz, ever fickle, lost his early enthusiasm for the celebrated holy man and persuaded him to move his *dargāh* away from the royal quarter to a site some distance east of the city where the tomb of the saint still stands and is still venerated. The rift between Fīrūz and Gīsū Darāz had important consequences, causing considerable tension between the sultan and his brother, Aḥmad, who later ascended the throne and moved the capital to a new site.

The Dargāh of Gīsū Darāz is a large complex of tombs, mosques, *madrasas,* rest-houses, courtyards and gateways and shows the significant role of the Chishtī saint in the religious history of south India. The *dargāh* was founded at the beginning of the fifteenth century, but the monuments date from many periods, up to the seventeenth century, and are built in a variety of styles.

The Tomb of Gīsū Darāz (d.1422) has a double-storeyed façade divided into regularly spaced arched recesses. The decoration is mostly confined to the elaborate parapet of foliated and trefoil design, the single fluted corner finials and the parapet of a frieze of indented squares. Doorjambs are in the Hindu pot-on-post design. Within the painted decoration of the dome is vivid. The canopy over the grave is decorated in mirror work and mother-of-pearl but is a later addition. The sixteenth- and seventeenth-centuries additions to the *dargāh* are built in the style of the 'Ādil Shāhī period. There is an inscription which refers to a gate built for the *dargāh* by Ibrāhīm Ādil Shāh in 1538. Afẓal Khān, the great minister of the 'Ādil Shāhī rulers Muḥammad 'Alī II and Sikandar, was so greatly attracted to Ḥazrat Gīsū Dārāz that he built a small Bījāpūr-style mosque with the typical clusters of finials, raised dome on petals and modelled brackets in the south court. Of interest also is the immense arch springing from two high towers in the southern corners of the court which also dates from the seventeenth century [Ill. 147]. The arch is ornamented with enlarged stucco roundels containing heraldic animals supported on large brackets. The interest in these seventeenth century additions is that they show the attraction the Dargāh of Gīsū Darāz had for later 'Ādil Shāhī rulers, who continued to build extensions and monuments until the end of the Sultanate.

All *dargāhs* in Īndia, including the Dargāh of Gīsū Darāz, are puzzling as studies of architecture. Buildings are crowded together and many different styles exist side by side, ranging from the fourteenth to the seventeenth centuries. Throughout India not only rulers but government officials wanted to be buried near a shaykh. The practice of royal patronage as seen in the Dargāh of Gīsū Dārāz by the additions in the south court built by Afẓal Khān in the mid-seventeenth century is not unique. Near the tombs of the early Bahmānī sultans, the Dargāh of Shaykh Junaydī, teacher of Ḥasan Bahmān and his son Muḥammad I, also bears the mark of the 'Ādil Shāhī dynasty. In the early sixteenth century, Yūsuf 'Ādil Khān, the founder of the Bījāpūr Sultanate, added a monumental gateway framed by two lofty circular minarets, which consists of a long two-storeyed façade with rows of arched openings. In Aland northwest of Gulbarga, the Dargāh of Ḥazrat Shaykh 'Alā' al-Dīn Ansārī, known also as Ladlay Sāhib, spiritual guide of Gīsū Darāz, also has two similar gateways probably built in the early sixteenth century by Yūsuf 'Ādil Khān.

South-east of the complex of Ḥazrat Gīsū Darāz is a smaller *dargāh* which commemorates another saint who lived in Gulbarga, Shāh Kamāl Mujārrad. The compound consists of a small plain tomb, built in typical late-fourteenth century style, a small mosque and two other structures. The mosque is probably of later date than the tomb and has a prayer chamber of fifteen bays, three rows of five aisles, with five hemispherical domes. The mosque provides an outstanding example of stucco decoration, the most elaborate seen in Gulbarga. Embellishing the façade above the five entrance arches are multi-lobed bands of richly carved stucco as well as roundels. The geometric and foliate forms are combined here in an exuberant display.

Two other structures, one planned around a central domed chamber entered through a portico, another consisting of a linear arrangement, ten arched cells surmounted by domes, lack any ornament. Their purpose is not entirely clear but they may have served as rest houses or *sarā'ī* or even as a stable for horses.

Between Gulbarga and Bīdar in Holkondā is another interesting *dargāh* known locally as the Dargāh of Shaykh Muḥammad Mashāyakh.[12] Five tombs are situated in an enclosure with a large entrance gateway on the eastern side and a wall mosque on the western side, and two tombs are located outside the enclosing walls.

The seven tombs were built at different periods. The earliest within the enclosure is the Tomb of Shaykh Muḥammad Mashayakh probably built in the mid-fourteenth century, since it displays the characteristics of that time, a square plan with a sloping walls, simple arch-shaped merlon cresting and fluted domed corner finials. There are three other square domed tombs, one in the south-east corner of the compound and two outside the enclosure walls of about the same date. The other three tombs are of a later date, two are square with double-storeyed façades, and a third is a fifteenth century octagonal tomb of a design unique in India.

There are three structures datable to the late fourteenth century, the two tombs outside the enclosure walls, the Tomb of Allū and Mallū, and the Tomb of Jalāl Khān. The Tomb of Allū is the only tomb in the Deccan known to be built entirely of brick. It has a curious basketwork motif on the band below the cresting.

Two later monuments, the Tomb of Ā'zam Khān and the Tomb of Khair Khān, display some interesting characteristics which tie them to later Bahmānī structures. The walls are perpendicular and the façade is double-storeyed, very similar to the mid-fifteenth century tombs of Āshtūr near Bīdar.

The Tomb of Dilāwar Khān [Ill. 148] is a tall domed octagonal structure with narrow pointed recessed arches set in rectangular panels on each side. The panels and recessed arches have black stone mouldings, which resemble those on the fifteenth century Tomb of 'Alā' al-Dīn in Bīdar. The design of the Ḥolkondā tomb appears to be purely Persian, an octagonal tomb tower as built in Iran from the twelfth to the fourteenth centuries. It is not clear how the design found its way tō Holkondā.

It is also not clear who lies buried in these seven tombs. Judging by their size, the cost of construction must have been considerable. Generally, *dargāhs* are located on elevated sites and it is not a common practice to have even royal tombs on the same level as the tomb of the saint. In Bīdar, for example, the Tomb of Ḥaẓrat Khalīl Allāh is situated on an elevation. The sultans of Bīdar chose to be buried lower than the shrine, and Āshtūr, the royal necropolis, lies in a valley below the venerated shrine. But in Holkondā the tombs within the enclosure wall of the *dargāh* are on the same level and not at some respectful distance below the revered tomb of the saint, as had been the custom.[13]

Another unwritten law appears to have been that the mosque in a *dargāh* is to be situated just west of the tomb of the saint. In Holkondā two tombs, the Tomb of Khayr Khān and the Tomb of Ā'zam Khān, were placed between the tomb of the saint and the mosque on its west.

Finally, it was not considered respectful to build tombs larger or more imposing than the mausoleum of the saint. In Holkondā this rule was also broken, the tombs built in the *dargāh* were more splendid than the tomb of the saint.

Apparently, the tombs in Holkondā were built by foreigners, most likely Iranians

[12]E. Schotten Merklinger, "Seven Tombs at Holkonda: A Preliminary Survey," *Kunst des Orients*, vol. X, nos. 1/2, pp.187-97 for a complete discussion of this group of monuments.

[13]Ibid., pp. 95-96.

ignorant of the rules of south India. That would also explain the design of the Tomb of Dilāwar Khān. As for the shaykh buried here so far removed from the centre of the Sultanate, perhaps he chose exile rather than submit to bondage.[14]

Although nothing is known about Shaykh Muḥammad Mashāyakh, he appears to have been venerated after his death by at least certain elements of the population. The men buried in Holkondā lavished money and care on their tombs and chose this site above others as their last resting place.

* * *

Twenty-five kilometres south of Gulbarga, on the Bhīma River, Fīrūz established Fīrūzābād, a second royal capital, in about 1400 which he abandoned some fifty years later. It is not clear why the sultan attempted to change the site of the capital nor why the plan was discarded only a half century later.[15]

Massive stone fortified walls, with engaged circular bastions, enclose the city on all but the west side. In the middle of each side are defensive gateways with vaulted entrances and barbican walls.

The largest single monument in Fīrūzābād is the Jāmi‘ Mosque west of the city centre, with a rectangular court and domed entrance gateway on the east side. The prayer hall consists of thirteen rows of five bays. Behind the mosque is the palace area, a number of courts bounded by high walls with some collapsed structures now inside.

The monuments of Fīrūzābād were built in a uniform style. The tapering walls, parapets, finials with bulbous tops, stilted arches, flat domes and pyramidal vaults are all features of the Bahmānī style in the early fifteenth century. The traces of stucco design are similar to the ornament on the Tomb of Fīrūz Shāh in Gulbarga.

* * *

After the death of Fīrūz, the capital of the Bahmānī Sultanate was transferred to Bīdar by Aḥmad I. Various reasons may have contributed to this decision, among them Bīdar's excellent position on the brink of a plateau nearly 60 m. above sea level providing a natural defence. But climatic conditions aside, the continuous conflict with Vijayanagar made it vital to have a capital located further north in a more central and safer location within the realm.

An era of comparative peace was ushered in by Aḥmad. He extended the borders of the Bahmānī Sultanate by fighting successful campaigns against the sultans of Mālwā and Gujarat, and the Rājā of Vijayanagar, annexing portions of the Konkan and Berār.

Besides being a successful military leader, Aḥmad was the first sultan to weaken Tughluq influence and to replace it with new ideas then reaching south India from Iran. He attracted several saints from Persia and as a result the Shī‘ā doctrine became more popular in the Deccan. Not surprisingly, the new religious atmosphere also brought with it Persian influences in many of the monuments built in the new capital.

Historians have been kind to the memory of ‘Alā' al-Dīn,the next sultan and Aḥmad's eldest son, who succeeded to the throne in 1435. Although self-indulgent

[14] E. Schotten Merklinger, op. cit., p. 43.

[15] On Firuzabad see Klaus Fischer, "Firozabad on the Bhima and its Environs," *Islamic Culture*, vol. XXXIX/ 4, pp. 246-55. Also, George Michell, "Firozabad: A Little Known Muslim Capital in the Deccan," *Marg*, vol. XXXVII, no. 3, pp. 86-87; and George Michell and Richard Eaton, *Firuzabad—Palace City of the Deccan*, Oxford, 1992.

and unable to control the army 'Alā' al-Dīn nevertheless did not neglect the more personal interests of his subjects. He built mosques and established public schools and other charitable institutions, the most important of which was an hospital in Bīdar staffed with Hindu and Muslim physicians. At Ni'matābād the sultan laid out a garden and built beautiful palaces trying to set an example which he hoped would be followed by the nobles.[16]

'Alā' al-Dīn died in 1458 and was succeeded by his eldest son, Humāyūn, whose reign was harsh and full of stress and rebellion among the entire population, especially the *āfāqīs* and *dakhnīs*. One of the most important acts of the reign was the appointment as prime minister of Maḥmūd Gāwān, a Persian destined to make history in the Deccan, where he stayed to serve the Bahmānī state loyally to the end of his life. Humāyūn's greatest architectural achievement is the spendid monument he had built over his father's remains.

A council of regency steered the affairs of state upon Humāyūn's death until the rule of the succeeding sultan, Muḥammad III (1463-82), when Khwāja Maḥmūd Gāwān emerged as a powerful force. The new prime minister skilfully held the balance between the *dakhnīs* and *āfāqīs*, distributing offices to both sides, and managed to win the support of the Hindu element of the population. Although foreign conflicts continued to trouble the Bahmānī Sultanate, Khwāja Gāwān succeeded in keeping effective control. The capital was decorated with many fine monuments, the most celebrated of which was the *madrasa* named after the prime minister. But the growing power of Maḥmūd Gāwān had long angered the jealous nobles who laid a plot, which resulted in 1481 in the minister's death.

The period of the following ruler, Maḥmūd (d.1518), saw the disintegration of the Bahmānī Sultanate. In the general turmoil of this reign, several powerful figures emerge in Bīdar, among them Yūsuf 'Adil and Niẓām al-Mulk, the future founders of the Bījāpūr and Aḥmadnagar Sultanates respectively, and Qāsim Barīd, the first ruler of the Barīdī dynasty. A Turkish slave of Muḥammad III, Qāsim Barīd forced the Bahmānī monarch to appoint him as prime minister, but he was not strong enough to keep in check the renegade generals who had begun to assert their autonomy. Disorder increased on all sides and finally led to the complete disintegration of the Bahmānī state.

The Solah Khambha Mosque occupies a prominent position in the fort. Built in 1327[17] although probably restored in later times, it is, therefore, the oldest building in Bīdar and the first mosque in the Deccan, constructed during the reign of Muḥammad Tughluq. In plan it has the usual open courtyard with a pillared sanctuary divided by circular columns into nineteen aisles and five bays each with a flat-domed ceiling. A high dome is placed over the bay in front of the pentagonal-shaped central *miḥrāb* composed of a tall, narrow stilted arch with vertical ribs and a small multifoil arch. The side niches are ribbed and cusped and have plaster decoration in the spandrels and above the apex.

The nineteen façade arches are uniform and each is supported on square masonry piers and therefore different from the circular columns of the interior. A flat dome on a raised circular drum with a frieze of trefoil merlon crowns the structure. In addition to the large dome, the roof consists of small domes hidden by the interlocking

[16]G.Yazdani, *Bidar: Its History and Monuments*, Oxford, 1947, p. 7.

[17]George Michell in "Bidar," *Marg*, vol. XXXVII, no. 3, p. 57, no. 1 states that due to a misreading of the inscription this monument is usually dated much later. See Z.A. Desai, "Architecture: The Bahmanis," *History of the Medieval Deccan*, edited by H.K.Sherwani and P.M. Joshi, Hyderabad,1974, vol. II, p. 248, n. 19.

parapet and the small corner finials.

The Jāmi' Mosque dates from the first decades of the sixteenth century. The mosque has a large court, enclosed by modern walls, and a prayer chamber of seven aisles divided by three bays. The pointed arches rise from plain piers. The *miḥrāb* has a pentagonal plan at the base and is covered by a tall dome, which has been compared with the lantern-shaped vaults of the Jāmi' al-Zaituna at Tunis and with several other early mosques in North Africa. On the exterior there are the usual *chhajja* on moulded brackets and a parapet of trefoil merlons, as well as bulbous-domed finials springing from lotus petals, a typical late Bahmānī feature.

At Āshtūr, a short distance northeast of Bīdar, are the tombs of the later Bahmānī sultans. These structures demonstrate the development of the architectural style of the fifteenth and early sixteenth centuries when Persian ideas began to influence local Indian forms. Most of the tombs are still square in plan, but the walls have lost their earlier slope and are now perpendicular, while the domes have started to assume a more bulbous shape.

The earliest structure of the group is the Tomb of Aḥmad I (d.1436). The large square domed chamber marks a departure from earlier mausolea having a façade of three rather than two storeys of arched pointed recesses, seven at the top and four each on the middle and lower storeys. The only exterior ornament is a series of calligraphic bands and plaster roundels in the spandels. The hemispherical dome at its point of springing has a trefoil parapet and eight corner turrets on each side of the drum.

The outstanding feature of the monument is the interior decoration. The walls and domes are covered in coloured paintings in Persian style[Ill. 149] and there is little doubt that Persian architects and craftsmen were being employed by the Bahmānī sultans of Bīdar.

The Persianizing tendency is also noticeable in the ṣūfī poems by Ni'mat Allāh al-Kirmānī found on the walls, in the calligraphic bands of the recessed niches, and along the rim of the dome, indicating that Aḥmad was strongly attracted, to the Shī'ā doctrine. The dome interior even contains painted bands graphically showing the connection of Ni'mat Allāh with the Saint Junayd al-Baghdādī and the *durūd*, a Shī'ā blessing on the Prophet and his descendents, the twelve *imāms*. The apex panel actually contains the names of Allāh, the Prophet and the immediate family members, 'Alī, Fātimā, Ḥasan, and Ḥusayn.

An equally strong Persian influence is seen on the next Āshtūr monument, the Tomb of 'Alā' al-Dīn (d.1458). The façades [Ill. 150] have fine arched recesses of unequal height placed around the large central niche. Of great interest are the carved black stone bands outlining the decorative tile panels and the four corners of the structure, running from the roof to the ground. Here for the first time appear both the true four-centered pointed Persian arches and traces of blue coloured tilework. The later Tomb of Maḥmūd (d.1518) has almost the same plan and dimensions as the Tomb of 'Ālā' al-Dīn, but reverts to the earliest method of having the façade divided into three rows of pointed arch recesses.

In addition to square tombs, the later Bahmānī sultans experimented with memorial structures built in other plans. The Chawkhandi, the Tomb of the Shī'ā saint, Khalīl Allāh(d.1460) [Ill. 151] [Plan 20] just west of the Ashtūr group of tombs, has an unusual plan. Entered through a large gateway with pointed arches, the saint's mausoleum is a square domes chamber standing within a double-storeyed

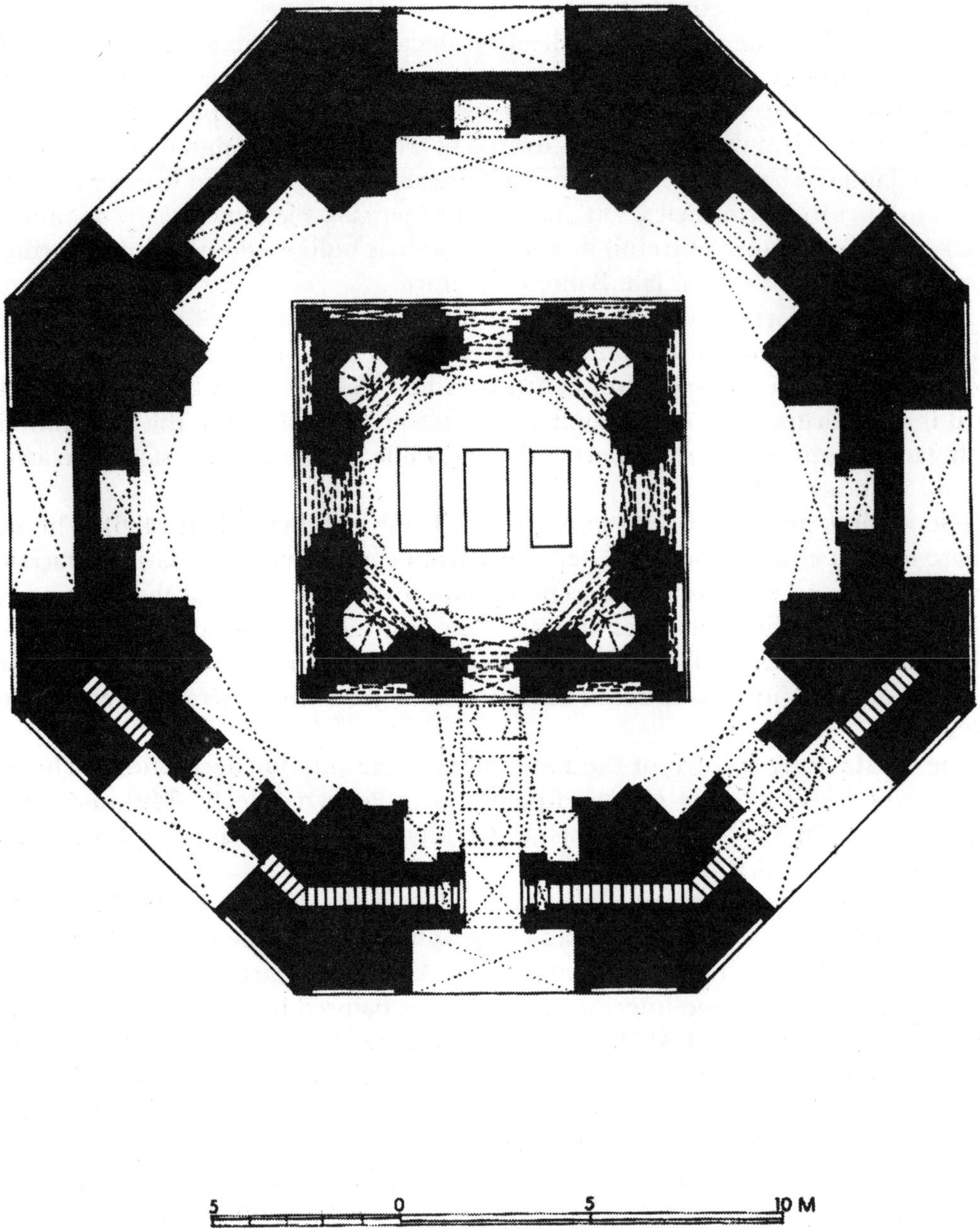

Plan 20. Bīdar, Tomb of Khalīl Allāh (Chawkhandi)

octagon. The outer octagonal shell has arched recesses flanked by panels that include diagonal squares, all outlined in carved black stone bands, and was probably intended to be covered in coloured tilework. Over the south doorway is an inscription written by a Persian, Mughīth al-Qārī al-Shīrāzī.[18]

Octagonal tombs were not frequently found in the Deccan. In fact, the only true octagonal tomb is in Holkondā. The Tomb of Dilāwar Khān is a tall, domed structure with narrow arched recesses set in rectangular panels on each side. No other domed octagonal tomb in this part of the Deccan was erected before the sixteenth century.[19]

[18]*Epigraphia Indo-Moslemica, 1927-8,* p.180; Yazdani, op. cit., p. 95, n. 3.

[19]E. Schotten Merklinger, "Seven Tombs at Holkonda," op. cit., pp. 194-95.

The Holkondā tomb must be dated to the sixteenth century and appears to be a tomb tower such as was found in all parts of Iran. Most of these towers are round or star-shaped and only a few are octagonal, the Gumbad-i 'Alī in Abarquh (1036), the fourteenth-century tomb of Qumm and the Imāmzāda Jafar at Isfahān dated 1341. The Tomb of Dilāwar Khān belongs stylistically to these octagonal tomb towers built in Iran from the eleventh to the fourteenth centuries. It is not clear how the design came to the Deccan. There do not appear to be any other such octagonal tomb towers in the Deccan, or for that matter, in India, either earlier or later than the fifteenth century example in Holkondā.

The only *madrasa* found in the Deccan, the Madrasa of Maḥmūd Gāwān [Ill. 152] in Bīdar, was completed in 1472 and is one of the most impressive monuments in India. The patron who brought this completely foreign idea to Bīdar was a Persian from Gilān, who was probably familiar with the Tīmūrīd *madrasa* in Khūrāsān and Transoxiana, monuments this *madrasa* resemble and which were probably used as its model.[20]

The *madrasa* plan [Plan 21] is typical of those developed in Tīmūrīd Persia in the fifteenth century and consists of four great arcaded *īwān* surmounted by domes raised high on circular or octagonal drums, axially placed in the centre of the four court façades. At the rear project are deep pentagonal chambers. The *īwān* are flanked with cells and living rooms for teachers, students and library facilities here in Bīdar, as nowhere else in the Islamic world, in three storeys, undoubtedly an Indian innovation noted first on the Tomb of Aḥmad in Bīdar and on some of the Lodī tombs in Delhi.

The *madrasa* is entered from the east side, where the façade is flanked by tall cylindrical domed corner minarets, only the northern one of which still stands [Ill. 153]. The minarets and the façades were ornamented with coloured tilework, some of which is still to be seen. There are stepped battlemented crenellations known as *kangūras*, panels of star-shaped patterns, circular scrolls ending in half-palmettes in profile and arabesques of white faience intertwined with turquoise scrolls bearing buds. The colours used are white, yellow, turquoise, light and dark blue. The minarets have a chevron pattern simulated to appear like brick laid in a decorative scheme. At the neck band of each storey is a calligraphic band with *Qur'ānic* texts in white, light green, light and dark blue tilework[Ill. 154].

Throughout the first half of the fifteenth century Persian decorators were working in Bīdar. On the Tomb of Aḥmad (1435)the artist signed himself Shukr Allāh of Qazwīn. On the Tomb of Khalīl Allāh(1460), there is a signature of Mughīth al-Qārī al-Shīrāzī. The Bīdar Madrasa inscription refers to Alī as-Ṣūfī[21] and the artist was probably responsible for decorating the entrance façade, but the court facades show no traces of tilework and must have been executed by lesser locally trained workmen.

It is unlikely that Maḥmūd Gāwān brought a trained architect to Bīdar from Samarkand to design the *madrasa.* 'Alī as-Ṣūfī, the master craftsman, decorated the entrance façade and corner minarets in a technique he probably learned from Mughīth of Shīrāz, perhaps his teacher. Most of the Tīmūrīd monuments of Samarkand were decorated with tilework by craftsmen from central Iran and it might, therefore, not be improbable that Mughīth himself learned the technique in the Tīmūrīd capital

[20]E. Schotten Merklinger, "The Madrasa of Maḥmūd Gāwān," *Kunst des Orients,* vol. XI, nos. 1/2, pp.146-57, for a discussion of the *madrasa.*

[21]Yazdani, op. cit., p. 95, n. 3.

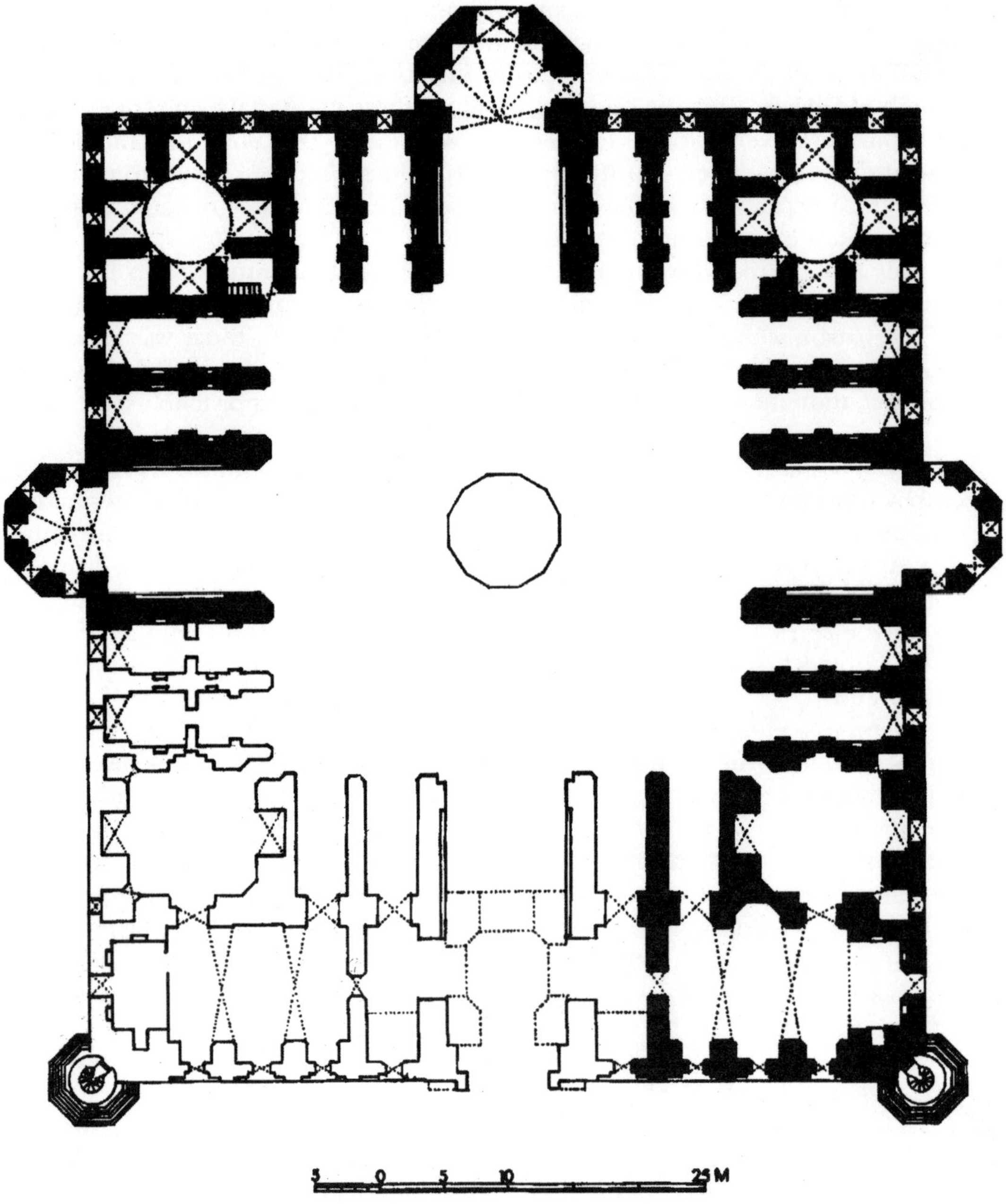

Plan 21. Bīdar, Madrasa of Maḥmūd Gāwān

of Transoxiana.

The Bīdar Madrasa is the only Indian Islamic monument with a four-*īwān* plan and could have been a prototype for a new type of mosque plan, the *madrasa*-mosque, such as was built in Persia. There is only one step from the four-*īwān madrasa* plan to the *madrasa*-mosque plan, which includes enlarging the court and using the *qibla īwān* as a prayer hall. This transition was successfully accomplished in Persia and

Central Asia to produce some of the greatest masterpieces of Islamic architecture. In India, however, the Bīdar Madrasa stands isolated, its plan a wholesale importation of a foreign form, never taking root on Indian soil, and thus having no further impact on architectural construction in India.

The rapid appearance and disappearance of the Bīdar Madrasa plan indicates once again that undilated importation and adoption of a foreign institution cannot happen without meeting the demands of the local population. Whatever the needs of Indian Muslims living in fifteenth century Bīdar might have been, the four-*īwān madrasa* religious institution as known in Tīmūrīd Persia did not satisfy them.

CHAPTER 13

The Deccan: The Bahmānī Successor States (1489-1687)

When the Bahmānī Sultanate disintegrated at the beginning of the sixteenth century, the Barīdī sultans were its direct successors in Bīdar. Amīr and his son Qāsim, as prime ministers, kept the last Bahmānī ruler, Maḥmūd (1482-1518), dependent. Upon the death of Maḥmūd, the rule of the great Bahmānī dynasty came to an end, although, in theory, puppet Bahmānī rulers remained on the throne until 1538. Real power was vested in the Barīdī ministers who now managed all affairs of state. The Bahmānī Sultanate lost much of its former territory and strength due to the numerous independent states which began to emerge, occupying territory previously held by the Bahmānī sultans. Yūsuf 'Ādil Shāh established the Bījāpūr Sultanate, Malik Aḥmad the Nizām Shāhī dynasty of Aḥmadnagar, Imād al-Mulk the principality of Burhānpūr and Thalner, Qāsim Barīd the Bīdar successor state, and Quṭb al-Mulk the Golkondā Sultanate.

Amīr Barīd was *de facto* ruler in Bīdar until 1543 when his son, 'Alī, named himself sultan. A cultered man fond of poetry, 'Alī was responsible for many improvements to Bīdar and its fort, and the rebuilding of a number of monuments, such are the Rangīn and Tarkish Maḥal. But the most outstanding accomplishment of 'Alī's reign was the construction of his own tomb.

After, 'Alī's death in 1580, five sultans followed to rule the independent Barīdī realm for another thirty-nine years. 'Alī, along with four other monarchs, successfully defeated the Hindu kingdom of Vijayanagar in the Battle of Talikota in 1565. But after this victory, the three allied Sultanates of Aḥmadnagar, Bījāpūr, and Golkondā became too powerful for the Barīdī rulers. In 1619 Bīdar was absorbed into the 'Ādil Shāhī Sultanate where it remained until 1656 to pass finally into the expanding Mughal Empire under Aurangzīb.

The necropolis [Ill. 155] in which the memorial structures of the Barīdī sultans are built is to the west of Bīdar. The Tomb of Qāsim Barīdī (d.1504) is a small structure with a plain conical-shaped dome. The tomb of his successor, Amīr I, was left incomplete, without a dome, on the sudden death of the sultan in 1543.

The Tomb of 'Alī I (d.1580)[Ill. 156] is the masterpiece of the series. The tall domed structure has a central arched opening flanked by two tiers of smaller arched recesses on its four sides, and five horizontal bands, now plain, but probably intended for coloured tilework decoration, above the entrances. The parapet and base of the dome both have trefoil merlons.

The interior of the domed tomb has rectangular panels with verses from the Persian poet Attar written by Khwajagi of Shirwan.[1] The bands of *Qur'ānic* texts in the upper parts

[1]G.Yazdani, *Bidar: Its History and Monuments*, Oxford, 1947, p. 152.

of the walls were written in *thuluth* by a master calligrapher, 'Abd al-Fattah[2] [Ill. 157].

The tomb is situated in the middle of a four-square (*chār-bāgh*) garden, entered on the south side through a gateway with low arches. The upper rooms are decorated with small multi-lobed niches. Beyond is a small mosque with three wide arches in triple planes, and two turrets with bulbous tops flanking the façade.

Imitating the Tomb of 'Alī on a smaller scale is the incomplete structure of his son, Ibrāhīm (d.1587). The importance of the Tomb of 'Alī Barīd is in its four open sides. The first example of this plan was used in a mausoleum in Merv in Tūrkestān, the mausoleum of the Imām Bāb cemetery, built in the tenth century.[3] There were also two mausolea in Tunis, the Sidi Bou Khrissan (1093) and the Msid al-Quubahm, typologically related to the preceding. The first extant with such a plan is the Tomb of the Samanīds in Bukhārā, dated before 943. The unusual plan of the Tomb of 'Alī appears to have been brought from Central Asia. While monuments open on all four sides were not unusual in early Islam, this plan was not popular in medieval Islam and its appearance in sixteenth century Bīdar remains unexplained.

* * *

Bījāpūr is not mentioned frequently in history texts before 1478, when, along with Mudgal and Rāichūr, it was assigned to the famous Bahmānī minister, Maḥmūd Gāwān. In 1481, after Gāwān's death, it was reassigned to Yūsuf 'Ādil Khān who became its provincial governor. Political and religious tension increased in the late fifteenth century and Yūsuf declared his independence in 1490 by establishing the 'Ādil Shāhī Sultanate, managing to resist Mughal onslaughts for nearly two-hundred further years. Finally, Bījāpūr was absorbed in the Mughal Empire in 1686.

Chroniclers claim that Yūsuf was the son of the Ottoman Sultan Murād II and brother of the illustrious Mehmet II, the conqueror of Constantinople.[4] There are tales of his clandestine travels to Persia to escape assassination attempts, and of his final voyage to the safety of the Bahmānī court in the Deccan where he soon distinguished himself as one of the Turkish slaves of Maḥmūd.

Almost immediately upon declaring his independence, Yūsuf, who had lived in Persia and there became an ardent Shī'ā, was the first Muslim ruler in India to introduce the Shī'ā doctrine. The move caused so much opposition among the other Muslim rulers of the Deccan that Yūsuf had finally to relent and to give up his championship of the Shī'ā cause. Neither he nor his successor were ever again sufficiently strong to implement this religious reform and the Sunnī doctrine remained the official faith in Bījāpūr.

Yūsuf died in 1510 and was followed in succession by Ismā'īl (1510-34), Ibrāhīm I (1535-58), Alī I(1558-80), the minor Ibrāhīm II (1580-1627), with a regency governed by the great dowager queen, Chānd Bībī, and Muḥammad (1627-56). The Bījāpūr sultans were almost continually engaged in warfare with the neighbouring Muslim states of the Deccan and with the Hindu Kingdom of Vijayanagar, which was finally defeated by the four Muslim Deccan sultanates in 1565. But, at the beginning of the seventeenth century a new threat from the north emerged. The Mughals invaded, besieged and finally conquered the 'Ādil Shāhī state in 1686.

During 'Alī I's long reign there was much building activity in the capital. The city walls, with five main gates flanked by bastions and approachable by drawbridges across

[2]Ibid.

[3]E. Schotten Merklinger, *Indian Islamic Architecture: The Deccan 1347-1686,* Warminster, 1981, p. 121.

[4]Mohamed Kasim Ferishta, *History of the Rise of the Mahomedan Power in India,* translated by John Briggs, New Delhi, 1981, vol. III, p. 1.

a moat, were completed in 1565, as were the forts of Shāhdrug, Dhārwar, Shāhanūr and Bankapūr.

In the citadel an assembly hall, the Gagan Maḥal [Ill. 158], once adorned with carved woodwork, was constructed. Its large central arch and the two narrower flanking arches have the same shape earlier introduced in the Jāmi' Mosque of Gulbarga. The bracket used on this monument is a fish, head down, with eyes and gill-covers and scales on the body, the round medallion supported on the tail. Such fish banners are still shown during Muḥarram celebrations in Hyderābād, where their possession was a coveted distinction in earlier times.[5] Muḥammad also built several small hunting villas in the village of Kumatgi, near Bījāpūr, on the walls of which some interesting paintings may be seen. But the most famous building of the reign is the Jāmi' Mosque(1576).

The next important ruler was 'Alī's nephew, who succeeded to the throne as Ibrāhīm II (1580-1627), and who ruled during the difficult period when the Mughals began to play a more important part in Deccan affairs. The loss of Berār in 1595 and the defeat of his own army at Sonepur shocked Ibrāhīm into making an alliance with Akbar, which was finalized by giving his own daughter in marriage to Akbar's son, the Viceroy of Berār. The sultan decided that from now on he would withdraw from further involvement in Deccan politics. Among the great monuments of the age of Ibrāhīm are the superb Mehtar Maḥal gateway and the Ibrāhīm Rawza, intended as the tomb of the sultan.

Ibrāhīm passed on to his son and successor, Muḥammad, a city which was a great centre of learning and culture. Bījāpūr was the home of the famous Muslim historian Muḥammad Kāsim Ferishta and the site of one of the most amazing monuments in the whole Islamic world, the Tomb of Muḥammad, known as the Gol Gumbad, the largest space ever covered by a single dome.

Two more contestants in the Deccan power struggle became a further threat during Muḥammad's final days. In addition to the Mughals, who finally forced Muḥammad to pay tribute in 1636, the Marathas, under Shivājī, defeated the Bījāpūr army in 1656 and annexed part of the 'Ādil Shāhī Sultanate. 'Alī II was compelled to pay tribute and to cede land both to the Mughals and the Marathas.

In 1672 'Alī II died and was succeeded by the last sultan of the line, Sikandar, a boy of five, who managed to continue ruling the weakened state for another fourteen years. In 1686 the 'Ādil Shāhī garrison finally surrendered to the great Mughal leader, Aurangzīb, who eventually conquered Bījāpūr, leaving only the Quṭb Shāhī Sultanate as an independent territory in the Deccan.

According to inscriptions there may have been more than three hundred mosques built during the 'Ādil Shāhī dynasty in Bījāpūr. Most of these are not congregational mosques and consist of either three or six bays with three arched façade entrances and no court.

The earliest datable mosque of the 'Ādil Shāhī period is Yūsuf's Old Jāmi' Mosque (1512) built during the reign of Ismā'īl.[6] Several features are seen here which are to become characteristic of the entire 'Ādil Shāhī period: the three façade arches are of varying widths; the central arch is wider than the two flanking it; the "Bījāpūr" dome sits on a high circular drum and like a bud springs out of a band of lotus petals; and at the corners, rather than minarets there now appear small crowned pavilions.

[5]John Burton-Page, "Bijapur," *Marg,* vol. XXXVII, no. 3, p. 63.

[6]*Epigraphia Indo-Moslemica, 1909-10,* p. 56; *Annual Report of Indian Epigraphy, 1964-5,* D 62.

Yūsuf's Old Jāmi' Mosque is built of poor quality plastered rubble, probably an indication that the early 'Ādil Shāhīs used few foreign masons and did not build with ashlar masonry until after the reign of 'Alī I, when the rulers acquired new wealth upon the defeat of the Hindu Kingdom of Vijayanagar in 1565.

By the mid-sixteenth century various devices are being used to emphasize the passage to the *miḥrāb.* The most common of these is the wider or more heavily decorated central arch. Another method to accent the central aisle also becomes popular about this time. The plan of Ibrāhīm's Old Jāmi' Mosque, the Mosque of Ā'īn al-Mulk and the Mosque of Ikhlās Khān does not change but in each the dome on a drum is replaced by other features. Ibrāhīm's Old Jāmi' Mosque has a tall *mīnār* over each of the piers flanking the central arch of the façade. The Mosque of Ā'īn al-Mulk instead has two small *chhatris* over the central piers, and four engaged *mīnārs* at the corners. The Mosque of Ikhlās Khān also has two brick minarets over the piers flanking the central arch and, in addition, a two-storeyed *chhatri* on the roof over the *miḥrāb,* instead of the usual dome.

Curiously the contemporary Tomb of Ā'īn al-Mulk has a splendid dome, although the accompanying mosque does not. It is not clear why architects and craftsmen of the mid-sixteenth century, although quite capable of constructing structurally sound domes, refused (or were forbidden) to do so.

In Ibrāhīm II's reign the rubble and plaster material used in construction was replaced by finely worked ashlar masonry. The Mosque of Malika Jahān Begam, wife of Ibrāhīm II, is the earliest ashlar structure and has complex vegetal, geometric and calligraphic ornament.

In addition to an hemispherical dome which springs out of a band of petals, the mosque is the first in Bījāpūr to have attached to the front corners two slim turrets, here ornamental appendages and not functional minarets. The turrets become an actual part of the mosque and their decoration is standardized, with leaves engirdling the shaft at different levels, as balconies once did, and with a bud at the crown. Hanging stone chains adorn the cornice, a device which later develops into the elaborate decoration of the Kālī Mosque in Lakshmeswar.

The Andā Mosque (1608)[7] [Ill. 159] is the only known example of a mosque built on the upper storey of a monument. The ground storey has no *miḥrāb* and was probably designated as a resthouse or *sarā'ī,* although it has been suggested that it might also have been intended for ladies.[8] The seclusion of women in Islam might indeed make a mosque on an upper level attractive.

In plan the Andā Mosque has the usual three bays and triple-arched façade plus an open terrace and a small court on the upper storey, which is also more ornate than the structure on the lower level. The dome of the mosque is melon-shaped and ribbed, the first of its kind in Bījāpūr. Four minarets, also with fluted domes, spring from the four roof corners, and there is a group of four minarets at the back over the *miḥrāb.*

While the Andā Mosque is situated on the upper storey of a structure, the Mosque of Afẓal Khān (1659) in the suburbs of Bījāpūr is an actual two-storeyed mosque with a *miḥrāb* in the *qibla* wall of both storeys, indicating that both levels were used for prayer. In Ākkalkot, in Gulbarga District, there is a small mosque, the Chhotī Mosque, with just one bay and one arched entrance passage, the only example of a mosque

[7]*Epigraphia Indo-Moslemica, 1909-10,* p. 59; *Annual Report of Indian Epigraphy, 1964-5,* D 275.

[8]Henry Cousens, *Notes on the Buildings and Other Antiquarian Remains at Bijapur,* Bombay, 1890, pp. 77-78.

built with this plan.

The small Mehtar Maḥal Mosque (1620) is built in the same plan with three bays and would pass without notice were it not for its famed Mehtar Maḥal gateway [Ill. 160], a tall square tower with two slender buttress-like minarets at the front corners, each with upper floors, balconies and oriel windows. The balconies are supported by very finely carved stone brackets made in imitation of woodwork [Ill. 161]. The stone used for the construction of the Mehtar Maḥal gateway is not the usual locally found trap, but a laminar limestone known as Kurnool limestone, found near Talikota, noted for its finely grained and hard texture, thereby allowing the intricate carving found on the perforated brackets.

Many stories circulate as to why this exquisite monument is called "Sweepers Gateway." The most convincing of these is the tale of the poor sweeper who was suddenly endowed with wealth and who, in bewilderment and thanks, built this small mosque and gateway, which took on the name of its patron.

The Mecca Mosque is dated to the reign of 'Alī II but the minarets of this monument are probably the only remaining parts of a very early mosque. On the east side a saint is buried, who, it is said, built the mosque about the end of the thirteenth century. The early structure was probably pulled down to erect the later monument on the same site and could perhaps have been the Jāmi' Mosque of the citadel in which Yusuf introduced the Shī'ā doctrine. During the very early years of Islam in India Muslims did not use Hindu temple material exclusively, as they were to do later, often finding their own material. The minarets of the Mecca Mosque attached to the corners of the eastern façade are built of rough simple bricks, probably by unskilled hands. The brackets here were of wood, supporting wooden balconies, pieces of which still remain. The minarets have spiral staircases rebuilt with stone as far as the roof. Beyond that level stone was not necessary and the old brick and wooden remains were left intact. The new mosque is said to have been built for ladies of the royal household, perhaps the reason why such a heavy enclosing wall was constructed all around. The Mecca Mosque has no *mimbar,* since in women's mosques there is none and no sermon is given since no man is allowed entry.

The plan followed for congregational mosques in Bījāpūr is that of the conventional hypostyle. But the Jāmi' Mosque (1576) [Ill. 162] is the only mosque in the Bījāpūr built in this orthodox plan, with a square court and one-bayed arcades on the north and south sides and probably an intended third on the eastern side had the mosque been finished as planned.

The monument is the largest religious structure in the Deccan, apparently intended as a memorial of the great victory of the Battle of Talikota in 1565, when the combined forces of the Deccan Muslim Sultanates defeated the great Hindu King Rāma Rājā of Vijayanagar. No monument of such dimensions had ever been built before, and it probably shows the wealth and power of the 'Ādil Shāhī Sultanate at this time. And every Deccan monarch up to and including Aurangzīb, who built the eastern gateway, contributed something to it. Strangely, the structure was never completely finished for only buttresses appear where tall minarets should have been, and there are no merlons to form a parapet to the façade.

Each of the arcades facing the court has arched openings [Ill. 163]. The prayer hall is divided into nine by five domed bays, those under the dome remaining open. The twelve surrounding piers support the dome, which is itself supported by an original vaulting system of two intersecting squares of arches running across the square hall between the piers and joining to form an octagonal space under the dome. This ingenious method of constructing the zone of transition, seen here for the first time will be used again in the much larger dome of the Gol Gumbad.[9] The large hemispherical dome is raised on a square clerestory and is crowned by a crescent, a device used frequently by the 'Ādil Shāhīs.

The central lobed *miḥrāb* (1636) is dated to the reign of Muḥammad,[10] and is covered with gilded paintings of tombs, minarets, censers, chains, niches with books, vases flowers, bands and medallions bearing inscriptions [Ill. 164]. Muḥammad's fondness for painting is certainly clear, although he confined himself here to subject-matter acceptable in a religious monument.

How, after two centuries of using other mosque plans in the Deccan, did the traditional hypostyle plan find its way back to Bījāpūr? Judging by the simplicity of his own tomb, 'Alī appears to have been an austere Muslim and it is not unlikely that he sought a return to the orthodox plan of early Islam.

Many tombs of the 'Ādil Shāhī sultans of Bījāpūr follow a plan not found earlier in Bahmānī or Barīdī tomb architecture. The new feature, to be used later for the most famous 'Ādil Shāhī structure, the Ibrāhīm Rawza, is a single or double arcade surrounding the square tomb chamber. The first royal memorial structure in Bījāpūr, the Tomb of 'Alī I (d.1580-81) is built on this plan, a tomb chamber surrounded by an arcade of five pointed arches on each side, the two end arches with wider spans than the three intermediate. The tomb also indicates that 'Ālī I thought little of his own glorification, since the structure is quite plain, the sultan probably intending it to have an austere look. Craftsmen were certainly available for their efforts are seen in the contemporary Jāmi' Mosque.

The Tomb of 'Alī I marks the beginning of another new trend, the burial of sultans in Bījāpūr, for the earlier 'Ādil Shāhī sultans had chosen Gogī, a distance from the capital, as the site of their final resting place. 'Alī built his tomb in the south-west part of Bījāpūr, inside the city walls, an unusual practice since tombs generally lie outside the city walls. The Bahmānī rulers followed this scheme first in Gulbarga, where the early royal tombs are south of the fort, the later ones east of the city, and in Bīdar some kilometres east of the city walls. The Barīdī sultans chose the western suburbs of Bīdar for their tombs. Up to this time the only tombs within city walls had been those of holy men. Perhaps this is the explanation of 'Alī's choice of site, since he presumably wished to be buried near the saint he venerated, for whom he built the Mosque and Tomb of Ḥazrat Sayyid 'Alī Shāhid Pīr. The mosque of this complex is of great interest due to the wagon-vaulted ceiling which covers the entire structure, the only such known example in Bījāpūr. The sanctuary is divided into three sections by two transverse arches which project slightly from the surface.

The Tomb of Ibrāhīm II (d.1626) [Ill. 165] also follows the new arrangement. This momument belongs to a group of complexes, a tomb, a mosque and a tank built on a plinth within a square enclosure, known as a *rawza.* The Ibrāhīm Rawza [Plan 22] lies a short distance west of Bījāpūr. An inscription over the door of the tomb gives the date of its construction as 1626 and states that the structure was intended as a tomb for Ibrāhīm's wife, Tāj Sultāna, but instead Ibrāhīm, dying before his wife, was buried

[9]E. Schotten Merklinger, "Possible Seljuk Influence on the Dome of the Gol Gumbad," *East and West,* vol. XXVIII, nos.1-4, 1978, pp. 257-61.

[10]*Epigraphia Indo-Moslemica, 1909-10,* p. 59.

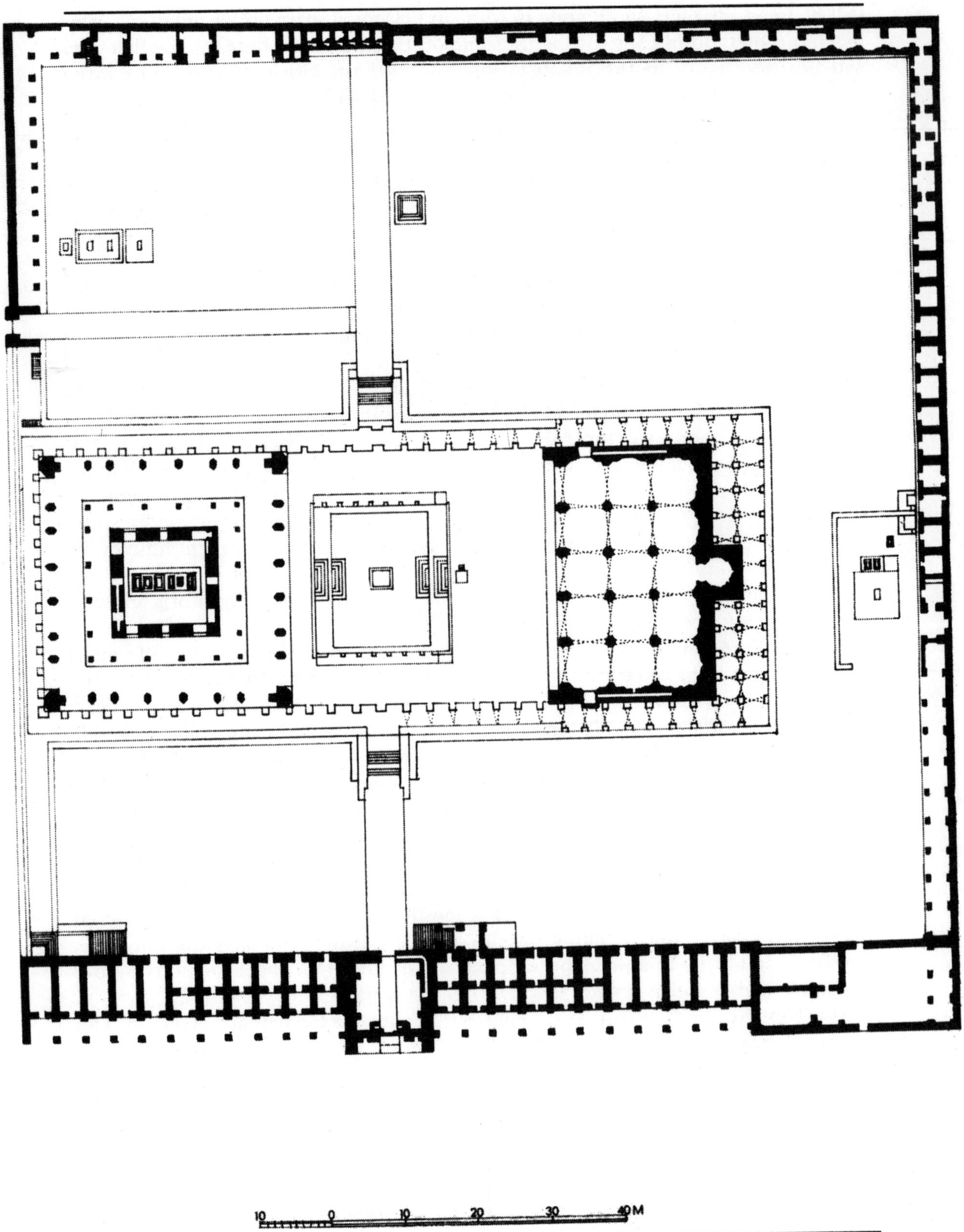

Plan 22. Bījāpūr, Ibrāhīm Rawza (after H. Cousens)

here.[11]

The two large structures set on a plinth face each other with a tank between them. The tomb on the east side is square and has a doorway flanked by fanlight windows originally fitted with masonry screens. It is surrounded by a pillared arcade of seven pointed arches [Ill. 166], the penultimate on each side narrower than the rest. The exterior walls on the tomb are elaborately decorated with shallow tracery of arabesques and interlaced extracts from the *Qur'ān*. The elegant dome is set in lotus pedals [Ill. 167].

The interior has a remarkable flat stone ceiling, which appears to be hanging, but is, in fact, composed of stone slabs set edge to edge and placed in strong mortar, the only support which binds them. Both the tomb and the mosque are noted for their deep cornices and their minarets. Under the cornice of the mosque are remnants of heavy chains with pendents each carved out of a single block of stone [Ill. 168].

The plan of having a tomb, a mosque on the western side and a cistern situated together on a plinth became very popular and was copied by royalty and ministers for their memorial structures. In Afẓalpur, Gulbarga District, there is another *rawza* of the mid-seventeenth century built with a similar plan by the famous Bījāpūr minister, Afẓal Khān. From about this time, there is another *rawza* in Bījāpūr constructed by the same minister, who apparently finished the mosque in his lifetime. The tomb remained unfinished when Afẓal Khān was apparently ordered away on the fatal expedition against Shivājī at Pratāpgad, where he lost his life. Astrologers told him that he would not return and the minister was so impressed by their predictions that he prepared for death, inscribing the date on his cenotaph and drowning his sixty-four wives. The mosque is unusual for being the only two-storeyed mosque in Bījāpūr, although it is not clear whether the upper storey was intended for the *zanāna*.

A very similar tomb with a surrounding arcade was built for Pīr Shaykh Hamīd Qādirī and Shaykh Latīf Allāh Qādirī, two ṣūfī saints who lived in Bījāpūr during the reign of Ibrāhīm II. The structure, however, is incomplete, since the arcade was only finished on the western and northern sides.

The Tomb of Jahān Begam (d.1660), wife of Muhammad, is another square structure surrounded by a double arcade, each side pierced with three pointed arches. The monument is a replica of the Gol Gumbad in size and design but the four central facade arches are left open here. There remains some doubt as to who is actually buried within, since two wives of Muḥammad lie beside him in the Gol Gumbad. Jahān Begam, if indeed she was a wife, must have been the third.

The huge unfinished Tomb of 'Alī II (d.1672) [Ill. 169] is also a square structure surrounded by a double arcade each of seven arches. In addition, there are some lesser known tombs which follow the same plan as the Tomb of Shāh Nawāz Khān and Ḥajjī Ḥasan.

Not all tombs built during the 'Ādil Shāhī period are constructed in the new plan. The old tradition was continued in several lesser known tombs in Bījāpūr, for instance the Tomb of Shāh 'Alī Ḥusayn with its dome almost hidden by wall cresting. The Tomb of Muḥammad Ḥusayni and the Tomb of Fātima, Ibrāhīm II's wet nurse, are all of simple proportions with arched openings or recessed arched panels on each side.

The most famous and majestic Bījāpūr monument following the simple square

[11] *Annual Report of Indian Epigraphy, 1964-5*, D 310.

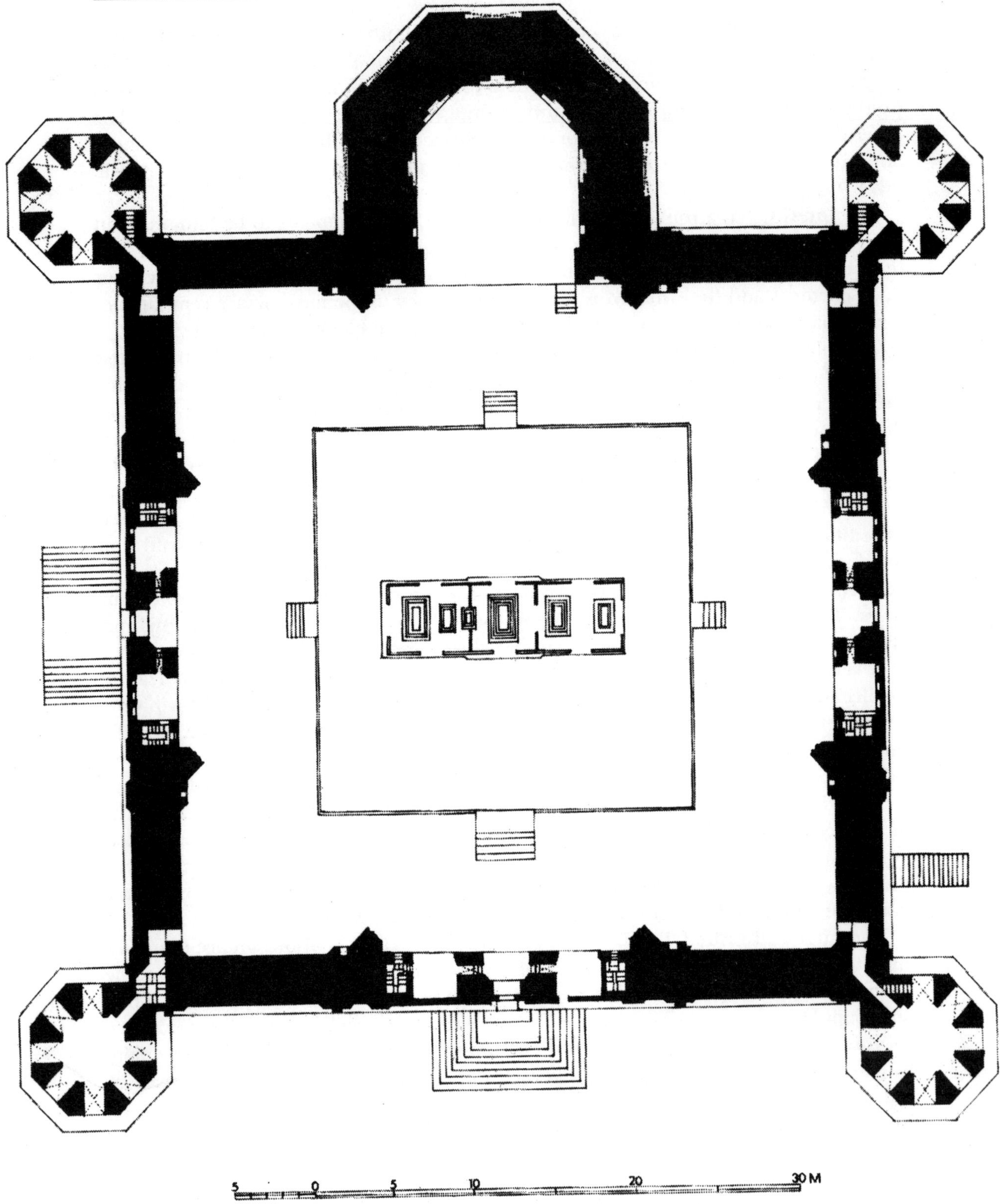

Plan 23. Bījāpūr, Gol Gumbad

plan is the Tomb of Muḥammad (d.1656) known as the Gol Gumbad [Ill. 170] [Plan 23]. A large hemispherical dome crowns the structure, with walls 60.35 m. in height, not including the once gilded finial on the dome top measuring over 2 m. The dome, built of bricks laid flat in lime mortar, is a rigid concrete shell with no voussoirs or lateral thrusts, resting, as it were, dead weight on the mass of masonry formed by the pendentives, each acting as a tie to the other, keeping the whole structure in equilibrium. This great dome, the largest curved space ever constructed, is supported internally by arches in intersecting squares, as in the Jāmi' Mosque. An engaged octagonal turret with seven open storeys and crowned by the usual Bījāpūr dome is located at each corner, with a winding interior staircase leading to each corner of the tower and to the flat roof between the corners and the dome. From here there is a passage through the thickness of the dome into the whispering gallery around the dome interior. The great cornice is supported by four tiers of brackets.

In the interior, on a raised platform in the centre of the mausoleum under the dome, are the cenotaphs of a grandson of Sultan Muḥammad, his younger wife, Arus Bībī, the sultan himself, his favourite mistress, Rhumba, his daughter, and his older wife, in this order from east to west. The real graves, as in nearly all Indian Muslim tombs, are in the crypt below.

The Athar Maḥal or Palace of Relics in Bījāpūr was constructed during the reign of Muḥammad. The monument claims no architectural distinction looking like a "great rectangular box laid over on its side, its lid open, and front turned towards the east".[12] Yet, it is one of the most sacred structures in Bījāpūr, since it is believed to enshrine two hairs from the Prophet's beard.

The interest in the monument is in the mural paintings in the interior which show floral arrangements in vases and urns, as well as petals, leaves and stems separately. There is also a room with some damaged figures which appear to be western imitations of oriental court life, perhaps done by Italian artists in the employ of Muḥammad, who had little knowledge of even the manners, customs and traditions of the Orient.[13] The artists simply painted Europeans and dressed them, as far as they were able, in Indian attire. The interest is not so much in the subject-matter, unusual as it was, but in the fact that they were allowed at all at this time in a sacred monument. It comes as no surprise, then, that the fanatical Aurangzīb is said to have been so enraged at seeing such paintings on the walls of a religious structure that he ordered the faces of all figures to be destroyed. The intolerant Mughal emperor was so enfuriated with the liberal religious climate of Bījāpūr that he could not rest until he had subdued this heretical Muslim Sultanate of the Deccan.

* * *

The old fort and city of Rāichūr are in the doab, the interfluvial area between the River Krishna and its principal tributary, the Tungabhadra.[14] For more than a hundred years the doab became a prize coveted by both the Muslim states of the Deccan and the Kingdom of Vijayanagar and it was not until after the defeat of the Hindū state in 1565 that the area was permanently joined to the 'Ādil Shāhī Sultanate, where it remained for over a century.

[12] H. Cousens, *Bijapur: The Old Capital of the Adil Shahi Kings*, Poona, 1923, p. 28.

[13] E. Scholten Merklinger, *Indian Islamic Architecture, The Decean 1347-1686*, p. 105.

[14] E. Schotten Merklinger, "The Mosques of Raichur: A Preliminary Classification," *Kunst des Orients*, vol. XII, nos. 1/2, pp. 79-94.

The fortress of Rāichūr was built in 1294, a date which coincides with the first Muslim incursions into the Deccan. The Muslim invaders reached Rāichūr in 1310 on their way south to capture Gulbarga in 1313. The history of Rāichūr in the following years is not known but it was probably included in the Delhi Sultanate during Muḥammad Tughluq's reign and by 1327, the founding of Vijayanagar, it was an important town. When the Bahmānī Sultanate declared its independence in 1347, Rāichūr was included in the province of Gulbarga. Of the inscriptions found in Rāichūr none bears a date earlier than the establishment of the Bījāpūr Sultanate in 1490. But parts of two monuments in Rāichūr Fort may belong to an earlier period.

The Ek Mīnār kī Mosque was built according to an inscription over the main entrance in the early sixteenth century during the reign of the second 'Ādil Shāhī ruler, Ismā'īl.[15] But the single minaret standing in the south east corner of the court appears to be an earlier structure [Ill. 171]. It was perhaps intended, like its great predecessor in Delhi, to serve a double purpose, as a victory tower and as a minaret for the use of the *mu'azzin.* The Rāichūr minaret consists of two storeys each with windows and surrounded with projecting balconies girded with stone balustrades, no doubt a later addition. Crowning it is an hemispherical dome in the Bahmānī style. A winding staircase leads to the top storey.

The curious plan of having one minaret standing detached from the prayer hall is a very old one, having been first used in the Mosque of al-Mutawakkil at Samārrā in the mid-ninth century, where it stands about 27 m. from the north wall. In the Mosque of Abū Dulūf in Samārrā, another freestanding minaret stands almost 10m. outside the north wall of the mosque enclosure.[16] In the later ninth century Ibn Tulun copied these Mesopotamian examples in his mosque in Cairo.

The design of the Rāichūr minaret resembles that of the two minarets that frame the eastern wall of the Mecca Mosque in Bījāpūr, probably built in the early fourteenth century, when Malik Kafūr, the great general of 'Alā' al-Dīn Khaljī, invaded south India. The Ek Mīnār probably dates from the same time.

The Daftari Mosque erected in 1498-99[17] of Hindu temple material is the first dated mosque of Rāichūr. A domed entrance leads to the court and prayer hall with a dome on an octagonal drum, resting on lintels and brackets supported on stone pillars. The prayer hall has three rows of four Chalukyan-type pillars which support a flat ceiling. The façade is decorated with a battlemented parapet and a cornice.

The only other mosque inscription before the Battle of Talikota belongs to the Ek Mīnār kī Masjid. It is entered from the south, through a flat-roofed gateway supported on eight Chalukyan-type temple pillars.

Mosque styles appear not to have changed immediately after the battle of Talikota, and earlier plans were apparently used until the end of the sixteenth century. The Jāmi' Mosque in Rāichūr Fort built twelve years after the Battle of Talikota in 1577-78[18] is in a hypostyle plan. It has two entrances, one on the east side, and the other on the south side, which appear to be the *maṇḍapa* of a temple, the flat roof supported on six stone Chalukyan-type pillars with square base and cruciform capitals. The prayer hall has three rows of four stone pillars supporting a flat ceiling.

One further mosque was built in this period. The Kālī Mosque, situated at the foot

[15]*Epigraphia Indo-Moslemica, 1962,* pp.61-62; *Annual Report of Indian Epigraphy, 1958-9,* D 141.

[16]K.A.C. Creswell, *Early Muslim Architecture*, Harmondsworth, 1958, p. 285.

[17]*Epigraphia Indo-Moslemica, 1962,* pp. 61-62.

[18]Ibid., *1963,* pp. 66, 72-75; *Annual Report of Indian Epigraphy, 1958-9,* D 136.

of the hill, is constructed of four Chalukyan-type black basalt pillars supporting a flat roof. The parapet is of simple arch heads with a row of brick moulding and corner finials below.

Two mosques belong to the last period of construction in Rāichūr. The large Jāmi' Mosque in Sarrāf Bāzār and the small Chowk Mosque both use a combination of Hindu temple pillars and arches. The Chowk Mosque is the final development of the Rāichūr style, since it has a dome supported on pendentives, a feature common on Bījāpūr but the only example found in Rāichūr. It is a three-bayed mosque with two temple pillars added to support a flat roof. This arrangement is the reverse of the usual mosque plan where the pillars are used to support the roof, and where the prayer hall has a screen thrown across to impress the worshipper with the force of Islam.

The Jāmi' Mosque in the Sarrāf Bāzār is dated by an inscription over the main gate to 1628-29[19] and to the reign of Muḥammad. Although use is still being made of temple pillars and a flat ceiling, this monument is larger and has a *maqsūra* composed of eleven arches supported on piers. The mosque therefore resembles the contemporary structures of Bījāpūr. The brackets supporting the *chhajja* are similar to those of other seventeenth century 'Ādil Shāhī mosques.

The early monuments in Rāichūr reveal that they were built by Hindu craftsmen who did not really understand Islamic structural methods and constructed, as they had in Delhi in the thirteenth century, in the only way they knew how, using the lintel-and-beam system with corbelled domes and Hindu columns.

In the seventeenth century the style changes. The Jāmi' Mosque in the Sarrāf Bāzār and Chowk Mosque show characteristics which lead to the conclusion that masons and architects were probably sent to Rāichūr from Bījāpūr. Although they could not construct mosques entirely in the Bījāpūr style, at least the façades, minarets, domes and the *maqsūra* were imitated.

* * *

Golkondā was the capital of a rich and powerful state ruled by the Quṭb Shāhī sultans between 1512 and 1687, when it, the last independent Sultanate of the Deccan, was finally annexed to the mighty Mughal Empire. Qulī Quṭb Shāh, founder of the dynasty, was a great military leader, who rose to power during the confusion which finally toppled the enfeebled Bahmānī Sultanate. The legacy he left to his successors was a strongly fortified citadel and a capital city with many splendid structures. Quṭb was a devout Shī'ā who attempted to introduce this doctrine as the state religion.

From the mid-sixteenth century on the Golkondā Sultanate was at the height of its power. Muḥammad Qulī Quṭb decided to change the capital from crowded Golkondā to Hyderābād, and made it his new administrative capital. The Chār Mīnār, a monumental gateway built at the crossing of the four principal streets, became the centre of the new chief city. From now onwards all government affairs were conducted in Hyderābād, although fortified Golkondā remained the commercial centre for the diamond industry.

By 1600, with the fall of Aḥmadnagar to the Mughals, only the 'Ādil Shāhī and Quṭb Shāhī Sultanates remained independent and able to fight their powerful adversary, the Mughal Emperors. A last period of peace and prosperity prevailed

[19]*Epigraphia Indo-Moslemica, 1963,* p. 76; *Annual Report of Indian Epigraphy, 1958,* D 147.

during the reign of Muḥammad Qulī Quṭb (1612-26) but with the accession of the next ruler, Abdullāh Quṭb (1626-72), the inevitable downfall of the dynasty began.

The last independent Sultanate of the Deccan was finally conquered in 1687 by Aurangzīb, who destroyed its impregnable fortress and most of its monuments. The only Quṭb Shāhī structures extant today around the former capital are a group of seven royal tombs and some small mosques and gates set in formal gardens, northwest of Golkondā.[20]

The architectural style of the Golkondā monuments is based on Bahmānī prototypes with more ornate stucco decoration. Most of the tombs are square double-storeyed structures situated on plinths, with the lower storeys extended by an arcaded verandah. The upper part generally has crenellated parapets with small turrets encircled by miniature arcaded galleries at the corners. The turrets are octagonal and crowned by cupolas rising from a band of lotus petals. Projecting cornices covered in stucco ornament are supported on brackets. The tombs are all crowned by a type of bulbous double-dome on a high drum also encircled by bands of petals.

The Tomb of Abdullāh (d.1672) [Ill. 172] is the most typical of the group. A massive two-storeyed monument, it has an upper storey crowned with a hanging balcony decorated with pierced panels and topped by finials and a parapet. The bulbous dome springs from a band of petal ornament on a high drum.

Other royal mausolea in Golkondā belong to Qulī Quṭb al-Mulk (d.1543), Ibrāhīm (d.1580), Muḥammad Qulī (d.1612), Muḥammad (d.1626) and his queen, Ḥayāt Bakhshī Begam (d.1667). The Tomb of Jamshīd (d.1550) [Ill. 173], the second Quṭb Shāhī ruler, has an octagonal plan and is divided in half by a balcony supported on Hindū-type brackets on two levels.

* * *

The city of Hyberābād was founded in 1591 when Muḥammad Qulī transferred the Quṭb Shāhī capital from Golkondā to a site 11 km west on the right side of the River Musi. Muḥammad Qulī loved great architecture and constructed many monuments in Hyderabad which show the Quṭb Shāhī style at its best. In addition to mosques, he built schools, hospitals, caravansarais and palaces and he tried to encourage the noblemen of his court to also give architectural patronage.

The finest civil structure in Hyderābād if not in all of India is the Chār Mīnār built in 1591 to serve as a triumphal archway to the royal palace, like the Tīn Darwāza in Aḥmadābād. The square structure has an arched opening in each of its four sides. Above there are two encircling arcades supported on carved brackets. A small arcaded

[20]In 1979 I spent time in Andhra Pradesh to visit sites where Quṭb Shāhī monuments supposedly existed according to inscriptions and old Gazetteers. While I did not manage to visit all the sites, I did track down a number of forgotten monuments. Foremost among these sites are Deverakonda, about 50 km south-west of Nalgonda, Elgandal, Komatur, Medak, Indol, and Patancheru. In Deverakonda are three monuments. By far the most interesting is the Shrine of Ḥajji Muḥammad Qādirī, an obviously early building built of Hindu temple spoils and *jālī* screens with cresting of an arch-head type. A *chhatri* tomb standing in the middle of a walled enclosure resembles those found in the Delhi area, as in Hauz Khas. There are also a mosque and a tomb with engrailed arches of probably a later date. In Elgandal there is a splendid mosque on top of the fort, a quite ornate structure with good minarets. There is also a smaller mosque in ruins in the fort below. Outside the fort area is an *'īdgāh* with very fine stucco decoration. In Bodhan, the Deval Mosque is a converted Hindu temple built on a temple site. There is another splendid Quṭb Shāhī mosque in Komatur probably of the sixteenth century, with a single hall and a triple arched façade, with two high minarets. It is built of ashlar to the *chhajja* and above that of brick and mortar. In Patancheru are two Quṭb Shāhī mosques with very good stucco work.

balcony and a pierced stone screen rise above the roof level. At each corner of the building is a tall *mīnār*, between which is a double arcaded balcony at roof level finished by two additional arcaded balconies. Each *mīnār* is crowned by a bulbous dome with petals at the base. The entire roof is open and has a small mosque at the west end. Near the Chār Mīnār are four wide arches built over four roads, called the Chār Kamān. From a balcony erected here, the Sultan watched the manoeuvres of his troops and gave audience to the people.

The Jāmi' Mosque built in 1597 by Muḥammad Qulī (1580-1612) near the Chār Mīnār has a double-aisled prayer hall overlooking the court. In the interior, large arches spring from heavy pillars to support the roof. Two rows each of seven arches, one above the other, complete the court façade. The lower seven openings, which cover the entire height of the façade, lead to the interior, while the upper arches are added for ornament. A cornice supported on brackets crowns the façade along with an ornamented parapet. At the two corners are circular pillars surmounted by short square turrets shaped like miniature tombs.

The famous Mecca Mosque is another congregational mosque which can accommodate over ten thousand worshippers. Its construction was started during the reign of Muḥammad Quṭb in 1617, but the work could not be completed by his successor due to Aurangzīb's Deccan campaigns. The three-bayed prayer hall has five by three bays, all domed except the central bay, which has a pointed vault. Intersecting arches spring from tall columns. The five-arched façade is crowned by a cornice supported on brackets. The northern and southern end are surmounted by two domes. Aurangzīb added two unusual minarets in front of the main entrance gate. Flanking the façade are two turrets surmounted by pillared kiosks and bulbous domes.

* * *

The Niẓām Shāhī dynasty, founded by Aḥmad Niẓām al-Mulk in 1490, ruled over the north-western provinces of the Bahmānī Sultanate for about a century and a half. Aḥmadnagar fell to Akbar in the year 1600 but two excellent statesmen, Malik Ambar and his son, managed to continue a form of independence for another four decades.

The Niẓām Shāhī sultans, as most other Muslim rulers in the Deccan, took an interest in art and architecture and were responsible for the construction of a number of interesting mosques, tombs and palaces in the newly founded city of Aḥmadanagar and in the less important neighbouring towns of Daulatābād and Khuldābād. Unfortunately, the Niẓām Shāhī sultans still await their architectural historian and very little of their activities in this sphere is known. It has even been felt that the architecture of the Niẓām Shāhīs was a poor relation to the magnificent monuments of Bījāpūr and Golkondā and that these rulers were more interested in laying out gardens around their monuments than in developing an elaborate system of ornament. Of the royal palaces little is left in the fort of Aḥmadnagar, where most of the structures were supposedly razed to the ground by the British. The surviving monuments in the fort and city were altered to make them suitable for the military.

The architectural style of the Niẓām Shāhīs, as that of the other states which evolved out of the former Bahmānī Sultanate, was based on the Bīdar monuments of the Bahmānīs. But the forms soon changed and the Nizām Shāhī style developed a character of its own based on indigenous sources and on the forms of Mālwā and Gujarat. The influence may best be noted in the building material and decoration.

Few original mosques remain, but it appears that they resemble the mosques of Berar rather than Bījāpūr or Golkondā. In general, the mosques are built on high plinths and have engaged square towers at the front corner. The roof of the prayer hall consists of one or more central dome and four *mīnārs* crowned by domed kiosks at the four corners. The most interesting feature of the Niẓām Shāhī mosques is a flying arch placed centrally above the roof on small *mīnārs*. This unique feature was originally used in structures with no central dome and was apparently designed to simulate the outlines of a dome.

Unfortunately, very little of great interest remains in the city of Aḥmadnagar, built in 1494 in the centre of the Niẓām Shāhī Sultanate. There are two monuments which may indicate what treasures sixteenth century Aḥmadnagar held. The earlier structure is the Tomb of Aḥmad Niẓām Shāh (d.1508), an ornately decorated monument situated in a walled enclosure.

The best example of a Nizām Shāhī mosque is the Damrī Mosque [Ill. 174] constructed by either Sāhir Khān or Shīr Khān, the two leading stone cutters then working on the Aḥmadnagar fort. It is locally told that the patron collected a small coin called *damaḍī* from the labourers and used the funds to build this mosque.

The mosque is small and is built of dry dressed ashlar masonry. It consists of a prayer hall of three by two bays with three arched openings on the north, west and south sides. The flat roof is supported on arches springing from octagonal bases. The prayer hall façade has a deep cornice on brackets encircling it and at each corner a square decorated tower used as a base for a slender minaret with an ornamental balcony. The battlemented parapet has double trefoil merlons. From the middle of the parapet wall spring square ornamented piers carrying two slender domed *mīnārs* which enclose a flying arc, where ordinarily a dome would have been placed. The side walls have two recessed arched windows and in the rear wall are three *miḥrābs* inscribed with *Qur'ānic* texts.

Tombs of the Nizām Shāhī sultans in Aḥmadnagar for the most part follow the design of later Bahmānī tombs, but with a more original treatment of wall surfaces and arch shapes. In plan most tombs are square with an hemispherical dome.

The first mausoleum, locally called Rūmī Khān's Tomb, was constructed in about the middle of the sixteenth century. Square in plan it is crowned by a large Lodī-type dome with four small flat-roofed kiosks at the corners and a parapet of trefoil merlons. The exterior walls are double-storeyed with pointed recessed arches. Dividing the two storeys is a series of string-courses and a band of blind merlon cresting. A high octagonal drum is extended upwards to form a battlemented octagonal terrace from which springs the circular drum supporting the fluted hemispherical dome. Of the corner lanterns only one remains.

The Tomb of Aḥmad[Ill. 175], the first Nizām Shāhī ruler (1490-1510), is one of the finest structure in Aḥmadnagar. Built of black stone, the square monument is crowned by an hemispherical dome. The façade has a row of large arched recesses framed in rectangular panels. A row of smaller arched niches, of varying designs, runs above it. Crowned by a cornice on brackets and a parapet of blind merlons punctuated by small finials, the monument in many features resembles a late Bahmānī structure.

The Tomb of Wakla has yet another design common in Bījāpūr and Golkondā. It consists of a domed double-storeyed square chamber surrounded by a verandah with five arches on each side.

*   *   *

Khuldābād, in Aurangābād District about 25km north-west of Aurangābād, is the burial ground of many saints who came to the Deccan as missionaries. The small town is known primarily for its two fourteenth century *dargāhs*, that of the Saint Zain al-Dīn and of Burhān al-Dīn Awliyā [Ill. 176]. There is also the sixteenth century Dargāh of Sayyid Rājī Qattāl. Around these *dargāhs* are the graves of many rulers of India, including that of the famous Mughal Emperor Aurangzīb. Here also are buried the later Niẓām Shāhī rulers and some of their ministers, as well as the last Quṭb Shāhī Sultan of Golkondā.

The last tomb of the Niẓām Shāhī dynasty is in Khuldābād. The Tomb of Malik Ambar (d.1626) [Ill. 177], who stemmed the tide of Mughal conquest in the Deccan while in the service of the Niẓām Shāhī sultans, has the same shape as other tombs but has exceptionally fine decoration on the exterior walls. The lower part has three cusped arches with ornamental niches carved on the piers at impost level, the upper part, nine narrow high arches. The middle arches on all four sides are filled with cusped and plain pierced arched masonry screens.

* * *

Fath Allāh Imād al-Mulk, governor of Berār under Muḥammad Bahmānī and his successors, declared his independence from the tottering Bahmānī Sultanate in 1490. He chose the Hindu fort of Gawilgarh, between the rivers Purna and Tāptī, as the citadel, and Elichpūr as the actual seat of government and capital of the new Imād Shāhī Sultanate. Gawilgarh consists of a strongly built fort pierced with ramparts and towers, one of which, the Burj-i Bahrām was built under the Niẓām Shāhīs to check Akbar's army.

Upon Imād al-Mulk's death in 1504, his son 'Alā' al-Dīn succeeded to the throne, but the Imād Shāhī dynasty did not long survive as a separate state, since Berār was conquered and annexed by the Niẓām Shāhī sultans of Aḥmadnagar in 1574, finally falling to the Mughal Emperors about two decades later. It is, therefore, not surprising that relatively few monuments were constructed during the short period of Imād Shāhī autonomy, which ended before the character of the architecture of the neighbouring states of Bījāpūr and Golkondā had even fully evolved. The fate of Berār was shared by the Niẓām Shāhī Sultanate of Aḥmadnagar, which lost part of its independence to the Mughals in 1600, yet managed to survive as a semi-autonomous region for another thirty-seven years.

During the short period of independence, the Imād Shāhī sultans constructed a number of palaces and mosques, mostly fallen into ruin or disappeared. Early surviving monuments remain only in Gawilgarh and Elichpūr, although, after the annexation of Berār by the Niẓām Shāhīs of Aḥmadnagar, minor monuments were also constructed in Fathkera, Malkapūr and Rohenker in Buldana district.

The extant Imād Shāhī buildings are all built of ashlar masonry and resemble the simple vigorous mosques of neighbouring Mālwā. Generally multi-domed and built on a high plinth, these monuments have engaged corner buttresses surmounted by either square *chhatris* or domed kiosks. Corner towers with simple geometric and floral decoration above the arcades are a distinctive feature of Berār architecture. The sides of the domed kiosks are filled with pierced masonry screens and are topped by a deep cornice on serpentine brackets, reminiscent of the Madrasa of Chanderī.

At the highest point of the Gawilgarh fort, Aḥmad Shāh Bahmānī originally built a Jāmi' Mosque, now in partial ruin but formerly a fine example of the local architecture.

Situated on a high plinth, the mosque consists of an open court surrounded by arcades on the north, south and east sides and a prayer hall on the west, with a large entrance gateway on the east side. The prayer hall was originally divided by square pillars into seven by three bays, of which only two front bays remain. The large central dome is supported on a circular drum and is decorated with a parapet of trefoil alternating with small domed finials. The seven arched openings of the court façade were flanked by two engaged *mīnārs* originally crowned by square kiosks filled with pierced masonry screens and crowned by a deep cornice supported on brackets. Of the two *mīnārs* only the one in the north-east corner remains. The only other façade decoration is a number of carved rosettes placed between the cornice brackets and on the arch spandrels. Traces of coloured tilework are noted on the monument.

Other surviving Imād Shāhī monuments are found in Elichpūr. The Jāmi' Mosque [Ill. 178] was extensively repaired in the reign of Aurangzīb but it has retained its Imād Shāhī character and resembles the Jāmi' Mosque of Gawilgarh.

The prayer hall is divided into four by eleven bays, the aisle nearest the façade originally crowned by eleven small domes. At the rear was a large central dome in front of the *miḥrāb*, which along with the other domes has collapsed. There are five *miḥrābs* in the *qibla* wall. In the arch spandels under the central dome are rosettes, which make up the only ornament.

The interest in the plan of the Jāmi' Mosque of Elichpūr is in the arrangement of its columns. Throughout, square double shafts support both squat and tall pointed arches. But the fourth and eighth dome in the façade aisle are supported by double sets of square columns. In addition, the double pillars originally supporting the large central dome are arranged to form a domed open space. Pointed arches spring from the eight surrounding pairs of pillars forming an octagon. Double columns were a Tughluq feature later used in Mālwā architecture. And the ingenious device of having a domed open space enclosed by an arched octagon in front of the *miḥrāb* dates back to the Mosque of Malik Mughīth in Māṇḍū.

The *'īdgāh* of Elichpūr [Ill. 179] was probably constructed in 1347. In plan, it is a wall mosque, with five recessed *miḥrābs*, crenellated at the top. At both corners, there are sloping towers crowned with double storeyed turrets. To the north of the central *miḥrāb*, there is an elevated domed *mimbar* in the shape of a square domed structure, pierced by three tall pointed arches on each side and encircled by a projecting cornice on brackets. It is crowned by a parapet but its original four corner finials have collapsed.

* * *

While most of the architecture of the Deccan dynasties was, of course, built at the capital cities, it comes as somewhat of a surprise to find quite a few structures of the period in outlying areas. Outside of Hyderābād and Golkondā, Quṭb Shāhī monuments, for instance, are found in such locations as Deverakoṇḍa, Tekmal(the Dargāh of Ḥusayn Pāshā)[Ill. 180], Elgandal, Komatur(the Jāmi' Mosque) [Ill. 181] and Patancheru. The same is true of the 'Ādil Shāhī dynasty where monuments are scattered over a large area and are found as far away as the Rāichūr doab, Dabhol, Dhārwār and Mysore. It must therefore be concluded that when the political climate was favourable, in the first half of the seventeenth century, the Deccan style of architecture as it developed in the capital cities was finally allowed to spread to some of the outposts of the Quṭb Shāhī and 'Ādil Shāhī Sultanates.

CHAPTER 14

Kashmīr (1339-1587)

Kashmīr came in contact with Muslim invaders for the first time in the eighth century, when two governors of Sind tried to invade the valley, but were able to reach only as far as the southern slopes of the Himalayas. Maḥmūd of Ghaznī was also unsuccessful in attempting to control the mountain kingdom in 1014 and in 1021. In the confusion following the Mongol withdrawal, Rinchana, son of the Tibetan Buddhist Ladhaki ruler, then living in Kashmīr, eventually did succeed in establishing Muslim rule. Under the influence of the Suhrawardī saint, Sayyid Sharaf al-Dīn, also known as Bulbul Shāh, Rinchana converted to Islam, took the name of Sadr al-Dīn and became the first sultan of Kashmīr. A real dynasty, however, was not established until 1339, when a Turkish soldier and adventurer, Shāh Mīr, ascended the throne with the title Sultan Shams al-Dīn. With him began the Shāh Mīr dynasty to rule in Kashmīr until 1561. Very little is known about Shams al-Dīn's successors, Jamshīd and 'Alā' al-Dīn. During the reign of the latter the capital was transferred to what is now Srinagar.

* * *

When the Muslims conquered Kashmīr in the fourteenth century they found a number of Hindu and Buddhist monuments, a few built of stone, but the majority almost of wood, the type of architecture associated principally with Muslim rule in Kashmīr. The mountains of Kashmīr have since ancient times been a continuous supply of timber. Unfortunately all early examples of the unusual early wooden building style have disappeared and it is only through later monuments that an idea of the early architecture may be formed.[1] Of the secular monuments there is only a brief reference to a wooden palace built by Zain al-'Ābidīn.

Kashmīrī masons working in wood used an old technique. A carefully squared log was placed horizontally on another, usually crosswise in the form of headers and stretchers, as in brickwork. In this method walls and piers for support were constructed, although pillars for carrying lighter loads were generally a single deodar tree trunk. The spaces between courses were filled with decorative brickwork or glazed tiles. The lack of sophistication in construction is also seen in the way logs were fastened to each other by a wooden pin, never a trace of joinery anywhere. There are no struts, trusses or even diagonal members for support, only dead weight supported by the mass below, a primitive system of construction borrowed from temple building. Furthermore, the brick insertions added extra weight to an otherwise already unstable system, and the structures often collapsed. Although the foundations of several

[1]Little is known about wooden architecture of Kashmīr. Brief descriptions may be found in Francois Bernier, *Travels in the Mughal Empire,* New Delhi, 1992; S. Lowenthal, "Some Persian Inscriptions Found in Srinagar," *JASB,* vol. XXXIII, Calcutta, 1864.

monuments of early Muslim rule remain, little or none of the superstructures have survived.

The typical wooden Kashmīrī monument is either a mosque or a tomb, the latter known as a *ziārat*, which often enshrines the remains of a saint. The design of mosques and tombs is identical and consists of a square structure in two or three storeys surmounted by a pyramidal roof projecting over the entire structure in three tiers. An additional element is added to the mosque between the roof apex and the spire, a square open pavilion for the *mu'azzin.* The waterproof roof covering generally consists of turf on birchbark laid on boards and supported in rafters, often enlivened with flowers such as irises. The pyramidal roofs and steeples in carved timber work recall earlier Buddhist monuments once found in the Kashmīr valley, today to be seen only in neighbouring Nepal.

The Mosque of Shāh Hamadān [Ill. 182] is a fine example of the wooden style of architecture. Set on the banks of the Jhelum River, the mosque was first built during the reign of Sikandar Budshāh (1389-1413) in memory of the Kubrawiyya Saint Mīr Sayyid Alī Hamadānī, who had migrated to Kashmīr in 1370 and who is said to have brought with him seven hundred followers. His influence did much to shape Muslim mystical thought in the recently Islamicized Kashmīr valley. Shāh Hamadānī died in 1385 in Swat, having helped to make large-scale conversions to Islam. It seems likely that the mosque in his honour was built by Sikandar, in whose reign the son of the saint, Sayyid Muḥammad, arrived in Kashmīr. Together the sultan and saint began a programme of Islamization, dismissing Hindus from government positions, introducing the Persian system of administration and destroying many temples including the famous Sun Temple at Martand. Many Muslims, displaced by Tīmūr's invasions of their homelands in Iran and Transoxiana, fled to Kashmīr at this time. Among these must have been artisans and architects who would have encouraged the sultan to begin new projects of religious and secular monuments.

The Mosque of Shāh Hamadān, built entirely of wood on a Hindu temple foundation, as most of the other wooden Kashmīrī structures, suffered from fire at various times,[2] but appears to represent accurately the original wooden style of the fifteenth century.

Apart from the cloisters which were added later, the mosque is a simple square and in plan virtually indistinguishable from the contemporary tombs of Kashmīr. The Mosque of Hamadān is two storeys in height, with a low three-tiered pyramidal roof, surmounted by an open pavilion over which rises the steeple and a finial. The lower part of the walls are formed of logs trimmed square and laid in alternate courses, the log ends producing a diaper pattern on the exterior[Ill. 183]. Under the eave is a heavy cornice corbelled out from the wall. Above the eave are arcades, verandahs and porticos once filled with wooden screens [Ill. 184]. The pyramidal roof is composed of rafters, with planks above covered with turf, and in-between layers of brick-back to make it waterproof. The interior is richly decorated and covered with panels of geometric patterns.

The Jāmi' Mosque of Srinagar [Ill. 185] is the largest and most imposing of all Kashmīrī mosques. It was founded by Sikandar But-shikan about 1400 and enlarged

[2]The foundations of the mosque were laid in the reign of Sultan Sikandar (1389-1413); it was burnt in 1480; then reconstructed and burnt again under Muḥammad Shāh (1484-86); and reconstructed by Abū al-Barst in the eighteenth century. Today Muslims and Hindus worship in it.

by Zain al-'Ābidīn, his son and successor, who added a *madrasa.* The original timber monument was destroyed three times by fire[3] and its present construction dates to the reign of the Mughal Emperor Aurangzīb, towards the end of the seventeenth century.

The Jāmi' Mosque most nearly corresponds to the orthodox plan, a square courtyard surrounded on four sides by wide arcades divided on three sides into four aisles, and on the east into three. The entire mosque is surrounded by a brick retaining wall relieved by a series of small arched openings on the upper portion. In the middle of the north, south and east sides are three projecting entrances of which the principal one is on the south side.

In the centre of the arcades surrounding the courtyard are four square arched entrances surmounted by pyramidal roofs from which rise steeples and finials[Ill. 186]. The archways on the north, south and east sides are supported on eight timber pillars, the ones found today modern unadorned substitutes standing in the original square limestone bases. The entrance on the western side is larger and has staircases in the side portions leading to the roof.

The extensive arcades are the most striking feature of this huge mosque. Composed of 378 timber pillars in all, each is made of a tall deodar trunk resting on a stone base. The fluted shafts rise to bracket capitals supporting the cross-beams of the flat timber ceiling. An arched *miḥrāb* is in the centre of the *qibla* wall. The courtyard is bisected by two paths planned in the manner of formal Mughal gardens. At the point of their intersection a small *bārādarī* has been built.

In Kashmīr masonry construction had all but been forgotten. Stone temple parts were recycled by the conquerors, as in all other parts of the subcontinent. Two early monuments built on the site of an old Hindu temple and other Hindu remains are the Tomb and Mosque of Madanī (1444), which belong to the reign of Zain al-'Ābidīn (1421-72). Both were constructed in memory of the same person probably built at about the same time.

The mosque is built on an Hindu stone plinth [Ill. 187], but its brick walls are Muslim. In plan it is square with the external walls pierced by trefoil arched windows. Some carved temple columns have been placed at the corner of the porch, at the sides of the windows and in the interior of the tomb. The entablature is Hindu in origin, and the large cornice and eaves are wooden, the latter decorated with a row of timber tongues projecting downward. The surmounting steepleless pyramidal roof is covered with turf on birchbark, two waterproofing agents, an element to become standard as the Kashmīrī style develops. The entrance is on the east side through an ogee-shaped elaborately carved doorway, flanked by two carved temple columns. The interior is plain, the carved timber ceiling supported on four wooden columns.

The Tomb of Madanī lies just north of the Mosque and is also built in part of recycled temple material. There is, however, a feature of great interest in this monument. The spandrel on its eastern face had an unusual type of tilework not found elsewhere in Srinagar, not commonly seen in India. It is possible that it did not belong to the original structure but to a later Mughal restoration, although this is by no means certain.

When stucco and brick began to lose their popularity as decorative media on Iranian

[3]The foundations were laid between 1398 and 1402; it was burnt in 1479; reconstructed in 1503; burnt again in 1620; reconstructed in 1605-27; burnt in 1674; and reconstructed by Aurangzīb between 1658-1707.

monuments during the fourteenth century, the use of mosaic faience became very popular. By Tīmūrīd times, during the fifteenth century, tile decoration virtually dominated the buildings on which it was applied.

In north India mosaic faience was almost unknown until after the invasion of Tīmūr at the end of the fourteenth century. The Lodīs used tile mosaics for the first time in the fifteenth century on some Delhi monuments, the Shīsh Gumbad, the Barā Gumbad and the mosque north of the Tomb of 'Īsā Khān near Humāyūn's Tomb.

The mosaic faience work of the Mughals was generally fired on separate tiles and then cut into the desired shapes, put together like a mosaic and stuck on the walls with mortar.[4] In pre-Mughal Multān and Sind there developed another type of tilework, cut into separate squares the different colours were fired together. But only a limited range of colours was used, light and dark blue, and occasionally yellow and brown.

The tiles of the Tomb of Madanī conformed to this Multānī and Sindī prototype but differed because of the brilliant use of colour. Also of great interest is the subject matter of the left spandrel of the east entrance archway. An animal, with the body of a leopard and the face and trunk of a human being is seen shooting with a bow and arrow at its own tail which ends in a dragons head.[5] Also in the panel is an onlooking fox amidst flowers and clouds. The background of the work is blue, the man's trunk red, the leopard's body yellow with light green spots, the fox reddish brown and the flowers of various colours. Other tiles were also used on this monument on the archway jambs and on a border above the *dado* where flowers, floral patterns and heads of donkeys and lions were interspersed.

The tilework of the Tomb of Madanī is little understood. In technique it does not conform to the feeble contemporary attempts of the Lodīs in Delhi. Nor does it fit in comfortably with early Mughal work. The only comparable work appears to have been in Multān and Sind, but how the technique arrived in Kashmīr remains unknown.

The subject matter of the tiles is an even greater puzzle. The beast in heraldic pose with human trunk might in fact be a Saggitarius[6] shooting at its own tail. But then we are faced with the even greater dilemma of how an astrological sign might find its way onto the eastern façade of this fifteenth century tomb in Kashmīr and who would have put it there. A lot of questions need to be answered before we can firmly date this most unusual mosaic decoration and put it in its proper art historical place.

The most attractive chapter of the Muslim history in Kashmīr was the reign of Zain al-'Ābidīn, a tolerant ruler and patron of the arts. The policy of Islamization started by his father, Sikandar But-shikan, was reversed by Zain al-'Ābidīn, commonly known as the "Great King." Allegedly after having been cured of a disease by a Hindu doctor, the sultan ordered that no further persecution of his Hindu subjects should be permitted.[7] But, once started, conversions to Islam did not stop and with the help of ṣūfīs continued throughout the fifteenth century, by which time the majority of Kashmīrīs had become Muslim. Simultaneously, however, Islam in Kashmīr was diluted

[4]W.H. Nicholls, *Archaeological Survey of Indian Report, 1900-7,* p.163 and J.R. Nichols, "Muḥammad Architecture," *Marg,* vol. VIII, no. 2, 1955, pp. 50-51.

[5]Ibid.

[6]I am indebted to Dr. Lisa Golombek of the Royal Ontario Museum, Toronto, Canada for this identification.

[7]Nicholls, op. cit., p. 162.

by non-Muslim practices and it has retained this eclectic character to the present day.

All of Zain al-'Ābidīn's tolerance did not stop him from using Hindu temple parts for constructing monuments. The sultan built both in brick and wood, as may be seen in the Tomb and Mosque of Madanī respectively. But one monument of his reign is fundamentally different from all other buildings in Kashmīr. The Tomb of Zain al-'Ābidīn's mother [Ill. 188], the wife of Sikandar But-shikan,[8] is constructed on a stone plinth originally belonging to a temple with a purely Hindu filleted torus cornice, enclosure wall and gateways. Only the brick superstructure appears to have been built in the fifteenth century. In plan, the plinth and monument are square with the angles replaced by rectangular projections recessed internally at the angles, over which are five domes, the central one larger. As on other brick monuments in Kashmīr, such as the Tomb of Madanī and a tomb on the island in Wular Lake, there are glazed and moulded blue tiles studded at intervals in the exterior walls, the semi-circular brick projections on the drum of the main dome, and the moulded brick string courses and sunken panels on the drum of the cupolas.

Zain al-'Ābidīn's weak successors were unable to match his achievements and, eventually, they were overpowered by crafty adventurers. In 1588 this corrupt state of affairs finally allowed Akbar to annex the enfeebled Kashmīr Sultanate to the Mughal Empire.

[8]See A. Cunningham, *JASB,* no. 2, Calcutta, 1848 and H.H. Cole, *Illustrations of the Ancient Buildings of Kashmir,* London, 1869.

Glossary

arabesque—a term used to designate denaturalized vegetal ornament, but which now also includes other Islamic ornament such as geometric, calligraphic and even figural. It is generally repetitious and fills the entire surface of the ornament.

amīr—(Arabic) title of military commanders who became military governors of the provinces they received as fiefs.

ashlar—masonry of square hewn stone.

chhajja—overhanging cornice, eave.

chhatri—small pavilions or kiosks which act as turrets on the roof.

dargāh—(Persian) in India refers to a Muslim shrine or tomb of a saint.

guldasta—small turret-like termination on the roof.

Hegira/Hijra—the emigration of the Prophet Muhammad from Mecca to Medina in September, AD 622. The Hijra era (written AH) is calculated from this lunar year.

'Īd—the two canonical Muslim festivals, the 'Īd al-Adhā (sacrificial festival) and the 'Īd al-Fitr (festival of the breaking of the fast).

īdgah—(Persian) term which refers to the prayer hall used for the two chief Muslim festivals.

Imām—the spiritual leader of the Islamic community. It also refers to the appointed leader of prayers in a mosque.

īwān—a vaulted hall with one side opening directly on the court.

jagir—a non-hereditary grant of land given by a ruler to a soldier or an official; a fief the Seljuqs and Mamluks called *iqta.*

jalī—lattice screen.

jāmi'—term applies to a mosque where the Friday prayer is conducted.

Khalīfa—(Caliph) (Arabic) the head of the orthodox Sunnī community.

Khānqāh—an endowed ṣūfi monastery governed by a shaykh.

khuṭba—the Friday service delivered in a *jāmi'* mosque.

Kufic—an early square ornate Arabic script which has erroneously attributed to Kufa in Iraq.

madrasa—a Muslim theological college.

maḥal—a palace.

manāra—(*mīnār* or minaret) a Muslim tower from which the call to prayer is generally but not always given.

maqsūra—an enclosure which protects the ruler in a mosque.

miḥrāb—a niche indicating the direction of Mecca (*qibla*) and hence of prayer.

mimbar—a pulpit in *jāmi'* mosques from which the Friday prayer is given.

mu'azzin—the official who gives the call to prayer in a religious institution.

Muḥarram—the first month of the Muslim year, a month of mourning the martyrdom of Ḥasan and Ḥusayn, the Prophet's grandsons. It is celebrated by pilgrimages to the sacred places of the Shī'ā, especially to Karbala. During this month the

passion play (*ta'ziyah*) reliving the death of the two early martyrs is performed.
ogee—a form of moulding or arch, the curves of which resemble the cyma reversa.
pendentive—a triangular surface by which a dome is supported on a square compartment.
pīr—an elder or shaykh, the spiritual leader of a ṣūfī monastery.
qibla—the direction of prayer (Mecca) which in India is to the west.
Qur'ān—the Muslim scriptures considered the revealed work of Allāh.
rawẓa—(Persian) a garden which in India refers to a large enclosure with a tomb and mosque.
riwāq—arcaded cloisters of a mosque.
ṣaḥn—the courtyard of a mosques.
shaykh—the spiritual leader of a ṣūfī monastery.
Shī'ā—a sect of Islam which recognized 'Alī and his family as the legitimate successors after the death of the Prophet and who, therefore, do not recognize the first three caliphs.
squinch—an arch placed diagonally at angles in the interior of moments to connect the dome to the square chamber below.
ṣūfī—(Arabic: wool which refers to the ascetic life symbolized by the woollen robe). It refers in Islam to a member of the spiritual orders which are united under a shaykh.
Sunnī— the orthodox Muslim sect.
ta'ziyah—in popular language the term refers to a copy of the tomb (*tābūt*) of Ḥusayn at Karbala. In general it refers to the passion play of the Shī'ā.
thuluth—an Arabic cursive script.
trabeate—the use of beams in construction as distinct from arches.
tughra—a calligraphic emblem which became a coat of arms of the state.
'ulamā'—a theologian appointed to an administrative post.
'urs—the anniversary of the death of a saint.

Bibliography

Chapter 1

Ahmad, Aziz, *Studies in Islamic Culture in an Indian Environment,* Oxford, 1964.
Bernier, Francois, *Travels in Hindustan (from 1655 to 1661),* Calcutta, 1904.
De Thevenot, Jean, *Indian Travels of Thevenot and Careri,* New Delhi, 1949.
Della Valle, Pietro, *Travels in India,* London, 1892.
Carre, Abbe, *The Travels of Abbe Carre (1672-74) to India and the Near East,* 2 vols., London, 1947.
Elliot, H.M., and J. Dowson, *The History of India as Told by its Own Historians,* 30 vols., Calcutta, 1960-63.
Elphinstone, M., *History of India,* London, 1905.
Ferishta, Mohamed Kasim, *Gulshan-i Ibrahimi,* translated as *History of the Rise of Mahomedan Power in India* by John Briggs, 4 vols., New Delhi, 1981.
Herklots, G.A., *Islam in India,* New Delhi, 1972.
Hollister, J.N., *The Shi'a in India,* London, 1953, reprint, New Delhi, 1979.
Ikram, S.M., *Muslim Civilisation in India,* New York, 1965.
Ishwari Prasad, *History of Medieval India,* Allahabad, 1927.
Lane-Poole, Stanley, *Medieval India Under Mohammadan Rule 712-1764,* Delhi, 1963.
Lannoy, Richard, *The Speaking Tree,* Oxford, 1971.
LeBon, Gustave, *Les Civilisations de l'Inde,* Paris, 1887.
Mujeeb, M., *Islamic Influence on Indian Society,* Meerut, 1972.
Nizami, K.A., *Studies in Medieval Indian History,* Aligarh, 1956.
Qureshi, I.H., *The Administration of the Sultanate of Delhi,* fifth edition, New Delhi, 1971.
Spear, Percival, *A History of India,* vol. II, Harmondsworth,1965.
Srivastava, A.L., *Medieval Indian Culture,* Agra, 1964.
Tavernier, Jean Baptiste, *Travels in India,* 2 vols., Calcutta, 1905, reprint, New Delhi,1995.
Thapar, Romila, *A History of India,* vol. I, Harmondsworth, 1966.
Titus, M.T., *Indian Islam,* London, 1930, reprint, New Delhi, 1979.
—, *Islam in India and Pakistan,* Calcutta, 1959.

Chapter 2

Brown, Percy, *Indian Architecture, Islamic Period,* fifth edition, Bombay, 1958.
Chaghatai, M. Abdullah, "The Sources of Pre-Mughal Architecture," *Journal of the Pakistan Society,* vol. VIII, 1960.
Davies, Philip, *Monuments of India,* vol. II, London, 1989.
Desai, Ziyauddin A., *Indo-Islamic Architecture,* New Delhi, 1970.
Diez, E., *Die Kunst Indiens,* Berlin, 1925.

Fergusson, James, *History of Indian and Eastern Architecture*, vol. II, London, 1910, reprint, New Delhi, 1998.
Havell, E.B., *The Ancient and Medieval Architecture of India: A Study of Indo-Aryan Civilization*, London, 1915.
—, *The Ideals of Indian Art*, London, 1920.
—, *Indian Architecture*, London, 1927.
Heam, E.R., *The Seven Cities of Delhi*, London, 1906, reprint.
Husain, A.B.M., *The Manara in Indo-Muslim Architecture*, Dacca, 1970.
Keene, H.G., *Handbook for Visitors to Delhi*, Calcutta, 1909.
LaRoche, E., *Indische Baukunst*, 6 vols., Berlin, 1921.
LeBon, Gustave, *Les Monuments de l'Inde*, Paris, 1893.
Marshall, John, "The Monuments of Muslim India," *Cambridge History Of India*, vol. III, Cambridge, 1922.
Nath, R., *History of Sultanate Architecture*, New Delhi, 1978.
—, *Islamic Architecture and Culture in India*, New Delhi, 1982.
Spear, Percival, *Delhi: Its Monuments and History*, Oxford, 1943.
Stephen, Carr, *The Archaeology and Monumental Remains of Delhi*, reprint, New Delhi, 1967.
Toy, Sidney, *The Fortified Cities of India*, London, 1965.
—, *The Strongholds of India*, London, 1957.
Wetzel, Friedrich, *Islamische Grabbauten in Indien der Zeit der Soldatenkaiser, 1320-1540*, Leipzig, 1918.
Yamamato, Y., M. Ara, and T. Tsukinowa, *Delhi: Architectural Remains of the Delhi Sultanate Period*, 3 vols., Tokyo, 1968-70 (in Japanese).

Chapters 3 and 4

Gold-Pearlroth, Anita, "The Formation of Indo-Islamic Architecture," unpublished Ph.D. dissertation, Institute of Fine Arts, New York University, 1976.
Khan, F.A., *Banbhore. A Preliminary Report of Recent Archaeological Excavations at Banbhore*, Karachi, 1963.
Lehmann, Fritz, "Architecture of the Early Sultanate Period and the Nature of the Muslim State in India," *Indica*, vol. XV, 1978, pp. 13-31.
Meister, Michael, "The Two-and-a-Half-Day Mosque," *Oriental Art*, vol. XVIII, 1972, pp. 57-62.
Naqvi, S.A.A., "Sultan Gharī, Delhi," *Ancient India*, no. 3, 1947.
Page, J.A., *An Historical Memoir of the Qutb*, Delhi, 1925, reprint, New Delhi, 1970.
Shokoohy, Mehrdad, *Bhadresvar, The Oldest Islamic Monuments in India*, Leiden, 1989.
—, and H. Natalie, "The Architecture of Baha al-Din Tughril in the Region of Bayana, Rajasthan," *Muqarnas*, vol. IV, 1987, pp. 114-32.
—, *Hisar-i Firuza: Sultanate and Early Mughal Architecture in the District of Hisar, India*, London, 1988.
Ved Prakash, "The Qutb Minar from Contemporary and Near Contemporary Sources," *Proceedings of the Indian History Congress*, vol. II, Ranchi, 1964.
Welch, Anthony, "Qur'an and Tomb: The Religious Epigraphs of Two Early Sultanate Tombs in Delhi," in F.M. Asher and G.S. Gai, eds., *Indian Epigraphy: Its Bearing on the History of Art*, New Delhi, 1985.

CHAPTER 5

Banerjee, J.M., *History of Firuz Shah Tughluq,* Delhi, 1967.
Husain, A.M., *Tughluq Dynasty,* New Delhi, 1976.
Madan, P.L., "Adilabad—A Dream of Muhammad bin Tughluq," *Islamic Culture,* vol. XXXVII, 1963.
Merklinger, E. Schotten, "Firuzabad, Capital of the Last Turkish Dynasty in India," *Proceedings of the Fourth Congress of Turkish Art,* Munich, 1989.
Page, J.A., *A Memoir of the Kotla Firuz Shah,* Delhi, 1937.
Waddington, Hilary, "Adilabad, a Part of the Fourth Delhi," *Ancient India,* vol. 1, no.1, 1946.
Welch, A., and H. Crane, "The Tughluqs: Master Builders of the Delhi Sultanate," *Muqarnas,* vol. 1, New Haven, 1983.

CHAPTER 6

Ara, Matsuoa, "The Lodhi Rulers and the Construction of Tomb-Buildings in Delhi," *Acta Asiatica,* vol. XLIII, 1982.
Asher, Catherine B., "From Anomaly to Homogeneity: The Mosque in Fourteenth to Sixteenth Century Bihar," in *Studies in Art and Architecture of Bihar and Bengal,* ed. G. Bhattacharya and Debala Mitra, Delhi, 1989.
—, "Legacy and Legitimacy: Sher Shah's Patronage of Imperial Mausolea," in K.P. Ewing, ed., *Sharī'at and Ambiguity in South Asian Islam,* Berkeley, 1988.
—, "The Mausoleum of Sher Shah Suri," *Artibus Asiae,* vol. XXXIX, 3/4, 1977.
—, "The Qila'-i Kuhna Mosque: A Visual Symbol of Royal Aspirations," *Chhavi,* 2, Benares, 1981.

CHAPTER 7

Ahmed, Shams-ud-Din, *Inscriptions of Bengal,* vol. IV, Rajshahi,1960.
Asher, Catherine B., *Islamic Monuments of Eastern India and Bangladesh,* Leiden, 1991.
Chakravarti, R.K., "Notes on Gaur and other Places in Bengal," in *Journal of Asiatic Society of Bengal,* vol. V, no. 7, 1910.
—, "Pre-Mughal Mosques of Bengal," *Journal of Asiatic Society of Bengal,* vol. VI, no. 5, 1910.
Crawford, D.G., "Satgaon and Tribeni," *Bengal Past and Present,* vol. III, 1909.
Creighton, H., *The Ruins of Gaur, Described and Represented in Eighteen Views with a Topographical Map,* London, 1817.
Dani, A.H., *Muslim Architecture in Bengal,* Dacca, 1961.
Francklin, W., *Ruins of Gaur,* 1912.
Hasan, Perween,"Sultanate Mosques and Continuity in Bengal Architecture," *Muqarnas,* New Haven, vol. VI, 1989, pp. 58-74.
Hasan, S.M., *The Adina Mosque at Hazrat Pandua,* Dacca, 1970.
—, *Mosque Architecture of Pre-Muslim Bengal,* sec. edn., Dacca, 1979.
—, *Muslim Monuments of Bangladesh,* Dacca, 1980.
Majumdar, R.C., *History of Medieval Bengal,* Calcutta, 1973.
Michell, George, ed., *The Islamic Heritage of Bengal,* Paris, 1984.
Ravenshaw, J.H., *Gaur: Its Ruins and Inscriptions,* London,1878.
Sarkar, J., ed., *The History of Bengal,* vol. II, Dacca, 1946, reprint, Patna, 1973.
Stewart, C., *History of Bengal,* reprint, Delhi, 1971.

Tarafdar, Momtazur Rahman, *Husain Shahi Bengal:1494-1538,* Dacca, 1965.
Annual Reports of the Archaeological Survey of India, Calcutta, 1902-3 to 1935-6, XV, 1882.
Annual Reports of Bengal Circle, 1900/1 to 1920/2.
Annual Reports of Eastern Circle, 1905/6 to 1920/1.
Annual Report on Indian Epigraphy, 1947/8 to present.

Chapter 8

Burgess, James, *The Muhammadan Architecture of Ahmadabad,* 2 vols., Archaeological Survey of India, New Imperial Series, vols. XXIV and XXXIII, London, 1900-1905.
—, *On the Muhammadan Architecture of Bharoch, Cambay, Dholka, Champanir, and Mahmudabad in Gujarat,* Archaeological Survey of India, New Imperial Series, vol. XXIII, London, 1896.
—, *A Revised List of Antiquarian Remains in Bombay Presidency,* vol. VIII, London, 1897.
Chaghatai, M.A., *Muslim Monuments of Ahmadabad Through their Inscriptions,* Poona,1934.
Commissariat, M.S., *A History of Gujarat,* vol. I, London, 1938; vol. II, Bombay, 1957.
Eastwick, E.B., "Champanir and Pawagadh" in *Indian Antiquary,* vol. IX, 1880, pp. 221-24.
Flood, F.B., "The Tree of Life as a Decorative Device in Islamic Window-Fillings: The Mobility of a Leitmotif," *Oriental Art,* vol. XXXVII, no. 4, Winter 1991/2, pp. 209-22.
Michell, G., and Snehal Shah, eds., "Medieval Ahmadabad,"*Marg,* vol. XXXIX, no. 3, 1988.
Misra, S.C., *The Mirat-i Sikandari: A History of Gujarat from Inception of the Dynasty of the Sultans of Gujarat to the Conquest of Gujarat by Akbar,* Baroda, 1961.
—, *Rise of Muslim Power in Gujarat,* Bombay, 1963, reprint, New Delhi, 1982.
Shokoohy, Mehrdad, *Bhadresvar, the Oldest Islamic Monuments in India,* Leiden, 1988.
—, "Muslim Architecture in Gujarat Prior to Islamic Conquest," *Marg,* vol. XXXIX, no. 4, 1988, p. 75.
Annual Reports of Archaeological Survey of India, Calcutta, 1902/3, 1904, 1925/26, 1929/30.
Baroda State Gazetteer, 2 vols., Bombay, 1923.
Bombay State Gazetteer, vols. I-IX, XIII, XIV.

Chapter 9

Abbott, John, *Sind, A Reinterpretation of the Unhappy Valley,* Karachi, 1977.
Aiken, E.H., *Gazetteer of the Province of Sind,* Karachi, 1907.
'Ali ibn Hamid, al-Kufi, *The Chachnameh, An Ancient History of Sind,* translated from the Persian by Mirza Khalichbeg Fredunbeg, Karachi, 1900-1902.
Billimoria, N.M., *Bibliography and Publications on Sind and Baluchistan,* Karachi, 1930, reprint, Lahore, 1977.
Blandford, William T., *The Geology of Western Sind,* Calcutta, 1880.
Burnes, Sir Alexander, *Travels in Bokhara,* London, 1835, reprint, Karachi, 1973.
—, *A Voyage on the Indus,* Karachi, 1973.
Burnes, James, *Narrative of a Visit to the Court of Sind at Hyderabad on the Indus,* Edinburgh, 1839.
Burton, Richard, *Scinde or the Unhappy Valley,* London, 1851, reprint, New Delhi, 1999.
—, *Sindh, and the Races that Inhabit the Valley of the Indus,* London, 1851, reprint, New Delhi, 1998.

—, *Sind Revisited,* London, 1877, reprint, New Delhi, 1998.
Carter, G.E.L., "Religion of Sind," *Indian Antiquary,* vols. XLVI and XLVII, 1917-18.
—, *A Short History of Sind,* Karachi, 1916.
Cousens, Henri, *The Antiquities of Sind,* Karachi, 1975.
—, *Portfolio of Illustrations of Sind Tiles,* London, 1906.
Dayarama, Gidumal, *Something About Sind,* Hyderabad, 1930.
Duarte, Adrian, *The Beggar Saint of Sehwan and other Sketches of Sind,* Karachi, 1974.
Fredunbeg, Mirza Khalichbeg, *The Chachnameh,* Karachi, 1900.
Haig, Major-General M.R., *The Indus Delta Country,* London, 1884, reprint, 1894.
Hughes, A.W., *A Gazetteer of the Province of Sind,* London,1874, reprint, 1876.
Jethmal, Parasram Gulraj, *Sind and Its Sufis,* Madras, 1924.
Kasim, Muhammad Mirza, *Tarikh-i Sind,* Moradabad, 1905.
Khan, Ansar Zahid, *History and Culture of Sind,* Karachi, 1980.
Khan, Muhammad Ishtiaq, *Archaeology of Sind,* Karachi, 1975.
Kuraishi, Muhammad Hamid, "Multan—Its Brief History and Persian and Arabic Inscriptions," *Epigraphia Indo-Moslemica, 1927-8,* pp. 1-16.
Lambrick, H.T., *Sind Before the Muslim Conquest,* Oxford, 1973.
—, *Sind: A General Introduction,* Hyderabad, 1964.
—, *Sir Charles Napier and Sind,* Oxford, 1952.
—, *The Terrorist,* London, 1972.
Majumdar, Nani Gopal, *Explorations in Sind,* Delhi, 1934.
Mayne, Peter, *The Saints of Sind,* London, 1956.
McMurdo, James, "An Account of the Country of Sindh, with Remarks on the State of Society, the Government, Manners and Customs of the People," vol. IX, pp. 2, 907-16, Calcutta, 1840.
Murray, John, *A Handbook of the Punjab, Western Rajputana, Kashmir and Upper Sind,* London, 1883.
Nock, J., "Rcport on the Road from Sinde, from Subzul to Shikarpoor," Calcutta, 1843, pp. 59-62.
Pathan, Mumtaz Husain, *The Arab Kingdom of al-Mansūrah in Sind,* Hyderabad, 1974.
—, *Sind: The Arab Period,* Hyderabad, 1978.
Pithavala, Manekji Bejanji, *Identification and Description of Some Old Sites in Sind,* Karachi, 1938.
—, *An Introduction to Sind: Its Wealth and Welfare,* Karachi, 1951.
—, *A Physical and Economic Geography of Sind and the Lower Indus Basin,* Hyderabad, 1959.
—, *Sind's Changing Map,* Karachi, 1938.
Postans, Thomas, *Personal Observations on Sindh,* 8 vols., London,1843, reprint, Karachi, 1973.
Pottinger, Sir Henry, *Travels in Belochistan and Sinde, Accompanied by a Geographical and Historical Account of Those Countries,* London, 1816.
Rahman, Mushtaque, *A Geography of Sind Province,* Karachi, 1975.
Raikes, Stanley Napier, *Memoir on the Thurr and Parkur Districts of Sind,* Bombay, 1856.
Riazul Islam, "The Rise of the Sammas in Sind," *Islamic Culture,* Hyderabad, 1948.
Ross, David, *The Land of the 5 Rivers and Sindh: Sketches Historical and Descriptive,* Lahore, 1976.
Sarkar, Sasanka Sekhar, *Ancient Races of Baluchistan, Punjab and Sind,* Calcutta, 1964.

Schimmel, Annemarie, "Sind Vor 1947," *Indo Asia,* Heft 1, 1979.
Siddiqi, M.H., *History of the Arghuns and Tarkhans of Sind,* Hyderabad, 1972.
Sorley, Herbert Tower, *The Gazetteer of West Pakistan: The Former Province of Sind including Khairpur State,* Lahore, 1968.
—, *Shah Abdul Latif Bhit: His Poetry, Life and Times,* Lahore, 1966.
Tattavi, Mir Ali Shir Qani, *History of Sind* (in Urdu), 1959.
Thakur, U.T., *Sindhi Culture,* Bombay, 1959.
von Orlich, Leopold, *Travels in India, Including Sinde and the Punjab,* translated from the German by H. Evans Lloyd, Lahore, 1976.
Archaeological Survey of India Reports, vol. VIII, 1897.
Gazetteer of the Province of Sind, vol. I, Bombay, 1927, Karachi, 1907-20, 1927.
Indian Antiquary, vol. XLVI, pp. 133, 205; vol. XLVII, p. 197.
Journal of Asiatic Society of Bengal.
Progress Report of the Archaeological Survey of India, Western Circle, Archaeology ending 31 March 1921.
Royal Asiatic Society Journal, vol.1, London, 1834, pp. 223-57.
Sind Gazetteer.
Sind Historical Society Journal.
Sind, Pakistan: An Introduction, Karachi, 1970.
Sind Quarterly ST 1637.

Chapter 10

Barnes, E., *Annual Report, Archaeological Survey of India, 1903-4,* Calcutta, 1906, pp. 30-45.
Day, U.N., *Medieval Malwa,* New Delhi, 1965.
Grade, M.B., *Guide to Chanderi,* Gwalior, 1928.
Jain, K.C., *Malwa Through the Ages,* Delhi, 1972.
Luard, C.E., *Gwalior State Gazetteer,* vol. 1, Gwalior, 1908, pp. 209-12.
"Mandu," *Marg,* vol. XII, Bombay, 1963.
Nath, R., *The Art of Chanderi,* New Delhi, 1979.
Sinh, Raghubir, *Malwa in Transition,* Bombay, 1936.
Yazdani, G., *Mandu, City of Joy,* Oxford, 1929.

Chapter 11

Cunningham, A., *Archaeological Survey of India Report,* vol. XI, Calcutta, 1880.
Fuhrer, A., and E. Smith, *The Sharqi Architecture of Jaunpur,* Archaeological Survey of India, New Imperial Series, vol. XI, Calcutta, 1889.
Nevill, H.R., *District Gazetteer of the United Provinces,* vol. XXVIII, *Jaunpur,* Allahabad, 1908.
Saeed, M.M., *The Sharqi Sultanate of Jaunpur: A Political and Cultural History,* Karachi, 1972.

Chapters 12 and 13

Bilgrami, S.H., and C. Willmott, *Historical and Descriptive Sketch of His Highness the Nizam's Dominions,* 2 vols., Bombay, 1884.
Burgess, J., *List of Antiquarian Remains in Bombay Presidency,* Archaeological Survey of Western India, Bombay, 1885.

—, *Provisional Lists of Architectural and other Archeological Remains in Western India*, Archaeological Survey of Western India, Bombay, 1875.

—, *Report on the Antiquities of Bidar and Aurangabad Districts*, Archaeological Survey of Western India, vol. III, London, 1878.

Campbell, C.A., *Glimpses of the Nizam's Dominions*, Philadelphia, 1898.

Cantrell, A.M., *An Account of the Ruins of Beejapoor*, Bombay, 1872.

Cousens, H., *The Architectural Antiquities of Western India*, London, 1926.

—, *Bijapur: The Old Capital of the Adil Shahi Kings*, Poona, 1923.

—, *Bijapur and Its Architectural Remains*, Archaeological Survey of Western India, New Imperial Series, vol. XXXVII, Bombay, 1916, reprint, 1976.

—, *List of Antiquarian Remains*, Archaeological Survey of India, New Imperial Series, vol. XXXI, Bombay,1900.

—, *Notes on the Buildings and Other Antiquarian Remains at Bijapur*, Bombay, 1890.

Eaton, R.M., *Sufis of Bijapur, 1300-1700: Social Roles of Sufis in Medieval India*, Princeton, 1978, reprint, New Delhi, 1996.

Ferishta, Mohamed Kasim, *Gulshan-i Ibrahimi*, translated as *History of the Rise of the Mahomedan Power in India* by John Briggs, 4 vols., Calcutta, 1966, reprint, New Delhi, 1981.

Gadre, Pramod B., *A Cultural Archaeology of Ahmadnagar During the Nizam Shahi Period (1494-1632)*, Delhi, 1986.

Ghauri, I.K.A., "The Central Structure of the Kingdom of Bijapur," *Islamic Culture*, vol. XLIV, 1970.

—, "Muslims in the Deccan: A Historical Survey," *Islamic Literature*, vol. XIII, 1967, pp. 25-38.

Gribble, J.D.B., *History of the Deccan*, 2 vols., London, 1896.

Haig, T.W., *Historic Landmarks of the Deccan*, Allahabad,1907.

Husaini, S.A.Q., *Bahman Shah*, Calcutta, 1960.

Ibrahim, Muhammad, *Rawdat al-Awliya-i Bijapur*, Hyderabad, 1896.

Merklinger, E. Schotten, *Indian Islamic Architecture: The Deccan:1347-1686*, Warminster, 1981.

—, "The Madrasa of Mahmud Gawan," *Kunst des Orients*, vol. XI, no. 1/2, pp. 146-57.

—, "The Mosques of Raichur: A Preliminary Classification," *Kunst des Orients*, vol. XII, no. 1/2, pp. 79-94.

—, "Possible Seljuk Influence on the Dome of the Gol Gumbad," *Proceedings of the Fifth International Congress of Turkish Art*, Budapest, 1979, pp. 613-27.

—, "Seven Tombs at Holkonda," *Kunst des Orients*, vol. X, no. 1/2, pp. 187-97.

Michell, G., ed., *Islamic Heritage of the Deccan*, Bombay, 1986.

—, and R. Eaton, *Firuzabad: Palace City of the Deccan*, Oxford, 1992.

—, and M. Zebrowski, *Architecture and Art of the Deccan Sultanates*, Cambridge, 1999.

Nasim, M., *Bijapur Inscriptions*, Memoirs of the Archaeological Survey of India, no. 49, Delhi,1936.

Radhey Shyam, *The Kingdom of Ahmadnager*, Delhi, 1966.

—, *The Kingdom of Khandesh*, Delhi, 1981.

—, *Life and Times of Malik Ambar*, Delhi, 1969.

Rao, K.M.V., *Glimpses of Dakkan History*, Bombay, 1951.

Sherwani, H.K., *The Bahmanis of the Deccan*, Hyderabad, 1953, reprint, New Delhi, 1985.

—, *History of the Quṭb Shāhī Dynasty*, New Delhi, 1974.

—, *Mahmud Gawan*, Allahabad, 1942.
—, *Muhammad Quli Qutb Shah*, Bombay, 1967.
—, and P.M. Joshi, eds., *History of the Medieval Deccan (1295-1724)*, vol. 1, Hyderabad, 1973; vol. II, Hyderabad, 1974.
Siddiqi, A.M., *History of Golkonda*, Hyderabad, 1956.
Siddiqi, M.S., *The Bahmani Sufis*, Delhi, 1989.
Sinha, S.K., *Medieval History of the Deccan*, Hyderabad,1964.
Tabataba Ali, *Burhan-i Ma'asir*, translated as *The History of the Bahmani Dynasty* by Major J.S. King, London, 1900.
Taylor, M., *Architecture of Beejapoor*, London, 1866.
—, *Sketches of the Deccan*, London, 1837.
Temple, Richard, *Journals Kept in Hyderabad, Kashmir, Sikkim and Nepal*, London, 1887.
Varma, D.C., *History of Bijapur*, New Delhi, 1974.
—, *Social, Economic and Cultural History of Bijapur*, Delhi, 1990.
Yazdani, G., "The Antiquities of Bidar," *Annual Report Archeological Survey of India, 1914-5*, Calcutta, 1920.
—, *Bidar: Its History and Monuments*, Oxford, 1947.
Yusuf, S., *Antiquarian Remains in Hyderabad State*, Archaeological Department of His Highness the Nizam's Dominions, Hyderabad, 1953.
Annual Report of the Archaeological Department of His Highness the Nizam's Dominions, Hyderabad, 1914-36.

Chapter 14

Bernier, Francois, *Travels in the Mughal Empire*, Calcutta, 1904, reprint, New Delhi, 1992.
Cole, H.H., *Illustrations of Ancient Buildings in Kashmir*, London, 1869.
Cunningham, A., *Journal of the Asiatic Society of Bengal*, no. 2, Calcutta, 1848.
Kak, R.C., *Ancient Monuments of Kashmir*, London, 1933.
Kaul, G.L., *Kashmir Through the Ages*, Srinagar, 1963.
Loewenthal, J., "Some Persian Inscriptions found in Srinagar," *Journal of the Asiatic Society of Bengal*, vol. XXXIII, Calcutta, 1864.
Mangat-Rae, Mary, "Wooden Mosques of Kashmir," *Oriental Art*, Autumn, 1967, pp. 263-270.
Nicholls, W.H., *Archaeological Survey of India, Annual Report, 1900-7*, Delhi.
Nichols, J.R., "Muhammad Architecture," *Marg*, vol. VIII, no. 2, 1955.

Index

Ill. 1. Delhi, Quwwat al-Islām Mosque.

Ill. 2. Delhi, Quwwat al-Islām Mosque, Aybak screen. (J. Fergusson)

Ill. 3. Delhi, Quwwat al-Islām Mosque, Aybak screen detail.

Ill. 4. Delhi, Quṭb Mīnār. (Roloff Beny/National Archives of Canada)

Ill. 5. Delhi, Quṭb Mīnār, detail of lowest storey.

decor seems on top of plain stone

Ill. 6. Delhi, Quṭb Mīnār, top storeys.

top storeys – conical

Ill. 7. Delhi, Quṭb Mīnār, calligraphic detail.

Ill. 8. Delhi, Quwwat al-Islām Mosque, Iltutmish, screen detail and calligraphy.

Ill. 9. Ajmer, Aḍhāī Din kā Jhoṃparā Mosque, dome interior.
(Roloff Beny/ National Archives of Canada)

once a Sanskrit college
converted to mosque 1199

Ill. 10. Ajmer, Aḍhāī Din kā Jhoṃparā Mosque, dome ceiling and shafts.
(Roloff Beny/ National Archives of Canada)

Ill. 11. Ajmer, Aḍhāī Din kā Jhoṃparā Mosque, screen.
(Roloff Beny/ National Archives of Canada)

Ill. 12. Ajmer, Aḍhāī Din kā Jhoṃparā Mosque, screen detail.
(Roloff Beny/ National Archives of Canada)

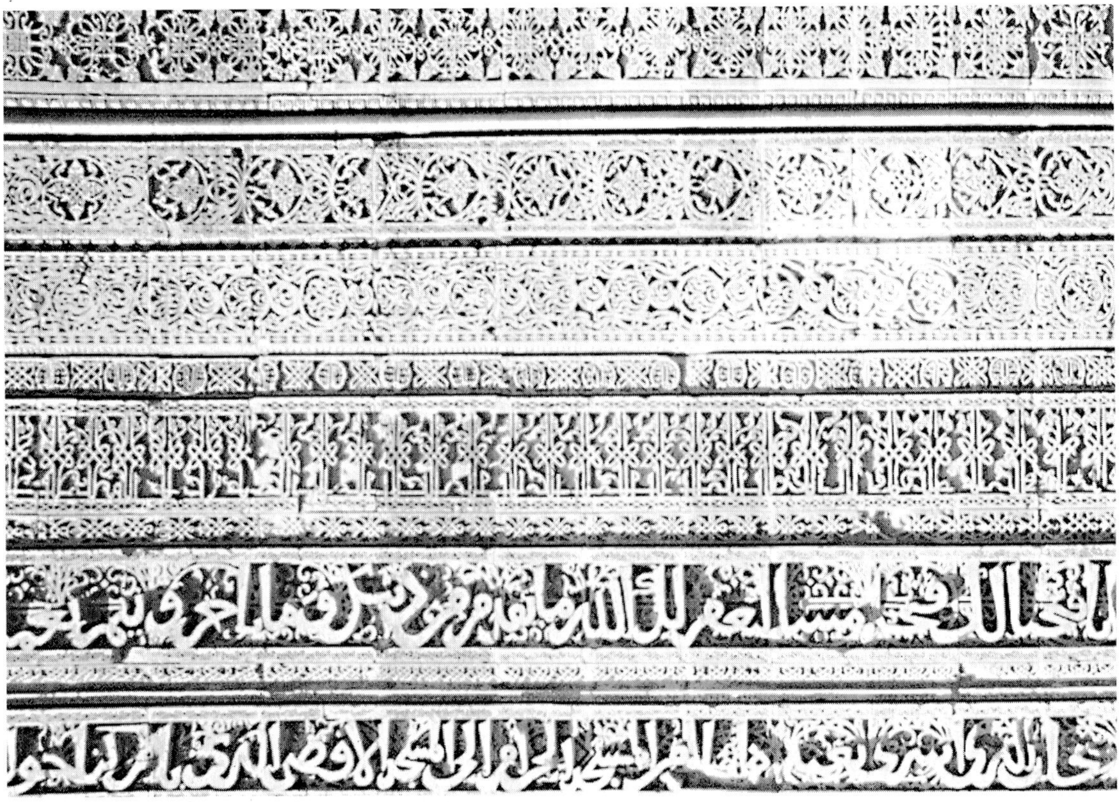

Ill. 13. Kaman, Chawrāsī Khambha, *qibla* wall.

1200

"84 Columns"

Ill. 14. Bayana, Ukha Mandir, exterior wall, east side.

c 1196 - 1210

Ill. 15. Delhi, Sultān Gharī Tomb. (Archaeological Survey of India)

Ill. 16. Delhi, Tomb of Iltutmish, interior, detail.

Ill. 17. Nagaur, Atarkin kā Darwāza.

Ill. 18. Nagaur, Atarkin kā Darwāza, detail.

Ill. 19. Delhi, Quwwat al-Islām Mosque, Alā'i Darwāza.

Ill. 20. Delhi, Quwwat al-Islām Mosque, Alā'i Darwāza, window grill.

Ill. 21. Delhi, Quwwat al-Islām Mosque, Alā'i Darwāza, pilaster panel detail.

Ill. 22. Delhi, Dargāh of Niẓām al-Dīn Awliyā, Jamā'at Khāna Mosque.

Ill. 23. Delhi, Tughluqābād, walls. (Roloff Beny/National Archives of Canada)

reign 1320–1325

Ill. 24. Delhi, Tomb of Ghiyāth al-Dīn Tughluq. (Archaeological Survey of India)

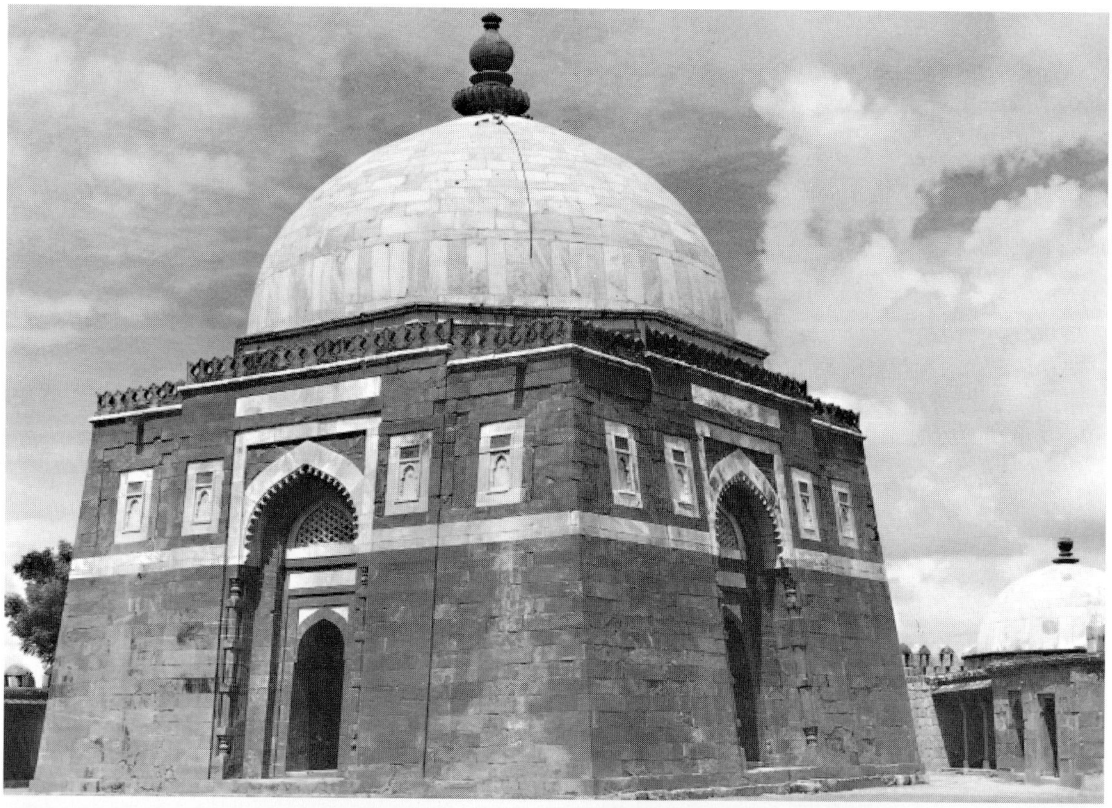

Ill. 25. Delhi, Tomb of Ghiyāth al-Dīn Tughluq, arch tympanum.

Ill. 26. Delhi, Bijay Mandal.

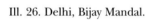

Tughluqd   1354   Ill. 27. Delhi, Kotlā of Fīrūz Shāh, entrance gateway.
            Firozabad

Ill. 28. Delhi, Kotlā of Fīrūz Shāh, stepped structure with Ashokan pillar.   palace from Topra in 1356.

Ill. 29. Delhi, Dargāh of Niẓām al-Dīn Awliyā, tank.

Ill. 30. Delhi, Tomb of Shāh Ālam in Wazīrābād.

Ill. 31. Delhi, Dargāh of Roshan Chirāgh-i Dillī, tomb.

Ill. 32. Delhi, Kalān Mosque, entrance gateway.

Ill. 33. Dèlhi, Kalān Mosque, prayer hall.

Ill. 34. Delhi, Khirkī Mosque, entrance gateway.
(Roloff Beny/National Archives of Canada)

Ill. 35. Delhi, Khirkī Mosque, a courtyard and arcades.
(Roloff Beny/National Archives of Canada)

Ill. 36. Delhi, Mosque in Dargāh of Shāh Ālam in Wazīrābād.

Ill. 37. Delhi, Madrasa of Fīrūz Shāh in Hauz Khās.

Ill. 38. Delhi, Tomb of Fīrūz Shāh Tughluq.

Ill. 39. Delhi, Chhotī Khān kā Gumbad.

Ill. 40. Delhi, Barā Gumbad.

Ill. 41. Delhi, Barā Gumbad, mosque.

Ill. 42. Delhi, Barā Gumbad, mosque pendentives.

Ill. 43. Delhi, Barā Gumbad, mosque, stucco decoration.

Ill. 44. Delhi, Tomb of Sikandar Lodī.

Ill. 45. Sassaram, Tomb of Shīr Shāh Sūr.

Ill. 46. Delhi, Tomb of ʿĪsā Khān. (Sketch of J. Fergusson)

Ill. 47. Delhi, Moth kī Mosque.

Ill. 48. Delhi, Moth kī Mosque, back view.

Ill. 49. Delhi, Jamālī Kamālī Mosque. (Archaeological Survey of India)

Ill. 50. Delhi, Jamālī Kamālī Mosque, squinches.

Ill. 51. Delhi, Qila'i Kuhna Mosque.

Ill. 52. Delhi, Qila'i Kuhna Mosque, *miḥrāb.*
(Roloff Beny/National Archives of Canada)

Ill. 53. Delhi, Shīr Mandal.

Bengal

Ill. 54. Pandua, Adina Mosque, central *īwān*.   1375 Sikandar Shah
(Roloff Beny/National Archives of Canada)

Ill. 55. Pandua, Adina Mosque, *qibla* wall carving.   → inner cutting room,
(Roloff Beny/National Archives of Canada)   not main qibla wall.

Ill. 56. Pandua, Adina Mosque, side arcade. 1375
(Roloff Beny/National Archives of Canada)

Ill. 57. Pandua, Eklakhi Tomb. ca 1433

Ill. 58. Pandua, Eklakhi Tomb, brick detail. 1433,

Ill. 59. Gaur, Dakhlī Darwāza. Bengal

Ill. 60. Gaur, Fīrūz Mīnār (T. Daniell).

Ill. 61. Gaur, Lattan Mosque.

Ill. 62. Gaur, Lattan Mosque, detail.

Ill. 63. Gaur, Lattan Mosque, detail.

Ill. 64. Gaur, Tantipara Mosque, dome pendentives.

Ill. 65. Gaur, Barā Sona Mosque.

Ill. 66. Gaur, Chhota Sona Mosque.

Ill. 67. Cambay, Jāmiʻ Mosque. 1325 Gujarat

Ill. 68. Dholkā, Hilāl Khān Qāzī Mosque. 1333 Gujarat

Ill. 69. Aḥmadābād, Jāmi‘ Mosque.

Ill. 70. Aḥmadābād, Jāmiʿ Mosque, central corridor, rotunda gallery.

Ill. 71. Aḥmadābād, Jāmiʿ Mosque, minaret decoration.

Ill. 72. Aḥmadābād, Jāmiʿ Mosque, balcony decoration.

Ill. 73. Aḥmadābād, Tomb of Aḥmad, perforated stone grill.

Ill. 74. Sarkej, Tomb of Ganj Bakhsh.

Ill. 75. Aḥmadābād, Mosque of Quṭb al-Dīn Shāh.

Ill. 76. Aḥmadābād, Mosque of Quṭb al-Dīn Shāh, buttress decoration.

Ill. 77. Aḥmadābād, Bībījī Mosque, façade.

Ill. 78. Usmānpūr, Mosque of Sayyid Usmān.

Ill. 79. Aḥmadābād, Tomb of Shāh Ālam.

Ill. 80. Aḥmadābād, Mosque of Rānī Rūpavatī, entrance.

Ill. 81 Aḥmadābād, Mosque of Rānī Rūpavatī, buttress decoration.

Ill. 82. Aḥmadābād, Mosque and Tomb of Rānī Sipari.

Ill. 83. Aḥmadābād, Mosque of Siddi Sayyid, window screen.
(Roloff Beny/National Archives of Canada)

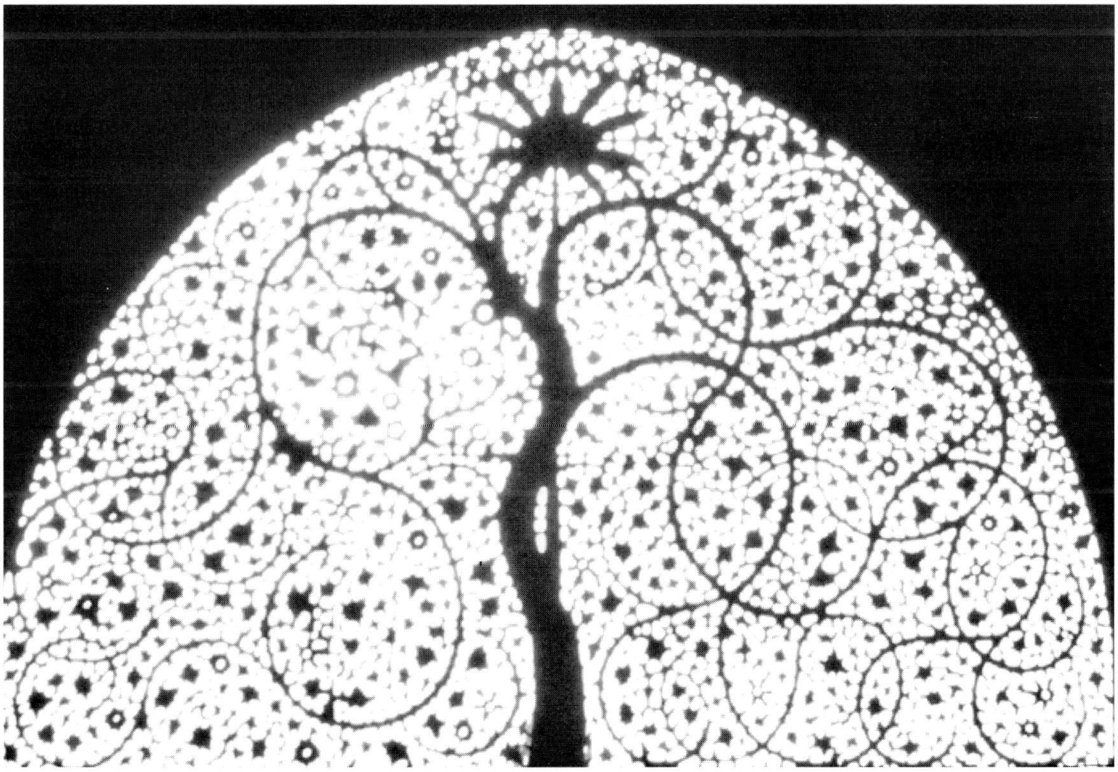

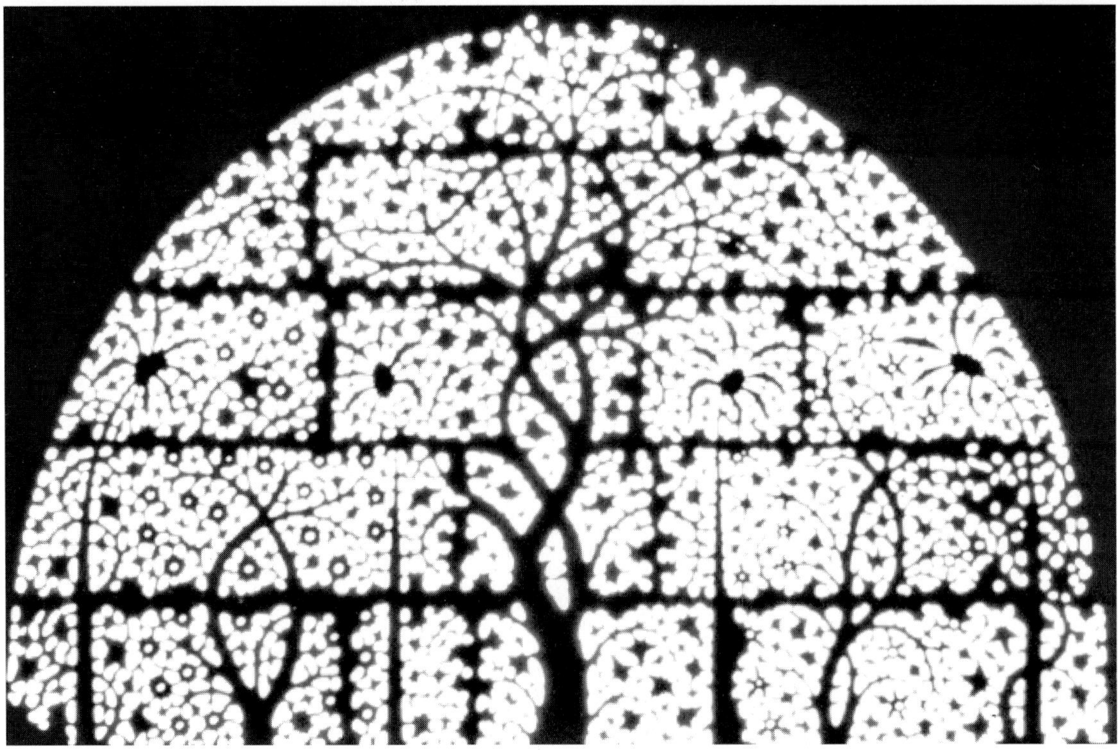

Ill. 84. Aḥmadābād, Mosque of Siddi Sayyid, window screen.
(Roloff Beny/ National Archives of Canada)

Ill. 85. Champanīr, Jāmi‘ Mosque, façade.

Ill. 86. Champanīr, Jāmi‘ Mosque, central corridor.

Ill. 87. Champanīr, Jāmi‘ Mosque, east façade with entrance pavilion.

Ill. 88. Nagaur, Shams Mosque.

Ill. 89. Jalor, Topkhāna Mosque.

Ill. 90. Makhli Hill, Tomb of Jam Niẓām al-Dīn.

Ill. 91. Makhli Hill, Tomb of Jam Niẓām al-Dīn, squinches.

Ill. 92. Makhli Hill, Tomb of Jam Niẓām al-Dīn, wall detail.

Ill. 93. Makhli Hill, Tomb of Jam Niẓām al-Dīn, *miḥrāb*.

Ill. 94. Makhli Hill, Tomb of Jam Niẓām al-Dīn, balcony window.

Ill. 95. Makhli Hill, Tomb of Jam Bābā.

Ill. 96. Makhli Hill, Tomb of Jam Bābā, wall detail.

Ill. 97. Makhli Hill, Tomb of Mīrzā ʿĪsā Khān II, general view.

Ill. 98. Makhli Hill, Tomb of Mīrzā ʻĪsā Khān II, double storeyed gallery.

Ill. 99. Makhli Hill, Tomb of Mīrzā ʻĪsā Khān II, pillars.

Ill. 100. Makhli Hill, Tomb of Mīrzā ʿĪsā Khān II, *miḥrāb.*

Ill. 101. Makhli Hill, Tomb of Dīwān Shurfa Khān.

Ill. 102. Makhli Hill, Tomb of Dīwān Shurfa Khān, dome interior.

Ill. 103. Makhli Hill, Tomb of Dīwān Shurfa Khān, *miḥrāb* wall.

Ill. 104. Chawkhandi, general view.

Ill. 105. Multān, Tomb of Shāh Rukn-i Ālam.

Ill. 106. Multān, Tomb of Shāh Rukn-i Ālam, wall decoration.

Ill. 107. Māṇḍū, Mosque of Malik Mughīs, exterior.

Ill. 108. Māṇḍū, Mosque of Malik Mughīs, interior.

Ill. 109. Māṇḍū, Jāmi' Mosque, gateway.

Ill. 110. Māṇḍū, Jāmi' Mosque, courtyard.
(Roloff Beny/National Archives of Canada)

Ill. 111. Māṇḍū, Jāmi‘ Mosque, *qibla* wall.
(Roloff Beny/National Archives of Canada)

Ill. 112. Maṇḍū, Tomb of Sultān Hūshang.
(Roloff Beny/National Archives of Canada)

Ill. 113. Māṇḍū, Tomb of Sultān Hūshang. (John Nankivell)

Ill. 114. Māṇḍū, Tomb of Sultān Hūshang, bracket detail.

Ill. 115. Māṇḍū, Delhi Darwāza.

Ill. 116. Māṇḍū, Hindola Maḥal, balcony.

Ill. 117. Māṇḍū, Hindola Maḥal, interior arches.

Ill. 118. Māṇḍū, general view with Jahāz Maḥal.

Ill. 119. Māṇḍū, Rūpamatī's Palace, domed pavilions.

Ill. 120. Chanderī, Jāmi' Mosque, prayer hall.

Ill. 121. Chanderī, Madrasa.

Ill. 122. Chanderī, Madrasa, interior squinches, pierced masonry screens.

Ill. 123. Chanderī, Shāhzādī-kā Rawza.

Ill. 124. Chanderī, Kūshak Maḥal, interior, intersecting vaults.

Ill. 125. Chanderī, Bādal Maḥal, gateway.

Ill. 126. Thalner, Five Tombs.

Ill. 127. Thalner, Octagonal Tomb no. 6.

Ill. 128. Thalner, Tomb no. 6, façade detail.

Ill. 129. Thalner, Tomb no. 3.

Ill. 130. Jaunpūr, Atālā Mosque. (T. Daniell)

Ill. 131. Jaunpūr, Atālā Mosque, arcade.

Ill. 132. Jaunpūr, Atālā Mosque, *miḥrāb*.

Ill. 133. Jaunpūr, Lāl Darwāza Mosque.

Ill. 134. Jaunpūr, Jāmi‘ Mosque, *īwān*.

Ill. 135. Jaunpūr, Jāmi‘ Mosque, courtyard arcade.

Ill. 136. Daulatābād, Chānd Mīnār. (Archaeological Survey of India)

Ill. 137. Gulbarga, Jāmiʻ Mosque. (J. Fergusson)

Ill. 138. Gulbarga, Jāmi' Mosque, main dome facing north-west.

Ill. 139. Gulbarga, Jāmi' Mosque, dome squinch.

Ill. 140. Gulbarga, Jāmi' Mosque, *miḥrāb*.

Ill. 141. Gulbarga, Jāmi' Mosque, squat arches.

Ill. 143. Gulbarga, Langar kī Mosque, interior.

Ill. 142. Gulbarga, Jāmi‘ Mosque, slim arches.

Ill. 144. Gulbarga, Langar kī Mosque, *miḥrāb,* tympanum.

Ill. 145. Gulbarga, Tomb of Fīrūz Shāh Bahmānī.

Ill. 146. Gulbarga, Tomb of Fīrūz Shāh Bahmānī, *miḥrāb*. (M. Zebrowski)

Ill. 148. Holkondā, Tomb of Dilāwar Khān.

Ill. 147. Gulbarga, Dargāh of Gīsū Darāz, ʻĀdil Shāhī gate. (M. Zebrowski)

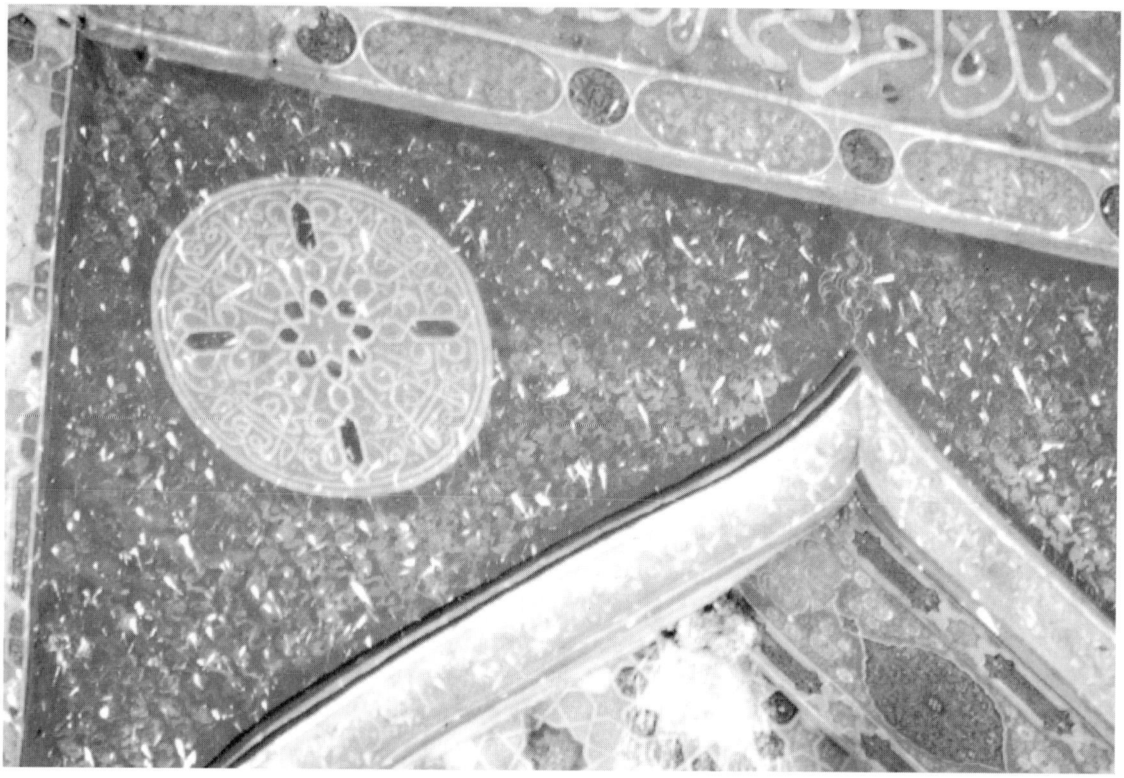

Ill. 149. Bīdar, Tomb of Aḥmad, interior, spandrel painting.

Ill. 150. Bīdar, Tomb of 'Alā' al-Dīn.

Ill. 151. Bīdar, Tomb of Khalīl Allāh (Chawkhandi).

Ill. 152. Bīdar, Madrasa of Maḥmūd Gāwān. (Captain Meadows Taylor)

Ill. 153. Bīdar, Madrasa courtyard. (A.J. Barry)

Ill. 154. Bīdar, Madrasa, mosaic faience ornament on minaret. (A.J. Barry)

Ill. 155. Bīdar, necropolis of Barīdī sultans. (Captain Meadows Taylor)

Ill. 156. Bīdar, Tomb of 'Alī I.

Ill. 157. Bīdar, Tomb of 'Alī I, interior, inscriptional panels.

Ill. 158. Bījāpūr, Gagan Maḥal. (J. Fergusson)

Ill. 159. Bījāpūr, Andā Mosque.

Ill. 160. Bījāpūr, Meḥtar Maḥal.

Ill. 161. Bījāpūr, Meḥtar Maḥal, brackets.

Ill. 162. Bījāpūr, Jāmi' Mosque.

Ill. 163. Bījāpūr, Jāmiʿ Mosque, interior.

Ill. 164. Bījāpūr, Jāmiʿ Mosque, *miḥrāb* detail.

Ill. 165. Bījāpūr, Tomb of Ibrāhīm II in Rawza.

Ill. 166. Bījāpūr, Tomb of Ibrāhīm II, pillared arcade.

Ill. 167. Bījāpūr, Tomb of Ibrāhīm II, dome.

Ill. 168. Bījāpūr, Mosque of Ibrāhīm II, cornice with chain.

Ill. 169. Bījāpūr, Tomb of ʿAlī II.

Ill. 170. Bījāpūr, Gol Gumbad.

Ill. 171. Rāichūr, Ek Mīnār kī Mosque, *mīnār*.

Ill. 172. Golkondā, Tomb of Abdullāh.

Ill. 173. Golkondā, Tomb of Jamshīd.

Ill. 174. Aḥmadnagar, Damrī Mosque.

Ill. 175. Aḥmadnagar, Tomb of Aḥmad Niẓām Shāh.

Ill. 176. Khuldābād, Dargāh of Burhān al-Dīn.

Ill. 177. Khuldābād, Tomb of Malik Ambar.

Ill. 178. Elichpūr, Jāmi' Mosque.

Ill. 179. Elichpūr, *'īdgāh.*

Ill. 180. Tekmal, Dargāh of Ḥusayn Pāshā.

Ill. 181. Komatur, Jāmiʿ Mosque.

Ill. 182. Srinagar, Mosque of Shāh Hamadān.

Ill. 183. Srinagar, Mosque of Shāh Hamadān, lower storey, diaper pattern.

Ill. 184. Srinagar, Mosque of Shāh Hamadān, upper verandah.

Ill. 185. Srinagar, Jāmi' Mosque.

Ill. 186. Srinagar, Jāmi‘ Mosque courtyard.

Ill. 187. Srinagar, Mosque of Madanī.

Ill. 188. Srinagar, Tomb of Zain al-ʿĀbidīn's Mother.
(Roloff Beny/ National Archives of Canada)